James Beattie

Selected Philosophical Writings

Edited and Introduced
by James A. Harris

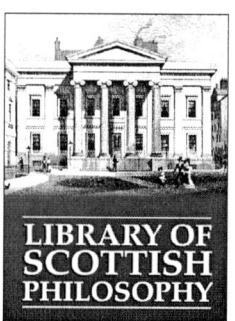

ia

IMPRINT ACADEMIC

Copyright © James A. Harris, 2004

The moral rights of the author have been asserted.
No part of any contribution may be reproduced in any form
without permission, except for the quotation of brief passages
in criticism and discussion.

Published in the UK by Imprint Academic
PO Box 200, Exeter EX5 5YX, UK

Published in the USA by Imprint Academic
Philosophy Documentation Center
PO Box 7147, Charlottesville, VA 22906-7147, USA

ISBN 0 907845 711

A CIP catalogue record for this book is available from the
British Library and US Library of Congress

Contents

Series Editor's Note. v
Introduction 1
Chronology. 15

MORALS

1. Introduction to *An Essay on Truth* 17
2. Of the Perception of Truth in General 27
3. Of the Rise and Progress of Modern Scepticism 38
4. On the Origins of the *Essay on Truth*:
   A letter to Thomas Blacklock. 56
5. On Memory 61
6. Beattie's Division of Moral Philosophy. 85
7. Of the Existence of God 88
8. A First Lesson in Religion 95
9. Of the Nature of Virtue. 97
10. Of the Origin of Civil Governments. 119
11. On Slavery 134

CRITICISM

12. On Poetry. 138
13. On Music. 152
14. Of Taste, and its Improvement. 161
15. Illustrations of Sublimity 183

Bibliography 203

Series Editor's Note

The principal purpose of volumes in this series is not to provide scholars with accurate editions, but to make the writings of Scottish philosophers accessible to a new generation of modern readers. In accordance with this purpose, certain changes have been made to the original texts:

- Spelling and punctuation have been modernized.
- In some cases, the selected passages have been given new titles.
- Some original footnotes and references have not been included.
- Some extracts have been shortened from their original length.
- Quotations from Greek have been transliterated, and passages in foreign languages translated, or omitted altogether.

Care has been taken to ensure that in no instance do these amendments truncate the argument or alter the meaning intended by the original author. For readers who want to consult the original texts, full bibliographical details are provided for each extract.

The Library of Scottish Philosophy was launched at the Third International Reid Symposium on Scottish Philosophy in July 2004 with an initial six volumes. Attractively produced and competitively priced, these appeared just fifteen months after the original suggestion of such a series. This remarkable achievement owes a great deal to the work and commitment of the editors of the individual volumes, but it was only possible because of the energy and enthusiasm of the publisher, Keith Sutherland and the outstanding work of Jon M.H Cameron, Editorial and Administrative Assistant to the Centre for the Study of Scottish Philosophy.

Acknowledgements

Grateful acknowledgement is made to the Carnegie Trust for the Universities of Scotland for generous financial support for the Library of Scottish Philosophy in general, and to George Stevenson for a subvention for this volume in particular.

Acknowledgement is also made to the University of Aberdeen Special Libraries and Collections for permission to reproduce the engraving of the Edinburgh Faculty of Advocates from *Modern Athens* (1829) and Raeburn's portrait of Beattie which hangs in the University's Chanonry Lodge.

Gordon Graham
Aberdeen, June 2004

Introduction

James Beattie was born in Laurencekirk, Kincardineshire, on 25 October 1735. As was usual in eighteenth-century Scotland, he went to university very young, and began his studies at Marischal College, Aberdeen, when only fourteen years old. This was the start of a life-long association with Marischal, then a separate institution from King's College. After five years as a schoolmaster in Fordoun, close to his native village, Beattie returned to Aberdeen in 1758 to teach in the city's Grammar School. In 1760 Beattie was appointed professor of moral philosophy and logic at Marischal, a position he occupied for the rest of his career. Also in 1760 he published the first of several books of poetry, the most notable of which was *The Minstrel* (1771, 1774), often said to anticipate some of the doctrines of Wordsworthian Romanticism. In the early years of his professorship, Beattie relied heavily on the lecture notes of his predecessor Alexander Gerard, but as time passed he stamped his course with his own character, decreasing the amount of 'pneumatology', or philosophy of mind, and focusing instead upon rhetoric and *belles lettres*. Many of his philosophical writings began life as lectures given to his students. His greatest success as a philosopher was with *An Essay on the Nature and Immutability of Truth*, a spirited and sometimes abusive attack on modern scepticism in general, and on David Hume in particular. The *Essay* appeared in 1770, and was a literary sensation, winning for its author honorary degrees from King's and Oxford, an audience with King George III, and a royal pension of £200 a year. 'We all love Beattie', said Dr Johnson in 1772. Beattie's personal life was, by contrast, often very unhappy. His wife Mary was afflicted with insanity, forcing the couple eventually to live apart; and his eldest son, James Hay, having been appointed joint professor with his increasingly ill father in 1787, died three years later. Beattie himself died at Aberdeen on 18 August, 1803.

Sir William Forbes notes in his *Life and Writings of James Beattie* that 'Dr. Beattie's philosophical writings may be properly divided into two classes, Morality and Criticism'.[1] Accordingly, this selection from Beattie's writings has two parts. As the reader will quickly perceive from Part One, moral philosophy is in the eighteenth century somewhat broader in scope than it is today. It was believed then that instruction in ethics needed to be preceded by a full analysis of the faculties of the human mind. Where 'natural philosophy' meant the study of nature, 'moral philosophy' meant the study of the mind in all its aspects, and so included study of such mental 'powers' as reason, judgment, memory, imagination, sympathy, and the five senses. In Beattie's day, people were just beginning to use the term 'psychology' as another name for the 'theoretical' (as opposed to 'practical') part of moral philosophy. 'Criticism', too, tends to be more ambitious and wide-ranging than present-day study of literature, and, in fact, also frequently strays into psychological territory. The eighteenth-century critic was often concerned to understand the manner in which a work operates upon the mind, and distinguished between styles of writing, and their respective merits, by examining the effects they had upon the reader. 'Criticism' is thus not primarily the study of intrinsic features of literary forms, nor interpretation of works in terms of authorial intention or cultural and social background, but instead a branch of rhetoric. Moreover, in his concern for how a work engages with the imagination and sentiments of its reader, the eighteenth-century critic is very often interested in the moral (in the narrower, modern sense of the word) qualities of a piece of writing. It was agreed that the function of any art form was to give pleasure, but it mattered that a work give the right kind of pleasure, pleasure in the right kind of thing, to the right degree. The critic's function was to ensure that his readers knew the right kind of pleasure when they felt it: it was, in other words, to cultivate good taste. A dedication to what we might call 'improvement' provides a means of linking Beattie's exercises in criticism with his moral philosophy. For moral

---

[1] Sir William Forbes, *An Account of the Life and Writings of James Beattie, LL.D.*, 2 vols., Edinburgh, 1806, vol. 2, p. 389.

philosophy, too, is first and foremost a practical science according to Beattie. Theoretical 'psychology' is valuable only to the extent that it yields a better understanding of the grounds and rewards of virtue. Both as a teacher and a writer, inculcating correct sentiments and habits is always Beattie's aim. He concluded his lecture course with a reminder to his students that 'the ultimate End of Man is Action; and that all Science which does not serve to make Men wiser and better, More profitable to themselves, Friends, and Country, is not only useless but also pernicious'.[2] This Introduction will show how the present selection from Beattie's writings on 'morals' and 'criticism' is lent unity by the importance Beattie attached to his role as educator and improver.

II

A central part of eighteenth-century Scottish intellectual life was the literary or philosophical club. It is difficult, in fact, to overemphasize the importance to the 'Scottish Enlightenment' of these informal, privately-organized, selective, and frequently short-lived societies, which met to discuss every kind of contemporary question, from the most abstract issues in Newtonian science to problems in agriculture and husbandry. In his first years as a professor in Aberdeen, Beattie was a member of the Aberdeen Philosophical Society, sometimes known as the 'Wise Club', founder members of which had included Thomas Reid, Professor of Moral Philosophy at Kings, George Campbell, Professor of Divinity at Marischal, and John Gregory, Professor of Medicine in the Old Town.[3] The Society concentrated its attention upon 'philosophical' subjects (thereby excluding questions in, for example, grammar, philology and history) and, especially, upon issues raised by the sceptical writings of Hume. In a famous letter of 1763, Reid, writing on behalf of the Society, tells Hume that if he is to 'write no more in morals politicks or metaphysicks, I am affraid we shall be

---

[2] Quoted from notes taken by one of Beattie's students in 1762/3 in Paul Wood, *The Aberdeen Enlightenment: The Arts Curriculum in the Eighteenth Century*, Aberdeen: Aberdeen University Press, 1995, p. 121.

[3] For an account of the activities of the Wise Club, see the introduction to H. Lewis Ulman (ed.), *The Minutes of the Aberdeen Philosophical Society 1758–1773*, Aberdeen: Aberdeen University Press, 1990.

at a loss for Subjects'.[4] But where Reid and Campbell were able to discuss and dissect Hume's arguments carefully and calmly, Beattie had a much more extreme and emotional reaction to Humean scepticism. He appears to have convinced himself that Hume was a threat to the order and happiness of society at large, and that his doctrines needed to be combated by something more forceful than either Reid's *Inquiry into the Human Mind on the Principles of Common Sense* (1764) or Campbell's *Dissertation on Miracles* (1762). As we have seen, Beattie's first interest had been in poetry and criticism, and he was prepared to admit to having 'neither head nor heart' for the work involved in undoing the confusions and sophistries of the sceptic: 'But when doctrines are published subversive of morality and religion; — doctrines, of which I perceive and have it in my power to expose the absurdity, my duty to the public forbids me to be silent; especially when I see, that, by the influence of fashion, folly, or more criminal causes, those doctrines spread wider every day, diffusing ignorance, misery, and licentiousness, where-ever they prevail'.[5] Unpublished writings, and the letter from Beattie to his friend Thomas Blacklock included here, show that he regretted the respect shown for Hume by other members of the Philosophical Society.[6]

Beattie's acute sense of the perniciousness of Hume's influence explains the extraordinary violence of some passages in the extracts from the *Essay on Truth* with which this selection opens (Selections 1–3). '[S]cepticism is now the profession of every fashionable inquirer into human nature', Beattie complains (p. 19). By 'scepticism' Beattie means, not a Lockean modesty about the extent of human knowledge, but an extreme form of doubt which recommends that, in view of the uncertainty of all things, we not believe anything at all. He interprets Hume as a proponent of this

[4] Paul Wood (ed.), *The Correspondence of Thomas Reid*, Edinburgh: Edinburgh University Press, 2002, p. 31.
[5] James Beattie, *An Essay on the Nature and Immutability of Truth in Opposition to Sophistry and Scepticism*, second edition, Edinburgh, 1771, p. 535.
[6] A satire entitled 'The Castle of Scepticism', dated 1767, gives vivid insight into Beattie's attitude towards the way Reid, Campbell and others treated Hume: see E.C. Mossner, 'Beattie's "The Castle of Scepticism": An Unpublished Allegory against Hume, Voltaire, and Hobbes', *University of Texas Studies in English* 27 (1948): 108–45.

radical kind of scepticism. Beattie's principal aim in the *Essay* is to show that such scepticism is absurd, and that, being absurd, it is plainly unjustified. We have the right to trust our natural belief in, for example, the existence of an external world of material substances, and the freedom of the will, and should not have our confidence in such beliefs undermined by the sophistry and word-juggling of writers like Hume. But this is not to say that Beattie thinks these basic beliefs can be *proven* to be true. We are as certain of their truth as it is possible to be of the truth of any principle, but not on the basis of rational argument. Rather, we *feel* them to be true, using what Beattie calls 'an instantaneous, instinctive, and irresistible impulse; derived neither from education nor from habit, but from nature; acting independently on our will, whenever its object is presented, according to an established law, and therefore properly called *Sense*; and acting in a similar manner upon all, or at least upon a great majority, and therefore properly called *Common Sense*' (p. 32). Beattie, then, is just as much a 'common sense philosopher' as Thomas Reid. Modern philosophy, for Beattie as for Reid, went wrong when Descartes argued that a belief should be rejected unless it can be given decisive justification. The subsequent slide into dangerous absurdity is charted in the excerpt entitled 'Rise and Progress of Modern Scepticism'. Beattie reads Hume in a way that is deeply uncharitable, and sometimes simply obtuse. It is nonsense to suggest that Hume's goal as a philosopher was to divest us of our natural beliefs, and Hume, not surprisingly, was made very angry by the *Essay on Truth*. He is said to have complained that he had 'not been used like a gentleman'. The letter from Beattie to Blacklock included here (Selection 4) gives some insight into the motivation behind the book.

The extract from the 'dissertation' 'Of Memory and Imagination' (Selection 5) shows that Beattie was capable of approaching subjects in moral philosophy coolly and accurately, even if he does not do so in the *Essay on Truth*. The extract tells us something about Beattie's positive conception of the proper method of analyzing the faculties of the mind: like many of his Scottish contemporaries (including Hume, in fact), Beattie believes that study of the mind should be based on 'Reflection, Consciousness, or Internal Sensation', and that psychology can proceed without investigation into the physical basis of thought. This extract is noteworthy also because it introduces a recurrent theme in Beattie's writings: the difference between human beings and animals. Beattie says that, unlike human beings, animals 'are affected, only or chiefly, with outward things; and seem incapable of what we call reflection of consciousness' (p. 62); he seeks to prove that, while animals have a faculty of memory, it is much inferior to human memory (pp. 80–81); and later on, he argues that animals have none of the 'secondary senses' necessary for aesthetic appreciation (p. 66). Furthermore, in the extract 'Of the Nature of Virtue', Beattie declares that conscience, the faculty by which we distinguish between virtue and vice, is 'peculiar to rational nature; brutes have nothing like it' (p. 99); and he begins the extract 'Of the Origin of Civil Government' with the claim that 'Man is the only political animal; that is, the only animal capable of government' (p. 120). Where Hume, for one, dwells on the similarities between man and animal, Beattie's concern is always with 'those powers, which form the glory, and indeed the distinguishing character of man; I mean, our capacities of speech, invention, and science, and those particulars in our frame, that entitle us to the denomination of moral, political, and religious beings' (p. 83). Moral philosophy, then, shows us that we have it in ourselves to be much more than merely sophisticated animals; and Beattie frequently moves quickly from the role of mental anatomist to the role of an instructor keen to suggest how to make the most of our distinctive powers. It will be seen that Beattie takes it as his task, not only to describe the faculty of memory, but also to tell the reader how memory can be cultivated and improved.

Largely for the benefit of his students, Beattie produced 'an Abridgment, and for the most part a very brief one' of his lecture course in moral philosophy, entitled *Elements of Moral Science* (1790–3). The Introduction to the *Elements* is included here (Selection 6) in order to help clarify Beattie's understanding of the subject he taught. It will be unsurprising to find Beattie (like every Scottish philosopher of his day) endorsing the Baconian definition of philosophy as 'The knowledge of nature applied to practical and useful purposes' (p. 86). It may be more unexpected that Beattie says that 'pneumatology', or '[t]he Speculative part of the philosophy of mind', comprises arguments for the existence and

Introduction 7

attributes of God as well as analysis of the human mind (p. 87). Beattie's version of the popular 'argument from design' is included here as representative of his style of natural theology (Selection 7), along with a passage from his biography of his son James Hay (Selection 8). It was in fact standard practice for a professor of moral philosophy to lecture on natural theology: this is not evidence of an unusual religiosity on Beattie's part. But it is, nevertheless, undoubtedly true that a vindication of religious belief was absolutely central to all of Beattie's teaching and writing. It mattered at least partly because, as Beattie put it in a passage from the *Elements* not included here, 'Atheism is utterly subversive of morality, and consequently of happiness... They therefore, who teach atheistical doctrines, or who endeavour to make men doubtful in regard to this great and glorious truth, THE BEING OF GOD, do every thing in their power to overturn government, to unhinge society, to eradicate virtue, to destroy happiness, and to promote confusion, madness, and misery'.[7] (It will be seen in the extract from the essay 'On Poetry and Music' included here (Selection 12) that Beattie objected to the way in which Swift in *Gulliver's Travels* represents his Houyhnhyms 'as patterns of moral virtue, as the greatest masters of reason, and withal as completely happy, without any religious ideas, or any views beyond the present life' (p. 150 fn.).) In underlining the importance of religious belief to virtue and happiness, Beattie is, once again, at one with most of his peers.[8] But religion for Beattie is always more than mere 'natural' religion: in a book not represented in this selection, *The Evidences of the Christian Religion: Briefly and Plainly Stated* (1786), Beattie insists on the 'importance and usefulness of Divine Revelation'.

Beattie's emphasis on the significance of revealed religion goes together with a belief in Original Sin. Human nature remains corrupted, and we therefore need the promise extended in the Bible to be sure of the possibility of regaining felicity. Yet Beattie is no Calvinist pessimist about our ability to undo, to some extent at

---

[7] James Beattie, *Elements of Moral Science*, 2 vols., Edinburgh, 1790–93, vol. I, pp. 375–6.
[8] I explore this issue in more detail in 'Answering Bayle's question: religious belief in the moral philosophy of the Scottish Enlightenment', in Steven Nadler and Daniel Garber (eds.), *Oxford Studies in Early Modern Philosophy: Volume I*, Oxford: Oxford University Press, 2003.

least, the results of the Fall. For one thing, he argues in favour of the natural freedom of the human will: we do not have to wait for a mysterious act of divine Grace before sin can be renounced.[9] For another thing, and as is shown in the passages included here from 'Of the Nature of Virtue' (Selection 9), he believes that the faculty of conscience remains healthy, and is 'the supreme regulating principle of human nature' (p. 100). Virtue, Beattie says, 'is the ultimate end for which man was made' (p. 100), and it is natural to us despite our corruption. Virtue, that is to say, is not for Beattie, as it is for the Calvinist, impossible for the 'natural man'. We deserve divine punishment, when we do, because we freely abuse what we are all given, not because we somehow inherit a curse on account of the sins of Adam. Also in this extract, Beattie engages with the eighteenth-century British debate concerning the means by which we distinguish between right and wrong, and seeks to reconcile the opposing parties by claiming that 'moral approbation is both an agreeable feeling, and also a determination of judgment or reason; the former following the other, as an effect follows the cause' (pp. 108–9). Beattie is particularly concerned to rebut the idea that 'moral sentiments are merely the effects of education' (see p. 110). He regards conscience as one of those faculties 'implanted in man by his Creator' (p. 113).

In Selection 10 Beattie discusses the origin of political society. He treats the question in two ways. He seeks to determine both 'what reasons, and by what steps is it probable, that men, not subject to government, would think of it, and submit themselves to it'; and also 'what may reasonably be presumed to have been the actual origin of government, according to the best lights that may be had from history, tradition, or conjecture' (p. 120). Like virtue, Beattie believes, political society is natural for human beings, and so Hobbes was wrong to argue that it is not. Government is artificial, but not unnatural (see p. 122). It is entered into freely, and freedom remains intact when government is established, though here freedom means neither the right to do as you please, nor being governed by laws of your own making. True liberty lies in

---

[9] See Beattie, *Elements of Moral Science*, vol. I, pp. 195–214. An account of Beattie on free will can be found in my *Of Liberty and Necessity: The free-will debate in eighteenth-century British philosophy*, Oxford: Oxford University Press, 2005, ch. 6.

being 'so governed by equitable laws, and so tried by equitable judges, that no person can be hindered from doing what the law allows, or have reason to be afraid of any person so long as he does his duty' (p. 130). And the British constitution has over the centuries been refined so as to guarantee such liberty. It will not be a surprise that Beattie was an enthusiast for the 1707 Act of Union that had united Scotland with England, nor that he was deeply hostile to the aims of the French Revolution. Yet Beattie was no mere unthinking conservative. His religious beliefs sometimes caused him to set himself against the views of the majority of his peers, as is shown by the short passage on slavery included here from the *Essay on Truth* (Selection 11).[10] Beattie refuses to accept that black people are naturally and inevitably inferior to white. Whatever differences there seem to be between the capacities of slaves and their masters, Beattie points out, are probably due to the conditions in which slaves are kept. It would be in the spirit of Britishness, he concludes, to abolish slavery altogether.

III

Beattie writes in a letter that his wish is 'rather to form the taste, improve the manners, and establish the principles, of young men, than to make them profound metaphysicians; I wish in a word, not to make Humes of them, or Leibnitzes, but rather, if that were possible, Addisons'.[11] As we have seen, Beattie took his role as a moralist seriously, but he does not regard virtue as in any sense requiring the repression of the passions and sentiments by reason or conscience. His task, as he sees it, is to promote the flourishing of all aspects of human nature, and the cultivation of the pleasure we naturally take in the beautiful and the sublime is, he thinks, a central part of that task. The persona Joseph Addison had adopted in *The Spectator* provided for Beattie, as for every enlightened person in eighteenth-century Britain, the model combination of virtue without abstinence, piety without bigotry, and taste

---

[10] There is a much longer treatment of slavery in the *Elements of Moral Science*: see vol. II, pp. 153–223.
[11] Cited by Wood, *The Aberdeen Enlightenment*, p. 126.

without pedantry.[12] Selection 12, taken from the essay 'On Poetry and Music, as they affect the Mind', sees Beattie expounding the mainstream view of his day that the proper goal of poetry is to give pleasure, and that it gives pleasure just in so far as it is 'natural', which is to say, just in so far as it represents or imitates accurately. This extract makes it clear that while Beattie is concerned with the morality embodied in a poem, and with poetry's capacity to 'instruct', he does not expect a poem to play the role of an improving tract. A short poem, for instance a lyric or an exercise in pastoral, need not concern itself with moral matters at all. But epic or drama, Beattie says, must 'touch the heart and exercise the conscience' (p. 140) if it is to succeed in giving us pleasure, since 'moral sentiments are so prevalent in the human mind, that no affection can long subsist there, without mingling with them, and being assimilated to their nature' (p. 140). What gives us most pleasure in a poem is therefore description of human affairs. Yet Beattie is careful to admit that a poem does not have to be 'an exact transcript of real existence' (p. 147) in order to succeed as imitation: it is enough if it be consistent with general experience, with popular opinion, and with itself. This emphasis upon the role of imitation in aesthetic pleasure raises the question of why we enjoy music, an art that is, according to Beattie, not usually imitative at all. Beattie's answer to this question is found in Selection 13, another extract from 'On Poetry and Music', where he argues that music pleases because 'certain melodies and harmonies have *an aptitude* to raise certain passions, affections, and sentiments in the soul' (p. 153). This in turn raises the further question of why different types of music develop in different places, even in different parts of the same country. Beattie's answer to this question, with reference to Scottish music, is also included here.

Beattie regarded a taste for the pleasures of the imagination as natural to human beings (and, as has been already noted, as absent in animals), but just as the moral sense has to be carefully tended so as to prevent corruption by prejudice and poor education, so also does taste. Taste and its improvement are Beattie's concerns in Selection 14. As usual, there is nothing particularly

---

[12] Beattie published (anonymously) his own edition of Addison's works: [James Beattie, ed.], *The Papers of Joseph Addison, Esq.*, 4 vols., Edinburgh, 1790.

original in Beattie's treatment of his topic here. He signals the influence upon his ideas of, not only Addison's *Spectator*, but also Francis Hutcheson, Alexander Gerard (his predecessor at Marischal) and Lord Kames.[13] While Beattie's general approach to the philosophy of mind is similar to that of Thomas Reid, one thing that differentiates Beattie's writings from Reid's is a concern for the role of 'habit' in the development of our beliefs and sentiments. Taste changes over time, Beattie observes: what was esteemed under the reign of Charles II is not what was valued under Queen Anne and George I; and 'Of late the publick taste seems to have been most effectively gratified by correct expression, and historical and philosophical inquiry' (p. 169). Changing habits and customs play an important role in determining what is found tasteful, as do 'constitutional differences'. The Enlightenment taken as a whole is often accused of being overly concerned with an unchanging and ubiquitous 'human nature', and with ignoring the role of history and geography in the determination of cultural practices and political institutions. There is some truth to this, but Beattie's concern with habit, with 'constitutional differences', and with geographical peculiarities (as in his discussion of Scottish music) illustrate the fact that a concern for faculties 'implanted in man by his Creator' could be combined with sensitivity to the difficulties in assuming that human beings are the same at all times and in all places.

It was mentioned above that Beattie's poetry is often seen as foreshadowing the Romanticism of William Wordsworth. There are what sound like anticipations of Wordsworth also in the essay 'On Poetry and Music', for instance where Beattie writes that 'some minds there are of a different make; who, even in the early part of life, receive from the contemplation of Nature a species of delight which they would hardly exchange for any other' (p. 143). There might seem to be something of the Romantic too in Selection 15, taken from Beattie's 'Illustrations of Sublimity'. Here Beattie makes it even clearer that the relation between poetry and morality is in his eyes far from straightforward. As he says, 'the test of sublimity is not moral approbation, but that pleasurable

---

[13] For selections from Hutcheson and Gerard see Jonathan Friday (ed.), *Art and Enlightenment: Scottish Aesthetics in the 18th Century* (Exeter: Imprint Academic, 2004).

astonishment wherewith certain things strike the beholder' (p. 185); and, because evil when depicted in the right way — for instance, as by Milton in his portrayal of Satan in *Paradise Lost* — has the capacity to astonish us pleasurably, 'we sometimes admire what we cannot approve' (p. 186). Shakespeare's tragedies similarly violate our natural sentiments, by causing us to take pleasure in horror; Beattie cites *Macbeth* as an example. The effect of the sublime in poetry is to elevate the mind, to push it up beyond the everyday, and beyond the realm of the merely natural, and thereby to provide proof that, to quote Beattie quoting Longinus, 'the whole world is not an object sufficient for the depth and rapidity of human imagination' (p. 201). It is only in the brief final paragraph of the dissertation that Beattie makes a claim for the moral value of the cultivation of a taste for the sublime. It would not do, however, to imagine that Beattie is consciously opposing the realm of the unencumbered free play of the aesthetic imagination to the more limited and prosaic moral domain. There is in fact nothing revolutionary, either in his conception of the sublime or in his claims about the value of early exposure to the beauties of nature. What is sometimes termed 'Pre-Romanticism' is often unimpeachably traditional in its values and aspirations. It has been claimed, in fact, that the only text of this period to which the label 'Pre-Romantic' could reasonably be applied is Wordsworth's own Preface to *Lyrical Ballads* (1800).[14]

IV

It has been emphasized here that Beattie is not properly regarded as an original thinker. One historian of the Scottish Enlightenment has argued that, in valuing Addisonian politeness over Humean 'metaphysics', Beattie departed from the mainstream of moral philosophy in eighteenth-century Scotland;[15] but to the extent that this is true, it does not signal a great deal of independence of mind on Beattie's part. His understanding of the nature of

---

[14] See P.W.K. Stone, *The Art of Poetry 1750–1820*, London: Routledge and Kegan Paul, 1967, ch. 9.

[15] See Wood, *The Aberdeen Enlightenment*, pp. 119–29; also 'Science and the Pursuit of Virtue in the Aberdeen Enlightenment', in M.A. Stewart (ed.), *Studies in the Philosophy of the Scottish Enlightenment*, Oxford: Clarendon Press, 1990.

virtue and taste was very far from innovative. Nor did Beattie want to be regarded as an innovator. He says in the *Essay on Truth* that if philosophers such as Descartes and Malebranche had given more attention to 'the ancients', 'they would have made a better figure in philosophy, and done more services to mankind' (p. 43); and he constantly refers to Greek and Roman writers, sometimes where one might expect him to refer to modern ones instead: the dissertation on the sublime is full of citations from Longinus, but never once refers the reader to Edmund Burke's *Philosophical Enquiry into the Sublime and the Beautiful* (1757). At every turn, Beattie simply echoes the dominant assumptions of his day, and this surely helps to explain his disappearance from the philosophical canon. There is nothing in his writings which presses questions that later philosophers were forced to answer. Another reason for his present obscurity is his intense concern for the practical, and declared hostility for the merely theoretical and speculative. By the time of Beattie's death, European philosophy, and American philosophy as well, was becoming increasingly technical and academic. Having for a brief period been as much the concern of the 'polite' man of letters as of the university professor, philosophy in the early decades of the nineteenth century retreated back into scholasticism, particularly with the arrival on the scene of the systems of Kant and Hegel. Psychology, moreover, eventually transformed itself into a 'proper' science, eschewing introspection and embracing the materialist theory of mind. As early as the *Treatise of Human Nature*, Hume had contrasted his 'anatomical' approach to the mind with the didactic approach of the moralist. Beattie's response was to claim that there is no distinction there; that when the mind is seen as it really is, it will be obvious that virtue and piety are what the mind is made for. The success of the *Essay on Truth* suggests that many of Beattie's contemporaries believed, or wanted to believe, the same. This was a Pyrrhic victory only, however: Hume may have lost the battle for popularity, but he won the larger war. Subsequently, anatomy triumphed over moralizing. Yet if one wants to understand the background against which Hume's startling innovations are seen in their proper light, Beattie is a good place to start.

Acknowledgments

The work on this volume was done during the tenure of a British Academy Postdoctoral Fellowship. I am extremely grateful to the late Roger J. Robinson for the help he gave me both in making the selections from Beattie's works and with the Introduction.

Chronology

1735	Born in Laurencekirk, Kincardineshire, 25 October
1749	Entered Marischal College, Aberdeen
1753	Graduated MA; began as a schoolmaster at Fordoun, Kincardineshire; also attending divinity classes at Aberdeen
1758	Moved to Aberdeen to teach in the Grammar School
1760	Published first book of poetry; appointed to chair of moral philosophy and logic at Marischal; invited to join the Aberdeen Philosophical Society (the 'Wise Club')
1763	First visit to London
1767	Married Mary Dun
1768	Birth of James Hay Beattie, 6 November
1770	Publication of *An Essay on the Nature and Immutability of Truth*; awarded LL.D. by King's College, Aberdeen
1771	Publication of *The Minstrel* (second volume published in 1774); second visit to London, meets Johnson and circle, Garrick, Reynolds
1773	Third visit to London; introduced to King George III; awarded honorary degree by University of Oxford; granted a royal pension of £200 per annum
1774	Refuses to apply for moral philosophy chair at Edinburgh, and declines positions in the Church of England
1775	Fourth visit to London; portrait painted by Reynolds
1776	Publication of a subscription volume containing the *Essay on Truth* and several other essays
1778	Birth of second son, Montagu, 8 July
1779	Supports moves to increase the freedoms of Scottish Roman Catholics
1780–1	Living apart from his wife because of her insanity
1783	Publication of *Dissertations, Moral and Critical*
1786	Publication of *Evidences of the Christian Religion*
1787	James Hay appointed joint professor with his father

1788	Joins agitation against the slave trade
1790	Death of James Hay, 19 November; publication of first volume of *Elements of Moral Science* (second volume published 1793)
1796	Death of Montagu, 14 March; retires from teaching in May; succeeded as professor of moral philosophy by George Glennie
1800	Partially paralysed by a stroke
1803	Dies at Aberdeen, 18 August

One

Introduction to 'An Essay on Truth'

To those who love learning and mankind, and who are more ambitious to distinguish themselves as men, than as disputants, it is a matter of humiliation and regret, that names and things have so oft been mistaken for each other; that so much of the philosopher's time must be employed in ascertaining the signification of words; and that so many doctrines, of high reputation, and of ancient date, when traced to their first principles, have been found to terminate in verbal ambiguity. If I have any knowledge of my own heart, or of the subject I propose to examine, I may venture to assure the reader, that it is no part of the design of this book, to encourage verbal disputation. On the contrary, it is my sincere purpose to avoid, and to do every thing in my power to check it; convinced as I am, that it never can do any good, and that it has been the cause of much mischief, both in philosophy and in common life. And I hope I have a fairer chance to escape it, than some who have gone before me in this part of science. I aim at no paradoxes; my prejudices (if certain instinctive suggestions of the understanding may be so called) are all in favour of truth and virtue; and I have no principles to support, but those which seem to me to have influenced the judgements of a great majority of mankind in all ages of the world.

Many will think, that there is but little merit in this declaration; it being as much for my own credit, as for the interest of mankind, that I guard against a practice, which is acknowledged to be always unprofitable, and generally pernicious. A verbal disputant! what claim can he have to the title of Philosopher! What has he to do with the laws of nature, with the observation of facts, with life and manners! Let him not intrude upon the company of men of science; but repose with his brethren Aquinas and Suarez, in the corner of some gothic cloister, dark as his understanding, and cold as his heart. Men are now become too judicious to be amused with words, and too *firm-minded* to be confuted with quibbles. — Many of my contemporaries would readily join in this apostrophe, who yet are themselves the dupes of some of the most egregious dealers in logomachy that ever perverted the faculty of speech. In fact, from some instances that have occurred to my own observation, I have reason to believe, that verbal controversy hath not always, even in this age, been accounted a contemptible thing: and the reader, when he comes to be better acquainted with my sentiments, will perhaps think the foregoing declaration more disinterested, than at first sight it may appear.

They who form opinions concerning the manners and principles of the times, may be divided into three classes. Some will tell us, that the present age transcends all that have gone before it, in politeness, learning, and good sense; will thank providence (or their stars) that their lot of life has been cast in so glorious a period; and wonder how men could possibly support existence amidst the ignorance and barbarism of former days. By others we are accounted a generation of triflers and profligates, sciolists in learning, hypocrites in virtue, and formalists in good-breeding; wise only when we follow the ancients, and foolish whenever we deviate from their footsteps. Such violent sentiments are generally wrong: and therefore I am disposed to adopt the notions of those who may be considered as forming an intermediate class; who, though not blind to the follies, are yet willing to acknowledge the virtues, both of past ages, and of the present. And surely, in every age, and in every man, there is something to praise, as well as something to blame.

When I survey the philosophy of the present age, I find much matter of applause and admiration. Mathematics, Natural Philosophy, and Natural History, in all their branches, have risen to a pitch of perfection, which does signal honour to human capacity, and far surpasses what the most sanguine projectors of former times had any reason to look for: and the paths to further improvement in those sciences are so clearly marked out, that nothing but honesty and attention seems requisite to ensure the success of future adventurers. Moral Philosophy and Logic have not been so fortunate: yet, even here, we have happily got rid of much pedantry and jargon; our systems have more the appearance of liberal sentiment, good taste, and correct composition, than those of the schoolmen; we disclaim (at least in words) all attachment to hypothesis and party; profess to study men and things, as well as books and words; and assert, with the utmost vehemence of protestation, our love of truth, of candour, and of sound philosophy. But let us not be deceived by appearances. Neither Moral Philosophy, nor the kindred sciences of Logic and Criticism, are at present upon the most desirable footing. The rage of paradox and system has transformed them (although of all sciences these ought to be the simplest and clearest) into a mass of confusion, darkness, and absurdity. One kind of jargon is laid aside; but another has been adopted, more fashionable indeed, but equally frivolous. Hypothesis, though verbally disclaimed, is really adhered to with as much obstinacy as ever. Words have been defined; but their ambiguity continues. Appeals have been made to experience; but with such misrepresentation and equivocation, as plainly show the authors to have been more concerned for their theory, than for the truth. All sciences, and especially Moral Philosophy, ought to regulate human practice: practice is regulated by principles, and all principles suppose conviction: yet the aim of our most celebrated moral systems is to divest the mind of every principle, and of all conviction; and, consequently, to disqualify man for action, and to render him as useless, and as wretched, as possible. In a word, Scepticism is now the profession of every fashionable inquirer into human nature; a scepticism which is not confined to points of mere speculation, but has been extended to practical truths of the highest importance, even to the principles of morality and religion. Proofs of all these assertions will appear in the sequel.

I said that my prejudices are all in favour of truth and virtue. To avow any sort of prejudice, may perhaps startle some readers. If it should, I must here entreat all such to pause a moment, and ask of their own hearts these simple questions. Are virtue and truth useful to mankind? Are they matters of indifference? Or are they pernicious? If any one finds himself disposed to think them pernicious, or matters of indifference, I would advise him lay my book aside; for it does not contain one sentiment in which he can be interested, nor one expression with which he can be pleased. But he who believes, that virtue and truth are of the highest importance, that in them is laid the foundation of human happiness, and that on them depends the very existence of human society, and of human creatures, — that person and I are of the same mind; I have no prejudices which he would wish me not to have: he may proceed; and I hope he will proceed with pleasure, and encourage, by his approbation, this honest attempt to vindicate truth and virtue; and to overturn that pretended philosophy, which supposes, or which may lead us to suppose, every dictate of conscience, and every impulse of understanding, questionable and ambiguous.

This sceptical philosophy (as it is called) seems to me to be dangerous, not because it is ingenious, but because it is subtle and obscure. Were it rightly understood, no confutation would be necessary; for it does in fact confute itself, as I hope to demonstrate. But many, to my certain knowledge, have read it, and admitted its tenets, who do not understand the grounds of them; and many more, swayed by the fashion of the times, have greedily adopted its conclusions, without any knowledge of the premises, or any concern about them. An attempt therefore to expose this pretended philosophy to public view, in its proper colours, will not, I hope, be censured as impertinent by any whose opinion I value: if it should, I shall be satisfied with the approbation of my own conscience, which will never reproach me for intending to do good.

I am sorry, that in the course of this inquiry, it will not always be in my power to speak of some celebrated names with that deference, to which superior talents, and superior virtue, are always entitled. Every friend to civil and religious liberty, every lover of mankind, every admirer of sincerity and simple manners, every heart that warms at the recollection of distinguished virtue, must consider Mr Locke as one of the most amiable, and most illustrious men, that ever our nation produced. Such he is, such he will ever be, in my estimation. The parts of his philosophy to which truth obliges me to object, are but few, and, compared with the extent and importance of his other writings, extremely inconsiderable. I object to them, because I think them erroneous and dangerous; and I am convinced, that their author, if he had lived to see the inferences that have been drawn from them, would have been first to declare them absurd, and would have expunged them from his works with indignation. Dr Berkeley was equally amiable in his life, and equally a friend to truth and virtue. In elegance of composition he was perhaps superior. I admire his virtues: I can never sufficiently applaud his zeal in the cause of religion: but some of his reasonings on the subject of human nature I cannot admit, without renouncing my claim to rationality. There is a Writer now alive, of whose philosophy I have much to say.[1] By his philosophy, I mean the sentiments he has published in a book called, *A Treatise of Human Nature*, in three volumes, printed in the year 1739; the principle doctrines of which he has since republished again and again, under the title of, *Essays Moral and Political*, &c.[2] Of his other works I say nothing; nor have I at present any concern with them. Virgil is said to have been a bad prose-writer; Cicero was certainly a bad poet: and this author, though not much acquainted with human nature, and therefore not well qualified to write a treatise upon it, may yet be an excellent politician, financier, and historian. His high merit in these three respects is indeed universally allowed: and if my suffrage could add any thing to the lustre of such distinguished reputation, I should here, with great sincerity and pleasure, join my voice to that of the public, and make such an encomium on the author of *the History of England* as would not offend any of his rational admirers.[3] But why is this author's character so replete with inconsistency! Why should his principles and his talents extort at once our esteem and detestation, our applause and contempt! That he, whose manners in private life are said to be so agreeable to many of his acquaintance, should yet, in the public capacity of an author, have given so much cause of just offence to all the friends of virtue and mankind, is to me matter of astonishment and sorrow, as well as of

---

[1] [Beattie means Hume.]

[2] [The third book of Hume's *Treatise* was in fact published in 1740. The 'principal doctrines' of the *Treatise* were republished, not in Hume's *Essays Moral and Political*, but rather in the *Enquiry concerning Human Understanding* (1748) and the *Enquiry concerning the Principles of Morals* (1751), both of which were reprinted (together with the *Essays*) in 1753–4 as *Essays and Treatises on Several Subjects*.]

[3] [Hume's *History of England* was published to great acclaim between 1754 and 1762.]

indignation. That he, who succeeds so well in describing the states of nations, should yet have failed so egregiously in explaining the operations of the mind, is one of those incongruities in human genius, for which perhaps philosophy will never be able to fully account. That he, who has so impartially stated the opposite pleas and principles of our political factions, should yet have adopted the most illiberal prejudices against natural and revealed religion; that he, who on some occasions hath displayed even a profound erudition, should at other times, when intoxicated with a favourite theory, have suffered affirmations to escape him, which would have fixed the opprobrious name of Sciolist on a less celebrated author; and, finally, that a moral philosopher, who seems to have exerted his utmost ingenuity in searching after paradoxes, should yet happen to light on none, but such as are all, without exception, on the side of licentiousness and scepticism: these are inconsistencies perhaps equally inexplicable; at least they are such as I do not at present choose to explain. And yet, that this author is chargeable with all these inconsistencies, will not, I think, be denied by any person of sense and candour, who has read his work with attention. His philosophy has done great harm. Its admirers, I know, are very numerous; but I have not as yet met with one person, who both admired and understood it. We are prone to believe what we wish to be true: and most of this author's philosophical tenets are so well adapted to what I fear I may call the fashionable notions of the times, that those who are ambitious to conform themselves to the latter, will hardly be disposed to examine scrupulously the evidence of the former. — Having made this declaration, which I do in the spirit of an honest man, I must take the liberty to treat this author with that plainness, which the cause of truth, the interests of society, and my own conscience, require. The same candour that prompts me to praise, will also oblige me to blame. The inconsistency is not in me, but in him. Had I done but half as much as he, in labouring to subvert principles which ought ever to be held sacred, I know not whether the friends of truth would have granted me any indulgence; I am sure they ought not. Let me be treated with the lenity due to a good citizen, no longer than I act as becomes one.

If it shall be acknowledged by the candid and intelligent reader, that I have in this book contributed something to the establishment of old truths, I shall not be much offended, though others should pretend to discover, that I have advanced nothing new. Indeed I would not wish to say any thing on these subjects, that has not often occurred to the common sense of mankind. In Logic and Morals, we may have new treatises, and new theories; but we are not now to expect new discoveries. The principles of moral duty have long been understood in these enlightened parts of the world; and mankind, in the time that is past, have had more truth under their consideration, than they will probably have in the time to come. Yet he who makes these sciences the study of his life, may perhaps collect particulars concerning their evidence, which, though known to a few, are unknown to many; may set some objects in a more striking light, than that in which they have been formerly viewed; may devise methods of confuting new errors, and exposing new paradoxes; and may hit upon a more popular way of displaying what has hitherto been exhibited in too dark and mysterious a form.

It is commonly acknowledged, that the science of human nature is of all human sciences the most curious and important. To know ourselves, is a precept which the wise in all ages have recommended, and which is enjoined by the authority of revelation itself. Can any thing be of more consequence to man, than to know what is his duty, and how he may arrive at happiness? It is from the examination of his own heart that he receives the first intimations of the one, and the only sure criterion of the other — what can be more useful, more delightful, and more sublime, than to contemplate the Deity? It is in the works of nature, particularly in the constitution of the human soul, that we discern the first and most conspicuous traces of the Almighty; for without some previous acquaintance with our own moral nature, we could not possibly have any certain knowledge of His. — Destitute of the hope of immortality, and a future retribution, how contemptible, how miserable is man! And yet, did not our moral feelings, in concert with what our reason discovers of the Deity, evidence the necessity of a future state, in vain should we pretend to judge rationally of that revelation by which life and immortality have been brought to light.

How then is this science to be learned? In what manner are we to study human nature? Doubtless by examining our own hearts and feelings, and by attending to the conduct of other men. But are not the writings of philosophers useful towards the attainment of this science? Most certainly they are: for whatever improves the sagacity of judgement, the sensibility of moral perception, or the delicacy of taste; whatever renders our knowledge of moral and intellectual facts more extensive; whatever impresses us with stronger and more enlarged sentiments of duty, with more affecting views of God and Providence, and with greater energy of belief in the doctrines of natural religion; – every thing of this sort either makes us more thoroughly acquainted, or prepares us for becoming more thoroughly acquainted, with our own nature, with the nature of other beings, and with the relations that they and we bear to one another. But I fear we shall not be able to improve ourselves in any one of these respects, by reading the modern systems of scepticism. What account then are we to make of those systems, and their authors? The following dissertation is partly designed as an answer to this question. But it has a further view. It proposes to examine the foundations of this scepticism, and to see whether these be consistent with what all mankind must acknowledge to be the foundations of truth; to inquire whether the cultivation of scepticism be salutary or pernicious to science and mankind; and whether it may not be possible to devise certain *criteria*, by which the absurdity of its conclusions may be detected, even by those who may not have leisure, or subtlety, or metaphysical knowledge, sufficient to qualify them for a logical confutation of all its premises. If it be confessed, that the present age has some tendency to licentiousness, both in principle and practice, and that the works of sceptical writers have some tendency to favour that licentiousness; it will also be confessed, that this design is neither absurd nor unreasonable.

A celebrated writer on human nature has observed, that 'if truth be at all within the reach of human capacity, it is certain it must lie very deep and abstruse': and a little after he adds, 'that he would esteem it a strong presumption against the philosophy he is going to unfold, were it so very easy and obvious'.[4] I am so far from adopting this opinion, that I declare, in regard to the few

---

[4] Hume, *A Treatise of Human Nature*, ed. David Fate Norton and Mary Norton, Oxford: Oxford University Press, 2000, pp. 3, 4.

things I have to say on human nature, that I should esteem it a very strong presumption against them, if they were not easy and obvious. Physical and mathematical truths are often exceedingly abstruse; but facts and experiments relating to the human mind, when expressed in proper words, ought to be obvious to all. I find, that those poets, historians, and novelists, who have given the most lively displays of human nature, and who abound most in sentiments easily comprehended, and readily admitted as true, are the most entertaining, as well as the most useful. How then should the philosophy of the human mind be so difficult and obscure? Indeed, if it be an author's determined purpose to advance paradoxes, some of which are incredible, and others incomprehensible; if he be willing to avail himself all he can of the natural ambiguity of language in supporting those paradoxes; or if he enter upon inquiries too refined for human understanding; he must often be obscure, and often unintelligible. But my views are very different. I only intend to suggest some hints for guarding the mind against error; and these, I hope, will be found to be deduced from principles which every man of common capacity may examine by his daily experience.

It is true that several subjects of intricate speculation are examined in this book: but I have endeavoured, by constant appeals to fact and experience, by illustrations and examples the most familiar I could think of, and by a plainness and perspicuity of expression which sometimes may appear too much affected, to examine them in such a way, that I hope cannot fail to render them intelligible, even to those who are not much conversant in studies of this kind. Truth, like virtue, to be loved, needs only to be seen. My principles require no disguise; on the contrary, they will, if I mistake not, be most easily admitted by those who best understand them. And I am persuaded, that the sceptical system would never have made such an alarming progress, if it had been well understood. The ambiguity of its language, and the intricacy and length of some of its fundamental investigations, have unhappily been too successful in producing that confusion of thought, and indistinctness of apprehension, in the minds both of authors and readers, which are so favourable to error and sophistry.

Few men have ever engaged in controversy, religious, political, or philosophical, without being in some degree chargeable with misconception of the adversary's meaning. That I have never erred in this way, I dare not affirm. But I am conscious of having done every thing in my power to guard against it. The greater part of these papers have lain by me for several years; they have been repeatedly perused by some of the acutest philosophers of this age, whom I have the honour to call my friends, and to whose advice and assistance, on this, as on other occasions, I am deeply indebted. I have availed myself all I could of reading and conversation; and endeavoured, with all the candour I am master of, to profit by every hint of improvement, and to examine to the bottom every objection, that others have offered, or myself could devise. And may I not be permitted to add, that every one of those who have perused this essay, has advised the author to publish it; and that many of them have encouraged him by this insinuation, to him the most flattering of all others, that by so doing, he would probably be of some service to the cause of truth, virtue and mankind? In this hope he submits it to the public. And it is this hope only that could have induced him to attempt polemical disquisition: a species of writing, which, in his own judgement, is not the most creditable; which he knows, to his cost, is not the most pleasing; and of which he is well aware, that it can hardly fail to draw upon him the resentment of a numerous, powerful, and fashionable party. But,

> *Welcome for thee, fair virtue! all the past;*
> *For thee, fair virtue! welcome even the last.*[5]

If these pages, which he hopes none will condemn who have not read, shall throw any light on the first principles of moral science; if they shall suggest, to the young and unwary, any cautions against that sophistry, and licentiousness of principle, which too much infect the conversations and compositions of the age; if they shall, in any measure, contribute to the satisfaction of any of the friends of truth and virtue; his purpose will be completely answered: and he will, to the end of his life, rejoice in the recollection of those painful hours which he passed in the examination of this most important controversy.

---

[5] [Alexander Pope, 'Epistle to Dr. Arbuthnot', ll. 358-9.]

Two

Of the Perception of Truth in General

On hearing these propositions — I exist; things equal to one and the same thing are equal to one another; the sun rose today; there is a God; ingratitude ought to be blamed and punished; the three angles of a triangle are equal to two right angles, &c — I am conscious that my mind readily admits and acquiesces in them. I say, that I believe them to be true; that is, I conceive them to express something conformable to the nature of things. Of the contrary propositions I should say, that my mind does not acquiesce in them, but disbelieves them, and conceives them to express something not conformable to the nature of things. My judgement in this case I conceive to be the same which I should form in regard to these propositions, if I were perfectly acquainted with all nature, in all its parts, and all its laws.

If I be asked what I mean by *the nature of things,* I cannot otherwise explain myself, than by saying, that there is in my mind something which induces me to think, that every thing existing in nature is determined to exist, and to exist after a certain manner, in consequence of established laws; and that whatever is agreeable to those laws is agreeable to the nature of things, because by those laws the nature of all things is determined. Of those laws I do not pretend to know any thing, except so far as they seem to be intimated to me by my own feelings, and by the suggestions of my own understanding. But these feelings and suggestions are such, and affect me in such a manner, that I cannot help receiving them, and trusting in them, and believing that their intimations are not fallacious, but such as I should approve if I were perfectly acquainted with every thing in the universe, and such as I may approve, and admit of, and regulate my conduct by, without danger of any inconvenience.

It is not easy on this subject to avoid identical expressions. I am not certain that I have been able to avoid them. And perhaps I might have expressed my meaning more shortly and more clearly, by saying, that I account that to be *truth* which the constitution of my nature determines me to believe, and that to be *falsehood* which the constitution of my nature determines me to disbelieve. Believing and disbelieving are simple acts of the mind; I can neither define nor describe them in words; and therefore the reader must judge of their nature from his own experience. We often believe what we afterwards find to be false; but while belief continues, we think it true; when we discover its falsity, we believe it no longer.

Hitherto we have used the word *belief* to denote that act of the mind which attends the perception of truth in general. But truths are of different kinds; some are certain, others only probable; and we ought not to call that act of the mind which attends the perception of certainty, and that which attends the perception of probability, by one and the same name. Some have called the former *conviction*, and the latter *assent*. All convictions are equally strong; but assent admits of innumerable degrees, from *moral certainty*, which is the highest degree, downward, through the several stages of *opinion*, to that suspense of judgement which is called *doubt*.[1]

We may, without absurdity, speak of probable truth, as well as of certain truth. Whatever a rational being is determined, by the constitution of his nature, to admit as probable, may be called *probable truth*; the acknowledgement of it is as universal as rational nature, and will be as permanent. But, in this inquiry, we propose to confine ourselves chiefly to that kind of truth which may be called certain, which enforces our *conviction*; and the belief of which, in a sound mind, is not tinctured with any doubt or uncertainty.

---

[1] [What Beattie says here, and in the next few paragraphs, is very much in the spirit of Book IV of Locke's *Essay concerning Human Understanding* ('Of Knowledge and Opinion').]

Of the Perception of Truth in General 29

The investigation and perception of truth is commonly ascribed to our rational faculties: and these have by some been reduced to two; reason, and judgement; the former being supposed to be conversant about certain truths, the latter chiefly about probabilities. But certain truths are not all of the same kind; some being supported by one sort of evidence, and others by another: different energies of the understanding must therefore be exerted in perceiving them; and these different energies must be expressed by different names, if we would speak of them distinctly and intelligibly. The certainty of some truths, for instance, is perceived intuitively; the certainty of others is perceived, not intuitively, but in consequence of a proof. Most of the propositions of Euclid are of the latter kind; the axioms of geometry are of the former. Now, if that faculty by which we perceive truth in consequence of a proof, be called *reason*, surely that power by which we perceive self-evident truth, ought to be distinguished by a different name. It is of little consequence what name we make choice of, provided that in choosing it we depart not from the analogy of language; and that, in applying it, we avoid equivocation and ambiguity. Some philosophers of note[2] have given the name of *Common Sense* to that faculty by which we perceive self-evident truth; and, as the term seems proper enough, we shall adopt it. But in a subject of this kind, there is great danger of our being imposed upon by words; we cannot therefore be too much upon our guard against that species of illusion. We propose to draw some important inferences from this doctrine of the distinction between Reason and Common Sense. Now these words are not always used in the strict signification we have here assigned them: let us therefore take a view of all the similar senses in which they are commonly used, and let us explain more particularly that sense in which we propose to use them; and thus we shall take every method in our power to secure ourselves against the impropriety of confounding our notions by the use of ambiguous and indefinite language. These philological discussions are indeed no

---

[2] [Beattie indicates that, in particular, he means French Jesuit Claude Buffier (1661–1737), author of *Traité des Premières Véritez et de la Source de nos Jugements* (*Treatise on First Truths and the Origins of our Judgements*) (1724), and Thomas Reid (1710–96), who published his *Inquiry into the Human Mind on the Principles of Common Sense* in 1764.]

part of philosophy; but they are very necessary to prepare us for it.

* * *

The word *reason* is used in several different senses. 1. It is used to signify that quality of human nature which distinguishes man from the inferior animals. Man is called a reasonable being, and the brutes are said to be irrational. But the faculty of reason, taking the word in a strict sense, is perhaps not more characteristical of the nature of man, than his moral faculty, or his imagination, or his power of artificial language, or his risibility. Reason, in this acceptation, seems to be a general name for all the intellectual powers, as distinguished from the sensitive part of our constitution. 2. Every thing that is called truth is sometimes said to be perceived by reason: by reason we are said to perceive, that the three angles of a triangle are equal to two right angles; and we are also said to perceive, by reason, that it is impossible for the same thing to be, and not to be. But these truths are of different kinds; and therefore the energies of understanding to which they are referred ought to be called by different names. 3. The power of invention is sometimes ascribed to reason. Thus Locke tells us, that it is reason which *discovers* and *arranges* the several intermediate proofs in an argument;[3] an office which, according to the common use of words, is to be referred, not to reason, but to imagination. 4. Reason, as implying a faculty not marked by any other name, is used by those who are most accurate in distinguishing, to signify that power of the human mind by which we draw inferences, or by which we are convinced, that a relation belongs to two ideas, on account of our having found, that these ideas bear certain relations to other ideas. In a word, it is that faculty which enables us, from relations or ideas that are known, to investigate such as are unknown; and without which we never could proceed in the discovery of truth a single step beyond first principles or intuitive axioms. And it is in this last sense we are to use the word *reason* in the course of this inquiry.

The term *common sense* is also used in several different significations. 1. Sometimes it seems to be synonymous with prudence.

---

[3] [See Locke, *Essay concerning Human Understanding*, IV.xvii.2.]

Thus we say, that a man possesses a large stock of common sense, who is quick in perceiving remote consequences, thence instantaneously determining concerning the propriety of present conduct. 2. Common sense, in certain instances, seems to be confounded with some of the powers of taste. We often meet with persons of strong sagacity in most of the ordinary affairs of life, and who are very capable of accurate reasoning, who yet, without any bad intention, commit the most egregious blunders with regard to decorum; both saying and doing what is offensive to their company, and inconsistent with their own character: and this we are apt to impute to a defect in common sense. But it seems rather to be owing to a defect in that kind of sensibility, or sympathy, by which we suppose ourselves in the situations of others, adopt their sentiments, and in a manner perceive their very thoughts; and which is indeed the foundation of good-breeding.[4] It is by this secret, and sudden, and (to those who are unacquainted with it) inexplicable, communication of feelings, that a man is enabled to avoid what would appear incongruous or offensive to others. They who are prompted by inclination, or obliged by necessity, to study the art of recommending themselves to others, acquire a wonderful facility in perceiving and avoiding all possible ways of giving offence; which is a proof, that this kind of sensibility may be much improved by habit: although there are, no doubt, in respect of this, as well as of all other modifications of perception, original and constitutional differences in the frame of different minds. 3. Some men are distinguished by an uncommon acuteness in discovering the characters of others: they seem to read the soul in the countenance, and with a single glance to penetrate the deepest recesses of the heart. In their presence, the hypocrite is detected, notwithstanding his specious outside; the gay effrontery of the coxcomb cannot conceal his insignificance; and the man of merit appears conspicuous under all the disguises of an unassuming and ungainly modesty. This talent is sometimes called *common sense*; but very improperly. It is far from being common; it is even exceedingly rare: it is to be found in men who are not remarkable for any other mental excellence; and we often see those who in other respects are judicious enough, quite

---

[4] See [Adam] Smith's *Theory of Moral Sentiments* [(1759)], Section 1 [('Of the Sense of Propriety')].

destitute of it. 4. Neither ought every common opinion to be referred to common sense. Modes in dress, religion, and conversation, however absurd in themselves, may suit the notions or the taste of a particular people: but none of us will say, that it is agreeable to common sense, to worship more gods that one; to believe that one and the same body may be in ten thousand different places at the same time;[5] to like a face the better because it is painted, or to dislike a person because he does not lisp in his pronunciation. Lastly, the term *common sense* has in modern times been used by philosophers both French and British, to signify that power of the mind which perceives truth, or commands belief, not by progressive argumentation, but by an instantaneous, instinctive, and irresistible impulse; derived neither from education nor from habit, but from nature; acting independently on our will, whenever its object is presented, according to an established law, and therefore properly called *sense*;[6] and acting in a similar manner upon all, or at least upon a great majority of mankind, and therefore properly called *common sense*. It is in this signification that the term *common sense* is used in the present inquiry.

That there is a real and essential difference between these two faculties; that common sense cannot be accounted for, by being called the perfection of reason, nor reason, by being resolved into common sense, will perhaps appear from the following remarks. 1. We are conscious, from internal feeling, that the energy of understanding which perceives intuitive truth, is different from that other energy which unites a conclusion with a first principle, by a gradual chain of intermediate relations. We believe the truth of an investigated conclusion, because we can assign a reason for our belief; we believe an intuitive principle, without being able to assign any other reason for our belief than this, that the law of our nature determines us to believe it, even as the law of our nature determines us to see a colour when presented to our open eyes at noonday. 2. We cannot discern any necessary connection between reason and common sense: they are indeed generally connected; but we can conceive a being endued with the one who is destitute of the other. Nay, we often find, that this is in fact the case. In

---

[5] [Beattie is alluding to the Catholic doctrine of transubstantiation.]

[6] For the circumstances that characterise a *sense*, see Dr [Alexander] Gerard's *Essay on Taste* [(1759)], Part 3, Sect. 1.

dreams, we sometimes reason without common sense. Through a defect of common sense, we adopt absurd principles; but supposing our principles true, our reasoning is often unexceptionable. The same thing may be observed in certain kinds of madness. A man who believes himself made of glass, may yet reason very justly concerning the means of preserving his supposed brittleness from flaws and fractures. Nay, what is still more to the purpose, we sometimes meet with persons, whom it would be injurious to charge with insanity, who, though defective in common sense, have yet, by conversing much with polemical writers, improved their reasoning faculty to such a degree, as to puzzle and put to silence those who are greatly their superiors in every other mental endowment. 3. This leads us to remark a third difference between these two faculties, namely, that the one is more in our power than the other. There are few faculties, either of our mind or body, more improvable by culture, than that of reasoning; whereas common sense, like other instincts, arrives at maturity with almost no care of ours. To teach the art of reasoning, or rather of wrangling, is easy; but it is impossible to teach common sense to one who wants it. You may make a man remember a set of first principles, and say that he believes them, even as you may teach one born blind to speak intelligibly of colours and light; but neither to the one, nor to the other, can you by any means communicate the peculiar feeling which accompanies the operation of that faculty which nature has denied him. A man defective in common sense may acquire learning; he may even possess genius to a certain degree: but the defect of nature he never can supply: a peculiar modification of scepticism, or credulity, or levity, will to the very end of his life distinguish him from other men. It would evidence a deplorable degree of irrationality, if a man could not perceive the truth of a geometrical axiom. Such instances are uncommon: but the number of self-evident principles cognizable by man is very great, and more vigour of mind may be necessary to the perception of some, than to the perception of others. In this respect, therefore, there may be great diversities in the measure of common sense which different men enjoy. Further, of two men, one of whom, though he acknowledges the truth of a first principle, is but little affected with it, and is easily induced to become sceptical in regard to it; while the other has a vivid perception of its truth, is deeply affected with it, and firmly trusts to his own feelings without doubt or hesitation; I should not scruple to say, that the latter possesses the greater share of common sense: and in this respect too, I presume the minds of different men will be found to be very different. These diversities are, I think, to be referred, for the most part, to the original constitution of the mind, which it is not in the power of education to alter. I acknowledge, however, that common sense, like other instincts, may languish for want of exercise; as in the case of a person who, blinded by a false religion, has been all his days accustomed to distrust his own sentiments, and to receive his creed from the mouth of a priest. I acknowledge also, that freedom of inquiry does generally produce a juster, as well as a more liberal, turn of thinking, than can ever be expected while men account it damnable even to think differently from the established mode. But from this we can only infer, that common sense is improvable to a certain degree. Or perhaps this only proves, that the dictates of common sense are sometimes over-ruled, and rendered ineffectual, by the influence of sophistry and superstition operating upon a pusillanimous and diffident temper. 4. It deserves also to be remarked, that a distinction extremely similiar to the present is acknowledged by the vulgar, who speak of mother-wit as something different from the deductions of reason, and the refinements of science. When puzzled with argument, they have recourse to their common sense, and acquiesce in it so steadily, as often to render all the arts of the logician ineffectual. 'I am confuted, but not convinced', is an apology sometimes offered, when one has nothing to oppose to the arguments of the antagonist, but the original undisguised feelings of his own mind. This apology is indeed very inconsistent with the dignity of philosophic pride; which, taking it for granted that nothing exceeds the limits of human capacity, professes to confute whatever it cannot believe, and, which is still more difficult, to believe whatever it cannot confute: but this apology may be perfectly consistent with sincerity and candour, and with that principle of which Pope says, that 'though no science, it is fairly worth the seven'.[7]

---

[7] ['Epistle to Burlington', l. 44.]

Of the Perception of Truth in General

Thus far we have endeavoured to distinguish and ascertain the separate provinces of *reason* and *common sense*. Their connection and mutual dependence, and the extent of their respective jurisdictions, we now proceed more particularly to investigate. — I ought perhaps to make an apology for these, and some other metaphorical expressions. And indeed it were to be wished, that in all matters of science, they could be laid aside; for the indiscreet use of them has done great harm, by leading philosophers to mistake verbal analogies for real ones; and often, too, by giving plausibility to nonsense, as well as by disguising and perplexing very plain doctrines with an affected pomp of high-sounding words and gaudy images. But in the philosophy of the human mind it is impossible to keep clear of metaphor, because we cannot speak intelligibly of immaterial things, without continual allusions to matter, and its qualities. All I need to say further on this head is, that I mean not by these metaphors to impose upon the reader, and that I shall do my utmost to prevent their imposing upon myself.

It is strange to observe, with what reluctance some people acknowledge the power of instinct. That man is governed by reason, and the brutes by instinct, is a favourite topic with some philosophers; who, like other froward children, spurn the hand that leads them, and desire, above all things, to be left at their own disposal. Were this boast founded in truth, it might be supposed to mean little more, than that man is governed by himself, and the brutes by their Maker.[8] But, luckily for man, it is not founded in truth, but in ignorance, inattention, and self-conceit. Our instincts, as well as our rational powers, are far superior, both in number and dignity, to those which the brutes enjoy; and it were well for us, on many occasions, if we laid our systems aside, and were more attentive in observing these impulses of nature in which reason has no part. Far be it from me to speak with disrespect of any of the gifts of God; every work of his is good; but the best things, when abused, may become pernicious. Reason is a noble faculty, and, when kept within its proper sphere, and applied to useful purposes, proves a means of exalting human creatures almost to the rank of superior beings. But this faculty

---

[8] 'And Reason raise o'er Instinct as you can, /In this 'tis God directs, in that 'tis Man' (Pope, *Essay on Man*, Epistle III, ll. 97–8).

has been much perverted, often to vile, and often to insignificant purposes; sometimes chained like a slave or malefactor, and sometimes soaring in forbidden and unknown regions. No wonder, then, if it has been frequently made the instrument of seducing and bewildering mankind, and of rendering philosophy contemptible.

In the science of body, glorious discoveries have been made by a right use of reason. When men are once satisfied to take things as they find them; when they believe Nature upon her bare declaration, without suspecting her of any design to impose upon them; when their utmost ambition is to be her servants and humble interpreters; then, and not till then, will philosophy prosper. But of those who have applied themselves to the science of Human Nature, it may truly be said, (of many of them at least), that too much reasoning hath made them mad. Nature speaks to us by our external, as well as by our internal, senses; it is strange, that we should believe her in the one case, and not in the other; it is most strange that supposing her fallacious, we should think ourselves capable of detecting the cheat. Common sense tells me, that the ground on which I stand is hard, material, and solid, and has a real, separate, independent existence. Berkeley and Hume tell me, that I am imposed upon in this matter: that the ground under my feet is really an idea in my mind; that its very essence consists in being perceived; and that the same instant it ceases to be perceived, it must also cease to exist: in a word, that *to be,* and *to be perceived*, when predicated of the ground, the sun, the starry heavens, or any corporeal object, signify precisely the same thing.[9] Now if my common sense be mistaken, who shall ascertain and correct the mistake? Our reason, it is said. Are then the inferences of reason in this instance clearer, and more decisive, than the dictates of common sense? By no means: I still trust to my common sense as before, and I feel that I must do so. But supposing the inferences of the one faculty as clear and decisive as the dictates of the other, yet who will assure me, that my reason is less

---

[9] [See Berkeley, *Principles of Human Knowledge*, Part I, Sections 1–4. In the *Enquiry concerning Human Understanding* Hume says that Berkeley's denials of material substances '*admit of no answer and produce no conviction*. Their only effect is to cause that momentary amazement and irresolution and confusion, which is the result of scepticism' (Section 12, Part 1; ed. Tom L. Beauchamp, Oxford: Clarendon Press, 2000, p. 116 fn.]

liable to mistake than my common sense? And if reason be mistaken, what shall we say? Is this mistake to be rectified by a second reasoning, as liable to mistake as the first? In a word, we must deny the distinction between truth and falsehood, adopt universal scepticism, and wander without end from one maze of error and uncertainty to another; a state of mind so miserable, that Milton makes it one of the torments of the damned;[10] — or else we must suppose, that one of these faculties is naturally of higher authority than the other; and that either reason ought to submit to common sense, or common sense to reason, whenever a variance happens between them. It has been said, that every inquiry in philosophy ought to begin with doubt; that nothing is to be taken for granted, and nothing believed, without proof.[11] If this be admitted, it must also be admitted, that reason is the ultimate judge of truth, to which common sense must continually act in subordination. But this I cannot admit; because I am able to prove the contrary by the most incontestable evidence. I am able to prove, that 'except we believe many things without proof, we never can believe any thing at all; for that all sound reasoning must ultimately rest on the principles of common sense, that is, on principles intuitively certain, or intuitively probable; and, consequently, that common sense is the ultimate judge of truth, to which reason must continually act in subordination'. — This I shall prove by a fair induction of particulars.

---

[10] [See *Paradise Lost*, Book II, ll. 555-69.]

[11] [Beattie is alluding to Descartes: see the first of the *Meditations*.]

Three

The Rise and Progress of Modern Scepticism

The Cartesian philosophy is to be considered as the ground-work of modern scepticism. The source of Locke's reasoning against the separate existence of the secondary qualities of matter, of Berkeley's reasoning against the existence of the material world, and of Hume's reasoning against the existence both of soul and body, may be found in the first part of the *Principia* of Descartes.[1] Yet nothing seems to have been further from the intention of this worthy and most ingenious philosopher, than to give countenance to error, irreligion, or licentiousness. He begins with doubting; but it is with a view to arrive at conviction: his successors (some of them at least) the further they advance in their systems, become more and more sceptical; and at length the reader is told, to his infinite pleasure and emolument, that the understanding, acting alone, does entirely subvert itself, and leaves not the lowest degree of evidence in any proposition whatsoever.[2]

---

[1] [Descartes's *Principles of Philosophy* was first published in Latin in 1644, and was translated into French in 1647. Part One contains a summary of the arguments put forward by Descartes in the *Meditations*. Presumably, Beattie alludes in particular to Descartes's deployment of the method of doubt.]

[2] [Beattie is quoting from Hume here: see the Conclusion to Book One of the *Treatise of Human Nature*: Norton and Norton (ed.), Oxford: Oxford University Press, p. 174. (All subsequent references to the *Treatise* will be to this edition.)]

The first thing a philosopher ought to do, according to Descartes, is to divest himself of all prejudices, and all his former opinions; to reject the evidence of sense, of intuition, and of mathematical demonstration; to suppose, that there is no God, nor heaven, nor earth; and that we have neither hands, nor feet, nor body; in a word, he is to doubt of every thing of which it is possible to doubt, and to be persuaded, that every thing is false which can possibly be conceived to be doubtful. Now there is only one point of which it is impossible to doubt, namely, that I, the person who doubts, am thinking. This proposition, therefore, *I think*, and this only, may be taken for granted; and nothing else whatsoever is to be believed without proof.

What is to be expected from this strange introduction? One or other of these two things must necessarily follow. This author will either believe nothing at all; or if he believe any thing, it must be upon the recommendation of false and sophistical reasoning. But Descartes is no sceptic in his moral reasonings: therefore, in his moral reasonings, he must be a sophister. Let us see whether we can make good this charge against him by facts.

Taking it for granted that he thinks, he thence infers, that he exists: *Ego cogito, ergo sum*. Now there cannot be thought where there is no existence; before he take it for granted that he thinks, he must also take it for granted that he exists. This argument therefore proceeds on a supposition, that the thing to be proved is true; in other words, it is a sophism, a *petitio principii*. Even supposing it possible to conceive thinking, without at the same time conceiving existence, still this is no conclusive argument, except it could be shown, that it is more evident to a man that he thinks, than that he exists; for in every true proof, a less evident proposition is inferred from one that is more evident. But, *I think,* and, *I exist,* are equally evident. Therefore this is no true proof. To set an example of false reasoning in the very foundation of a system, can hardly fail to have bad consequences.

Having in this manner established his own existence, our author next proceeds to prove the veracity of his faculties; that is, to show, by reasoning, that what he thinks true is really true, and that what he thinks false is really false. He would have done better to have taken this also for granted: the argument by which he attempts to prove it, does more honour to his heart than to his understanding. It is indeed a sophism of the same kind with the former, in which he takes that for granted which he proposes to prove. It runs thus. We are conscious, that we have in our minds the idea of a being infinitely perfect, intelligent, and powerful, necessarily existent, and eternal. This idea differs from all our other ideas in two respects: it implies the notions of eternal and necessary existence, and of infinite perfection; it neither is, nor can be, a fiction of the imagination; and therefore exhibits no chimera or imaginary being, but a true and immutable nature, which must of necessity exist, because necessary existence is comprehended in the idea of it. Therefore there is a God, necessarily existent, infinitely wise, powerful, and true, and possessed of all perfection. This Being is the maker of us and of all our faculties; he cannot deceive, because he is infinitely perfect; therefore our faculties are true, and not fallacious . . .

I object not to this argument for the divine existence, drawn from the idea of an all-perfect being, of which the human mind is conscious; though perhaps it is not the most unexceptionable method of evincing that great truth. I allow, that when a man believes a God, he cannot, without absurdity and impiety, deny or question the veracity of his own faculties; and that to acknowledge a distinction between truth and falsehood, implies a persuasion, that certain laws are established in the universe, on which the natures of all created things depend, which (to me at least) is incomprehensible, except on the supposition of a supreme, intelligent, directing cause. But I acquiesce in these principles, because I take the veracity of my faculties for granted; and this I feel myself necessitated to do, because I feel it to be the law of my nature, which I cannot possibly counteract. Proceeding then upon this innate and irresistible notion, that my faculties are true, I infer, by the justest reasoning, that God exists; and the evidence for this great truth is so clear and convincing, that I cannot withstand its force, if I believe anything else whatsoever.

Descartes argues in a different manner. Because God exists, (says he), and is perfect, therefore my faculties are true. Right. — But how do you know that God exists? I infer it from the second principle of my philosophy, already established, *Cogito, ergo sum*. — How do you know that your inference is just? It satisfies my reason. — Your argument proceeds on a supposition, that what satisfies your reason is true? It does. — Do you not then take it for granted, that your reason is not a fallacious, but a true faculty? This must be taken for granted, otherwise the argument is good for nothing. — And if so, your argument proceeds on a supposition, that the point to be proved is true. In a word, you pretend to prove the truth of our natural faculties, by an argument which evidently and necessarily supposes their truth. Your philosophy is built on sophisms; how then can it be according to common sense?

As this philosopher doubted where he ought to have been confident, so he is often confident where he ought to doubt. He admits not his own existence, till he thinks he has proved it; yet his system is replete with hypotheses taken for granted, without proof, almost without examination. He sets out with the profession of universal scepticism; but many of his theories are founded in the most unphilosophical credulity. Had he taken a little more for granted, he would have proved a great deal more: he takes almost nothing for granted, (I speak of what he professes, not of what he performs); and therefore he proves nothing. In geometry, however, he is rational and ingenious; there are some curious remarks in his discourse on the passions; his physics are fanciful and plausible; his treatise on music perspicuous, though superficial: a lively imagination seems to have been his chief talent, want of knowledge in the grounds of evidence his principal defect.

We are informed by Father Malebranche, that the senses were at first as honest faculties as one could desire to be endued with, till after they were debauched by original sin; an adventure, from which they contracted such an invincible propensity to cheating, that they are now continually lying in wait to deceive us.[3] But there is in man, it seems, a certain clear-sighted, stout, old faculty, called *reason*, which, without being deceived by appearances, keeps an eye upon the rogues, and often proves too cunning for them. Malebranche therefore advises us to doubt with all our might. 'If a man has only learned to doubt', says he, 'let him not

[3] [Beattie is referring to the discussion of the senses in Book One of Nicolas Malebranche's *Search after Truth* (1674–5). In fact, Malebranche argues that our senses 'are not as corrupt as might be imagined': it is, rather, the human will that was perverted by Adam's sin (see I.v.2-3: Malebranche, *The Search after Truth*, ed. and trans. Thomas M. Lennon and Paul J. Olscamp, Cambridge: Cambridge University Press, 1997, pp. 19-24).]

imagine that he has made an inconsiderable progress'.[4] Progress! In what? — In science? Is it not a contradiction, or at least an inconsistency, in terms, to say that a man makes progress in science by doubting? If one were to ask the way to Dublin, and to receive for answer, that he ought first of all to sit down; for that if he had only learned to sit still, he might be assured, that he had made no inconsiderable progress in his journey; I suppose he would hardly trouble his informer with a second question.

It is true, this author makes a distinction between the doubts of passion, brutality, and blindness, and those of prudence, distrust, and penetration: the former, says he, are the doubts of Academics and Atheists; the latter are the doubts of the true philosopher. It is true also, that he allows us to give an entire consent to the things that appear entirely evident. But he adopts, notwithstanding, the principles of Descartes' first philosophy; that we ought to begin our enquiries with universal doubt, taking only our own consciousness for granted, and thence inferring our existence, and the existence of God, and proving, from the divine veracity, that our faculties are not fallacious. Wherever it is possible that a deluding spirit may deceive us, there, says Malebranche, we ought to doubt; but a deluding spirit may deceive us wherever our memory is employed in reasoning; therefore, in all such reasonings, there may be error. In a word, there may be error in reasoning of every kind; for without memory there can be no reasoning: but in the truths discovered by a single glance, such as this; that two and two make four, it is not possible, he says, for a deluding god, however powerful, to deceive him. — It is easy to see, that such doctrines must lead either to sophistry, or to universal scepticism, or rather to both. For if a demonstrated conclusion may be false for any thing I know to the contrary, an axiom may be so too: my belief of the first is not less necessary than my belief of the last. Intuition is, of all evidence, the clearest, and most immediately convincing; but demonstration produces absolute certainty, and full conviction, in the mind of him who understands it. — Malebranche, indeed, acknowledges, that we may reason when once we know that God is no deceiver: but this, he says, must be known at one glance, (that is, I suppose, intuitively), or it

---

[4] *Search after Truth* I.xx.3 (Lennon and Olscamp ed. and trans., p. 86).

cannot be known at all; for all reasoning on this subject may be fallacious.

But I do not pretend to unfold all the false and sceptical principles of this author's philosophy. To confess the truth, I do not well understand it. He is generally mystical, often, if I mistake not, self-contradictory; and his genius is strangely warped by a superstitious veneration for the absurdities of Popery. He rejects the evidence of sense, because it seems repugnant to his reason; he admits the truth of transubstantiation, though certainly repugnant both to reason and sense. Of Aristotle, and Seneca, and the other ancient philosophers, he says, that their lights are nothing but thick darkness, and their most illustrious virtues nothing but intolerable pride. Fy, M. Malebranche! Popery, with all its absurdities, requires not from it adherents so uncandid, and so illiberal, a declaration.... If Descartes, and his disciple Malebranche, had studied the ancients more, and indulged their own imagination less, they would have made a better figure in philosophy, and done much more service to mankind. But it was their aim to decry the ancients as much as possible: and ever since their time, it has been too much the fashion, to overlook the discoveries of former ages, as altogether unnecessary for advancing the improvement of the present. Malebranche often inveighs against Aristotle, in particular, with the most virulent bitterness; and affects, on all occasions, to treat him with supreme contempt. Had this great ancient employed his genius in the subversion of virtue, or in establishing tenets incompatible with the principles of natural religion, he would have deserved the severest censure. But Malebranche lays nothing of this kind to his charge; he only finds him guilty of some speculative errors in natural philosophy. Aristotle was not exempted from that fallibility which is incident to human nature; yet it would not be amiss, if our modern wits would study him a little, before they venture to decide so positively on his abilities and character. It is observable, that he is most admired by those who best understand him. Now, the contrary is true of our modern sceptics: they are most admired by those who read them least, and who take their characters upon trust, as they find them delivered in coffeehouses and drawing-rooms, and other places of fashionable conversation, whose doctrines do so much honour to the virtue and good sense of this enlightened age.

* * *

Nothing was further from the intention of Locke, than to encourage verbal controversy, or advance doctrines favourable to scepticism. To do good to mankind, by enforcing virtue, illustrating truth, and vindicating liberty, was his sincere purpose: and he did not labour in vain. His writings are to be reckoned among the few books, that have been productive of real utility to mankind. But candour obliges me to remark, that some of his tenets seem to be too rashly admitted, for the sake of a favourite hypothesis. That some of them have promoted scepticism, is undeniable. He seems indeed to have been sensible, that there were inaccuracies in his work; and candidly owns, that 'some hasty and indigested thoughts on a subject never before considered, gave the first entrance to his *Essay*; which, being begun by chance, was continued by entreaty, written by incoherent parcels, and after long intervals of neglect resumed again, as humour or occasion permitted'.[5]

The first book of his *Essay*, which, with submission, I think the worst, tends to establish this dangerous doctrine; that the human mind, previous to education and habit, is as susceptible of any one impression as of any other: a doctrine which, if true, would go near to prove, that truth and virtue are no better that human contrivances; or, at least, that they have nothing permanent in their nature, but may be as changeable as the inclinations and capacities of men; and that, as we understand the term, there is no such thing as common sense in the world. Surely this is not the doctrine that Locke meant to establish; but his zeal against innate ideas, and innate principles, put him off his guard, and made him allow too little to instinct, for fear of allowing too much. This controversy, so far as it regards moral sentiment, we have examined in another place.[6] At present we would only observe, that if truth be any thing permanent, which it must be if it be any thing at all, those perceptions or impulses of understanding by which we become conscious of it, must be equally permanent; which they

---

[5] John Locke, *An Essay concerning Human Understanding*, ed. Peter Nidditch, Oxford: Clarendon Press, 1975, p. 7.
[6] [In a footnote to the *Elements of Moral Science*, Beattie says he wrote a treatise 'on the universality of moral sentiment' in 1767. The work was never published, but its 'general principles' are contained in Selection 9.]

could not be, if they depended on education, and if there were not a law of nature, independent of man, which determines the understanding in some cases to believe, in others to disbelieve. Is it possible to imagine, that any course of education could ever bring a rational creature to believe, that two and two are equal to three, that he is not the same person today he was yesterday, that the ground he stands on does not exist? Could make him disbelieve the testimony of his own senses, or that of other men? Could make him expect unlike events in like circumstances? Or that the course of nature, of which he has hitherto had experience, will be changed, even when he foresees no cause to hinder its continuance? I can no more believe, that education could produce such a depravity of judgement, than that education could make me see all human bodies in an inverted position, or hear with my nostrils, or take pleasure in burning and cutting my flesh. Why should not our judgements concerning truth be acknowledged to result from a bias impressed upon the mind by its Creator, as well as our desire of self-preservation, our love of society, our resentment of injury, our joy in the possession of good? If these judgements be not instinctive, I should be glad to know how they come to be universal: the modes of sentiment and behaviour produced by education are uniform only where education is uniform; but there are many truths which have obtained universal acknowledgement in all ages and nations. If these judgements be not instinctive, I should be glad to know how men find it so difficult, or rather impossible, to lay them aside. The false opinions we imbibe from habit and education, may be, and often are, relinquished by those who make a proper use of their reason; and the man who thus renounces his former prejudices, upon conviction of their falsity, is applauded by all as a man of candour, sense, and spirit; but if one were to suffer himself to be argued out of his common sense the whole world would pronounce him a fool.

The substance, or at least the foundation, of Berkeley's argument against the existence of matter, may be found in Locke's Essay, and in the *Principia* of Descartes. And if this argument be conclusive, it proves that to be false which every man must necessarily believe every moment of his life to be true, and that to be true which no man since the foundation of the world was ever capable of believing for a single moment. Berkeley's doctrine attacks the most incontestable dictates of common sense; and pretends to demonstrate, that the clearest, most decisive, and most general, principles of conviction, are certainly fallacious.

Mr Hume, more subtle, and less reserved, than any of his predecessors, has gone still greater lengths in the demolition of common sense; and in its place has reared a most tremendous fabric of doctrine; upon which, if it were not for the flimsiness of its materials, engines might easily be erected, sufficient to overturn all belief, science, religion, virtue, and society, from the very foundation. He calls this work, *A Treatise of Human Nature; being an Attempt to Introduce the Experimental Method of Reasoning into Moral Subjects*. This is, in the style of Edmund Curll, a taking title-page;[7] but alas! 'Fronti nulla fides [Place no trust in appearances]!' The whole of this author's system is founded on a false hypothesis taken for granted; and whenever a fact contradictory to that false hypothesis occurs to his observation, he either denies it, or labours hard to explain it away. This, it seems, in his judgement, is experimental reasoning: in mine, it is just the reverse.

He begins his book with affirming: that all the perceptions of the human mind resolve themselves into two classes; impressions, and ideas; that the latter are all copied from the former; and that an idea differs from its correspondent impression only in being a weaker perception. Thus, when I sit by the fire, I have an impression of heat, and I can form an idea of heat when I am shivering cold; in the one case I have a stronger perception of heat, in the other a weaker. Is there any warmth in this idea of heat? There must, according to Mr Hume's doctrine; only the warmth of the idea is not quite so strong as that of the impression. For this profound author repeats it again and again, that an idea is by its very nature weaker and fainter than an impression, but is in every other respect (not only similiar, but) the same.[8] Nay, he goes further, and says, that whatever is true of the one must be acknowledged concerning the other;[9] and he is so confident of the truth of this maxim, that he makes it one of the pillars of his philosophy.

---

[7] [Edmund Curll (1675–1747) was an English bookseller notorious for publishing obscene books. He is satirized by Pope in Book II of *The Dunciad*.]

[8] *Treatise of Human Nature*, I.iii.1 (p. 52).

[9] *Treatise of Human Nature*, I.i.7 (p. 18).

To those who may be inclined to admit this maxim on his authority, I would propose a few plain questions. Do you feel any, even the least, warmth in the idea of a bonfire, a burning mountain, or the general conflagration? Do you feel more real cold in Virgil's Scythian winter, than in Milton's description of the flames of hell? Do you acknowledge that to be true of the idea of eating, which is certainly true of the impression of it, that it alleviates hunger, fills the belly, and contributes to the support of human life? If you answer these questions in the negative, you deny one of the fundamental principles of Mr Hume's philosophy. We have, it is true, a livelier perception of a friend when we see him, than when we think of him in his absence. But this is not all: every person of a sound mind knows, that in the one case we believe, and are certain, that the object exists, and is present with us; in the other we believe, and are certain, that the object is not present. This, however, Mr Hume must deny; for he maintains, that an idea differs from an impression only in being weaker, and in no other respect whatsoever.

That every idea should be a copy and resemblance of the impression whence it is derived; — that, for example, the idea of red should be a red idea; the idea of a roaring lion should be a roaring idea; the idea of an ass, a hairy, long-eared, sluggish idea, patient of labour, and much addicted to thistles; that the idea of extension should be extended, and that of solidity solid; — that a thought of the mind should be endued with all, or any, of the qualities of matter, — is, in my judgement, inconceivable and impossible. Yet Mr Hume takes it for granted; and it is another of his fundamental maxims. Such is the credulity of Scepticism!

If every idea be an exact resemblance of its correspondent impression, (or object; for these terms, according to this author, amount to the same thing);[10] — if the idea of whiteness be white, of solidity solid, and of extension extended, as the same author allows;[11] — then the idea of a line the shortest that sense can perceive, must be equal in length to the line itself; for if shorter, it would be imperceptible; and it will not be said, either that an imperceptible idea can be perceived, or that the idea of an imper-

---

[10] *Treatise of Human Nature*, I.iv.2 (p. 138).
[11] *Treatise of Human Nature*, I.iv.5 (p. 157).

ceptible object can be formed: — consequently the idea of a line a hundred times as long, must be a hundred times as long as the former idea; for if shorter, it would be the idea, not of this, but of some other shorter line. And so it clearly follows, nay it admits of mathematical demonstration, that the idea of an inch is really an inch long; and that of a mile, a mile long. In a word, every idea of any particular extension is equal in length to the extended object. The same reasoning holds good in regard to the other dimensions of breadth and thickness. All ideas, therefore, of solid objects, are (according to Hume's philosophy) equal in magnitude and solidity to the objects themselves. Now mark the consequences. I am just now in an apartment containing a thousand cubic feet, being ten feet square, and ten high; the door and windows are shut, as well as my eyes and ears. Mr Hume will allow, that, in this situation, I may form ideas, not only of the visible appearance, but also of the real tangible magnitude of the whole house, of a first-rate man of war, of St Paul's cathedral, or even of a much larger object. But the solid magnitude of these ideas is equal to the solid magnitude of the objects from which they are copied: therefore I have now present with me an idea, that is, a solid extended thing, whose dimensions extend to a million cubic feet at least. The question now is, where is this thing placed? For a place it certainly must have, and a pretty large one too. I should answer, in my mind; for I know not where else the ideas of my mind can be so conveniently deposited. Now my mind is lodged in a body of no extraordinary dimensions, and my body is contained in a room ten feet square and ten feet high. It seems then, that, into this room, I have it in my power at pleasure to introduce a solid object a thousand, or ten thousand, times larger than the room itself. I contemplate it a while, and then, by another volition, send it packing, to make way for another object of equal or superior magnitude. Nay, in no larger vehicle than a common post-chaise, I can transport from one end of the kingdom to the other, a building equal to the largest Egyptian pyramid, and a mountain as big as Etna, or the peak of Tenerife. — Take care, ye disciples of Hume, and be very well advised before you reject this mystery as impossible and incomprehensible. It is geometrically deduced from the principles, nay from the first principles, of your master. By denying this, you give his system such a stab as it cannot possibly survive.

Say, you candid and intelligent, what are we to expect from a logical and systematic treatise, founded on a supposition, that a part may be ten or a hundred thousand times greater than the whole? Shall we expect truth? Then it must be inferred by false reasoning. — Shall we expect sound reasoning? Then surely the inferences must be false. — Indeed, though I cannot much admire this author's sagacity on the present occasion, I must confess myself not a little astonished at his courage. A witch going to sea in an egg-shell, or preparing to take a trip through the air on a broomstick, would really be a surprising phenomenon; but it is nothing to Mr Hume, on such a bottom, 'launching out (as he somewhere expresses it) into the immense depths of philosophy'.[12]

To multiply examples for the confutation of so glaring an absurdity, is really ridiculous. I therefore leave it to the reader to determine, whether, if this doctrine of solid and extended ideas be true, it will not follow, that the idea of a roaring lion must emit audible sound, almost, if not altogether, as loud, and as terrible, as the royal beast in person could exhibit; — that two ideal bottles of brandy will intoxicate as far at least as two genuine bottles of wine; — and that I must be greatly hurt if not dashed to pieces, if I am so imprudent, as to form only the idea of a bomb bursting under my feet. For hath not our author said, that 'impressions and ideas comprehend all the perceptions (or objects) of the human mind; that whatsoever is true of the one must be acknowledged concerning the other; nay, that they are in every respect the same, except that the former strike with more force than the latter?'

The absurdity and inconceivableness of the distinction between objects and perceptions, is another of our author's capital doctrines. 'Philosophers', says he, 'have distinguished between objects, and perceptions of the senses: but this distinction is not comprehended by the generality'.[13] Now how are we to

---

[12] [*Treatise of Human Nature*, I.iv.7 (p. 171).]

[13] *Treatise of Human Nature*, I.iv.2 (pp. 134, 139). The word *perception* (and the same is true of the words *sensation, smell, taste,* and many others) has, in common language, two, and sometimes three, distinct significations. It means, 1. The thing perceived. Thus we speak of the *taste* of a fig, the

know, whether this distinction be conceived and acknowledged by the generality? If we put the question to any of them, we shall find it no easy matter to make ourselves understood, and, after all, perhaps be laughed at for our pains. Shall we reason *a priori* about their sentiments and comprehensions? This is often Mr Hume's method; but it is neither philosophical nor fair. Will you allow me to reckon myself one of the generality? Then I declare, for my own part, that I do comprehend and acknowledge this distinction, and have done so ever since I was capable of reflection. I remember, when a child, to have had my fingers scorched with burning coals, and stung by bees: but I never confounded the object with the perception; I never thought that the pain I felt could either make honey or melt lead. — The instance, you say, is somewhat equivocal. — Well, then, I hope the following is explicit enough.

Suppose me to address the common people in these words: 'I see a strange sight a little way off; but my sight is weak, so that I see it imperfectly; let me go nearer, that I may have a more distinct sight of it'. — If the generality of mankind be at all incapable of distinguishing between the object and the perception, this incapacity will doubtless discover itself most, when ambiguous words are used on purpose to confound their ideas; if their ideas on this subject are not confounded even by ambiguous language, there is reason to think, that they are extremely clear, distinct, and accurate. Now I have here proposed a sentence, in which there is a studied ambiguity of language; and yet I maintain, that every person of common sense, who understands English, will instantly, on hearing these words, perceive, that by the word *sight* I mean, in the first clause, the thing seen; in the second, the power, or per-

---

smell of a rose. 2. The power or faculty perceiving; as when we say, 'I have lost my *smell* by a severe cold, and therefore my *taste* is not so quick as usual'. 3. It sometimes denotes that impulse or impression which is communicated to the mind by the external object operating upon it through the organ of sensation. Thus we speak of a *sweet* or *bitter taste,* a *distinct* or *confused,* a *clear* or *obscure, sensation* or *perception.* Most of our sceptical philosophers have either been ignorant of, or inattentive to, this distinction: Malebranche, indeed, seems to have had some notion of it; but either I do not understand this author, or there is a strange obscurity and want of precision in almost every thing he says. Mr Hume's philosophy does not allow this to be a rational distinction; so that it is impossible to know precisely what he means by the word *perception* in this and many other places. I have proved, however, that this assertion is false, whatever sense (consistent with common use) we affix to the word.

haps the organ, of seeing; in the third, the perception itself, as distinguished both from the percipient faculty, and from the visible object.[14] If one of the multitude, on hearing me pronounce this sentence, were to reply as follows; 'The sight is not at all strange; it is a man on horseback: but your sight must needs be weak, as you are lately recovered from sickness: however, if you wait a little till the man and horse, which are now in the shade, come into the sunshine, you will then have a much more distinct sight of them': — I would ask: is the study of any part of philosophy necessary to make a man comprehend the meaning of these two sentences? Is there any thing absurd or unintelligible either in the former or in the latter? Is there any thing in the reply, that seems to exceed the capacity of the vulgar, and supposes them to be more acute than they really are? If there be not, and I am certain there is not, here is

---

[14] To every person of common sense this distinction is in reality and practice quite familiar. But as the words we use in expressing it are of ambiguous signification, it is not easy to write about it so as to be immediately understood by every reader. The thing seen or perceived is something permanent and external, and is believed to exist whether perceived or not; the faculty of seeing or perceiving is also something permanent in the mind, and is believed to exist whether exerted or not: but what I here call *the perception itself* is temporary, and is conceived to have no existence but in the mind that perceives it, and to exist no longer than while it is perceived; for in being perceived, its very essence does consist: so that *to be*, and *to be perceived*, when predicated of it, do mean precisely the same thing. Thus, I just now see this paper, which I call the external object: I turn away, or shut my eyes, and then I see it no longer, but I still believe it to exist; though buried an hundred fathoms deep in the earth, or left in an uninhabitable island, its existence would be as real, as if it were gazed at by ten thousand men. Again, when I shut my eyes, or tie a bandage over them, or go into a dark place, I see no longer; that is, my faculty of seeing exerts itself, or is acted upon, no longer; but I still believe it to remain in my mind, ready to act, or to be acted upon, whenever it is again placed in the proper circumstances; for no body supposes that by shutting our eyes, or going into a dark place, we annihilate our faculty of seeing. But, thirdly, my *perception* of this paper is no permanent thing; nor has it any existence, but while it is perceived; nor does it at all exist but in the mind that perceives it: I can put an end to, or annihilate it, whenever I please, by shutting my eyes; and I can at pleasure renew it again by opening them. — It is really astonishing, that so many of our modern philosophers should have overlooked a distinction, which is of so great importance, that if we were unacquainted with it, a great part of human language would seem to be perfect nonsense. Such an oversight would be unpardonable in a dictionary-maker; but, I know not how it is, some of our philosophers have been admired and celebrated for their acumen in committing it.

an unquestionable proof, that the vulgar, and indeed all men whom metaphysic has not deprived of their senses, do distinguish between the object perceived, the faculty perceiving, and the perception or impulse communicated by the external object to the mind through the organ of sensation. What though all the three are sometimes expressed by the same name? This only shows, that accuracy of language is not always necessary for answering the common purposes of life. If the ideas of the vulgar are sufficiently distinct notwithstanding, what shall we say of that philosopher, whose ideas are really confounded by this inaccuracy, and who, because there is no difference in the signs, imagines that there is none in the things signified! That the understanding of such a philosopher is not a vulgar one, will be readily allowed; whether it exceeds, or falls short, let the reader determine.[15] This author's method of investigation is no less

---

[15] Mr Hume is not always consistent with himself in affirming, that the vulgar do not comprehend the distinction between perceptions and objects. 'It is not', he says, 'by arguments, that children, peasants, and the greatest part of mankind, are induced to attribute objects to some impressions, and deny them to others' [*Treatise of Human Nature*, I.iv.2 (p. 129)]. — So! it seems the greatest part of mankind do acknowledge a distinction between objects and perceptions. 'Accordingly we find, that all the conclusions which the vulgar form on this head, are directly contrary to those which are confirmed by philosophy'. — The more shame to that philosophy! say I. — 'For philosophy informs us, that every thing which appears to the mind, is nothing but a perception, and is interrupted, and dependent on the mind; whereas the vulgar confound perceptions and objects', — that is, I suppose, do not distinguish the former from the latter. — How! In the last sentence it was said, that the greatest part of mankind do distinguish between impressions (which are a species of perceptions) and objects, — 'and attribute a distinct continued existence to the very things they feel or see'. — So, now again the objects have a distinct continued existence; that is, are something different from perceptions, which every body knows have no continued existence. Here Mr Hume, within the compass of half a page, contradicts himself, and contradicts that contradiction, and finally acquiesces in the first contradiction. To hunt such a writer through so many shiftings and doublings, is not worth the reader's while nor mine. I hope we both know how to employ our time to better purpose. How often our author may affirm and deny, and deny and affirm, this doctrine, in the course of his work, I neither know nor care: it is certain, that, upon the whole, he holds the distinction between objects and perceptions to be *unreasonable,* (p. 129), *unphilosophical,* (p. 129), and *unsupported by the evidence of sense,* (p. 126). — And indeed, when this distinction, as we have explained it, is acknowledged, and attended to,

extraordinary than his fundamental principles. There are many notions in the human mind, of which it is not easy perhaps to explain the origin. If you can describe in words what were the circumstances in which you received an impression of any particular notion, it is well; Mr Hume will allow, that you may form an idea of it. But if you cannot do this, then, says he, there is no such notion in your mind; for all perceptions are either impressions or ideas, and it is not possible for us so much as to conceive anything specifically different from ideas and impressions;[16] now all ideas are copied from impressions; therefore you can have no idea nor conception of any thing of which you have not received an impression. — All mankind have a notion of power or energy. No, says Mr Hume; and impression of power or energy was never received by any man, and therefore an idea of it can never be formed in the human mind. If you insist on your experience and consciousness of power, it is all a mistake; his hypothesis admits not the idea of power, and therefore there is no such idea.[17] — All mankind have an idea of self. That I deny, says Mr Hume; I maintain, that no man ever had, or can have, an impression of self; and therefore no man can form any idea of it.[18] If you persist, and say, that certainly you have some notion or idea of yourself: — My dear Sir, says he, you do not consider, that this assertion contradicts my hypothesis of impressions and ideas; how then is it possible it should be true! This, it seems, is experimental reasoning!

But though Mr Hume deny, that I have any notion of self, surely he does not mean to affirm, that I do not exist, or that I have no notion of myself as an existent being. In truth, it is not easy to say what he means on this subject. Most philosophical subjects become obscure in the hands of this author; for he has a notable talent at puzzling his readers and himself: but when he treats of consciousness, of personal identity, and of the nature of the soul, he expresses himself so strangely, that his words either have no

---

all Berkeley's pretended demonstration of the non-existence of matter, and all Hume's reasonings against the existence of both matter and spirit, appear to be no better than a play upon words. For this key unlocks that whole mystery of sophism and quibble.

[16] *Treatise of Human Nature*, I.ii.6 (p. 49).

[17] *Treatise of Human Nature*, I.iii.14 (p. 108).

[18] *Treatise of Human Nature*, I.iv.6 (p. 164).

meaning, or imply a contradiction. 'The question', says he 'concerning the substance of the soul is unintelligible'.[19] — Well, Sir, if you think so, you may let it alone. — No; that must not be neither. 'What we call a *mind*, is nothing but a heap or collection of different perceptions (or objects) united together by certain relations, and supposed, though falsely, to be endowed with perfect simplicity and identity.[20] — If any one, upon serious and unprejudiced reflection, thinks he has a different notion of himself, I must confess I can reason with him no longer. All I can allow him is, that he may be in the right as well as I, and that we are essentially different in this particular. He may perhaps perceive something simple and continued, which he calls *himself*; though I am certain there is no such principle in me. But setting aside some metaphysicians of this kind', — that is, who feel and believe, that they have a soul, — 'I may venture to affirm of the rest of mankind, that they are nothing but a bundle or collection of different perceptions, which succeed each other with inconceivable rapidity, and are in a perpetual flux and movement. — There is properly no simplicity in the mind at one time, nor identity in different [times], whatever natural propension we may have to imagine that simplicity and identity. — They are the successive perceptions only that constitute the mind'.[21]

If these words have any meaning, it is this: My soul (or rather that which I call my soul) is not one simple thing, nor is it the same thing today it was yesterday; nay, it is not the same this moment as it was the last; it is nothing but a mass, collection, heap, or bundle, of different perceptions, or objects, that fleet away in succession, with inconceivable rapidity, perpetually changing, and perpetually in motion. There may be some metaphysicians to whose souls this description cannot be applied; but I (Mr Hume) am certain, that this is a true and complete description of my soul, and of the soul of every other individual of the human race, those few metaphysicians excepted.

That body has no existence, but as a bundle of perceptions, whose existence consists in their being perceived, our author all

---

[19] *Treatise of Human Nature*, I.iv.5 (p. 163).
[20] *Treatise of Human Nature*, I.iv.2 (p. 137).
[21] *Treatise of Human Nature*, I.iv.6 (pp. 164–5).

along maintains. He now affirms, that the soul, in like manner, is a bundle of perceptions, and nothing else. It follows, then, that there is nothing in the universe but impressions and ideas; all possible perceptions being comprehended in those two classes. This philosophy admits of no other existence whatsoever, not even of a percipient being to perceive these perceptions. So that we are now arrived at the height of human wisdom, that intellectual eminence, from whence there is a full prospect of all that we can reasonably believe to exist, and of all that can possibly become the object of our knowledge. Alas! What has become of the magnificence of external nature, and the wonders of intellectual energy, the immortal beauties of truth and virtue, and the triumphs of a good conscience! Where now the warmth of benevolence, the fire of generosity, the exultations of hope, the tranquil ecstasy of devotion, and the pang of sympathetic delight! All, around, above, and beneath, is one vast inanity, or rather an enormous chaos, encompassed with darkness universally and eternally impenetrable. Body and spirit are utterly annihilated; and there remains nothing (for we must again descend into the gibberish of metaphysic) but a vast collection, bundle, mass, or heap, of unperceived perceptions.

Such, if Mr Hume's words have any meaning, is the result of his system. And what is this result? If he or his admirers can prove, that there is a possibility of expressing it in words which do not imply a contradiction, I will not call it nonsense. If he or they can prove, that it is compatible with any one acknowledged truth in philosophy, in morals, in religion natural or revealed, I will not call it impious. If he or they can prove, that it does not arise *from common facts misrepresented,* and *common words misunderstood,* I shall admit that it may have arisen from accurate observation, candid and liberal inquiry, perfect knowledge of human nature, and the enlarged views of true philosophic genius.

Four

On the Origins of the 'Essay on Truth'

A Letter to Thomas Blacklock[1]

... Perhaps you are anxious to know what first induced me to write on this subject; I will tell you as briefly as I can. In my younger days I read chiefly for the sake of amusement, and I found myself best amused with the classics, and what we call the *belles lettres*. Metaphysics I disliked; mathematics pleased me better; but I found my mind neither improved nor gratified by that study. When Providence allotted me my present station, it became incumbent on me to read what had been written on the subject of morals and human nature: the works of Locke, Berkeley, and Hume, were celebrated as masterpieces in this way; to them, therefore, I had recourse. But as I began to study them with great prejudices in their favour, you will readily conceive how strangely I was surprised to find them, as I thought, replete with absurdities: I pondered these absurdities; I weighed the arguments, with which I was sometimes not a little confounded; and the result was, that I began at last to suspect my own understanding, and to think that I had not capacity for such a study. For I could not conceive it possible that the absurdities of these authors were so great as they seemed to me to be; otherwise, thought I, the

---

[1] [This letter is dated 9 January, 1769. Thomas Blacklock was an author and poet, blind from birth, whom Beattie had befriended in 1765. They remained friends until Blacklock's death in 1792.]

world would never admire them so much. About this time some excellent antisceptical works made their appearance, particularly Reid's *Inquiry into the Human Mind*.[2] Then it was that I began to have a little more confidence in my own judgment, when I found it confirmed by those of whose abilities I did not entertain the least distrust. I reviewed my authors again, with a very different temper of mind. A very little truth will sometimes enlighten a vast extent of science. I found that the sceptical philosophy was not what the world imagined it to be, nor what I, following the opinion of the world, had hitherto imagined it to be, but a frivolous, though dangerous, system of verbal subtlety, which it required neither genius, nor learning, nor taste, nor knowledge of mankind, to be able to put together; but only a captious temper, an irreligious spirit, a moderate command of words, and an extraordinary degree of vanity and presumption. You will easily perceive that I am speaking of this philosophy only in its most extravagant state, that is, as it appears in the works of Mr Hume. The more I study it, the more am I confirmed in this opinion. But while I applauded and admired the sagacity of those who had led me into, or at least encouraged me to proceed in, this train of thinking, I was not altogether satisfied with them in another respect. I could not approve that extraordinary adulation which some of them paid to their arch-adversary. I could not conceive the propriety of paying compliments to a man's *heart*, at the very time one is proving that his aim is to subvert the principles of truth, virtue, and religion; nor to his *understanding*, when we are charging him with publishing the grossest and most contemptible nonsense.[3] I thought I then foresaw, what I have since found to happen, that this controversy would be looked upon rather as a trial of skill between two logicians, than as a disquisition in which the best interests of mankind were concerned; and that the world, especially the fashionable part of it, would still be disposed to pay

---

[2] [Published in 1764, this was the first major work of the 'common sense' school of philosophy.]

[3] [There is a letter from Reid to Hume (dated 18 March 1763) in which Reid declares that he will always be Hume's 'disciple' in metaphysics, and tells Hume that to his 'friendly adversaries' in Aberdeen, his company 'would, though we are all good Christians, be more acceptable than that of Saint Athanasius' (Paul Wood (ed.), *The Correspondence of Thomas Reid*, Edinburgh: Edinburgh University Press, 2002, p. 31.]

the greatest deference to the opinions of him who, even by the acknowledgement of his antagonists, was confessed to be the best philosopher and the soundest reasoner. All this has happened, and more. Some, to my certain knowledge, have said, that Mr Hume and his adversaries did really act in concert, in order mutually to promote the sale of one another's works; as a proof of which they mention not only the extravagant compliments that pass between them, but also the circumstance of Dr Reid and Dr Campbell[4] sending their manuscripts to be perused and corrected by Mr Hume before they gave them to the press. I, who know both the men, am very sensible of the gross falsehood of these reports. As to the affair of the manuscripts, it was, I am convinced, candour and modesty that induced them to it. But the world knows no such thing; and, therefore, may be excused for mistaking the meaning of actions that have really an equivocal appearance. I know likewise that they are sincere, not only in the detestation they express for Mr Hume's irreligious tenets, but also in the complements they have paid to his talents; for they both look upon him as an extraordinary genius, a point on which I cannot agree with them. But while I thus vindicate them from imputations, which the world from its ignorance of circumstances has laid to their charge, I cannot approve them in every thing; I wish they had carried their researches a little farther, and expressed themselves with a little more firmness and spirit. For well I know, that their works, for want of this, will never produce that effect which (if all mankind were cool metaphysical reasoners) might be expected from them. There is another thing in which my judgment differs considerably from that of the gentlemen just mentioned. They have great metaphysical abilities; and they love the metaphysical sciences. I do not. I am convinced that this metaphysical spirit is the bane of true learning, true taste, and true science; that to it we owe all this modern scepticism and atheism; that it has a bad effect upon the human faculties, and tends not a little to sour the temper, to subvert good principles, and to disqualify men for the business of life. You will now see wherein my

---

[4] [George Campbell, Principal of Mariscal College, Aberdeen (and later Professor of Divinity), whose *Dissertation on Miracles* (1762) was indeed read and commented upon by Hume before publication — as was Reid's *Inquiry*.]

views differ from those of the other answerers of Mr Hume. I want to show the world, that the sceptical philosophy is contradictory to itself, and destructive of genuine philosophy, as well as of religion and virtue; that it is in its own nature so paltry a thing, (however it may have been celebrated by some) that to be despised it needs only to be known; that no degree of genius is necessary to qualify a man for making a figure in this pretended science; but rather a certain minuteness and suspiciousness of mind, and want of sensibility, the very reverse of true intellectual excellence; that metaphysics cannot possibly do any good, but may do, and actually have done, much harm; that sceptical philosophers, whatever they may pretend, are the corrupters of science, the pests of society, and the enemies of mankind. I want to show, that the same method of reasoning which these people have adopted in their books, if transferred into common life, would show them to be destitute of common sense; that true philosophers follow a different method of reasoning; and that, without following a different method, no truth can be discovered. I want to lay before the public, in as strong a light as possible, the following dilemma: our sceptics either believe the doctrines they publish, or they do not believe them; if they believe them, they are fools — if not, they are a thousand times worse. I want also to fortify the mind against this sceptical poison, and to propose certain criteria of moral truth, by which some of the most dangerous sceptical errors may be detected and guarded against.

You are sensible, that, in order to attain these ends, it is absolutely necessary for me to use great plainness of speech. My expressions must not be so tame as to seem to imply either a diffidence in my principles, or a coldness towards the cause I have undertaken to defend. And where is the man who can blame me for speaking from the heart, and therefore speaking with warmth, when I appear in the cause of truth, religion, virtue, and mankind? I am sure, my dear friend Mr Blacklock will not; he, who has set before me so many examples of this laudable ardour; he, whose style I should be proud to take for my model, if I were not aware of the difficulty, I may say the insuperable difficulty, of imitating it with success. You need not fear, however, that I expose myself by an excess of passion or petulance. I hope I shall be animated, without losing my temper, and keen, without injury to good manners. In a word, I will be as soft and delicate as the subject and my conscience will allow. One gentleman, a friend of yours,[5] I shall have occasion to treat with much freedom. I have heard of his virtues. I know he has many virtues; God forbid I should ever seek to lessen them, or wish them to be found insincere; I hope they are sincere, and that they will increase in number and merit every day. To his virtues I shall do justice; but I must also do justice to his faults, at least to those faults which are public, and which, for the sake of truth and of mankind, ought not to be concealed or disguised. Personal reflections will be carefully avoided; I hope I am in no danger of falling into them, for I bear no personal animosity against any man whatsoever; sometimes I may perhaps be keen; but I trust I shall never depart from the Christian and philosophic character.

---

[5] [Beattie means Hume.]

Five

On Memory

If we were engrossed by corporeal things only, and never thought of attending to what passes in our minds, we should be in a great measure ignorant of the nobler part of our frame, as well as of those principles of morality and science, which are the glory of human nature, and the chief source of human happiness. Reflection, consciousness, or internal sensation, is that faculty whereby we attend to our own thoughts, and to those various operations, which the mind performs without the aid of bodily organs. In feeling, we use the eye; in hearing, the ear; in smelling and tasting, the nose and tongue; and every part of our body is an instrument of touch: but, when we employ ourselves in recollection, invention, or investigation; when we exert our consciousness in regard to the feelings, pleasant or painful, that accompany our several passions and emotions; or when we meditate upon the morality of human conduct: — in these, and the like cases, the mind does not seem to act by the intervention of any bodily part: nay, of these, and other intellectual energies, we cannot but think, that a pure spirit may be much more capable than we. Accordingly, though mankind have at all times had a persuasion of the immortality of the soul, the resurrection of the body is a doctrine peculiar to Christianity, and met with no little opposition even in the Apostolic age: a proof, that, to mere human reason, it is more natural to think of the soul existing without the body, than to believe, that a re-union of these two substances after death is necessary to the happiness and perfection of the former.

It is true, that the mind and the body do mutually and continually operate upon, and affect, each other. Reason is perverted by disease; nay, by the quantity and quality of what we eat and drink. Wounds on the head have impaired both the memory and the understanding. Anger, sorrow, and other violent emotions of the mind, produce sensible and disagreeable effects on the body: and cheerfulness and hope, benevolence and piety, are equally conducive to the welfare of our mental and corporeal frame. Intense thinking is apt to discompose the head and the stomach; and, if too long continued, may prove fatal to health, or even to reason. Extreme anxiety is said to have changed the colour of the hair from black to white. Nay, it is well known, that, when certain evil humours predominate in the body, certain evil thoughts never fail to infest the soul; and that melancholy, and other sorts of madness, may sometimes be cured by physical applications. From these, and from many other facts of the same kind that might be mentioned, we may warrantably conclude, that, in the present life at least, the mind, in the exercise even of these powers of reflection or consciousness, is not independent of the body. But we know, on what particular organs the soul depends for its knowledge of sound and colour, taste and smell: whereas, with what part of the body, memory, for example, or reason, or imagination, is connected, we know not: neither can we explain these faculties, by experiments made upon matter; or in any other way, than by attending to what passes in our minds.

This mode of attention seems to be one of those peculiarities that distinguishes man from the inferior animals. Brutes see, and hear, and smell, and touch, and taste, no less acutely, and some of them more acutely, than we. But they are affected, only or chiefly, with outward things; and seem incapable of what we call reflection or consciousness. They sometimes look, as if they were thinking; but I know not, whether we ever see them act in consequence of having deliberated: their impulses to action are sudden, and appear for the most part to be the effect of some bodily sensation. To a certain degree they are docile, and acquire experience; but all is, or seems to be, the result of habit co-operating with instinct. Give a brute his food, the society of his fellows, and the means of security and rest; give him, in a word, those external things, which the inborn propensities of his nature require; and nothing can be wanting to his felicity: memory will not torment him with former evils, nor imagination with those that are to come. But in the midst of affluence and peace, and with every thing to gratify corporeal sense, man is often wretched: the reflections of his mind, the consciousness of what he has done, the remembrance of past, and the anticipation of future calamity; to say nothing of the evil passions of pride, envy, and malevolence; may poison all the gifts of fortune, and make him sensible, that human happiness and misery depend upon the soul, and not upon the body; upon what we *think* (if I may so express myself), rather than upon what we *feel*. I will not say, however, that all the inferior animals are void of reflection. The more sagacious among them do give some faint indications of such a power: but they probably possess it in no higher degree, than is barely necessary to their preservation. Whereas, if we consider what sort of creature man would be, if he had no faculties but the outward senses, we shall be satisfied, that from these internal powers both his dignity and his happiness arise.

Of these, as well as of the outward senses, there is considerable variety. Memory, imagination, reason, abstraction, conscience, are faculties of the human soul, as well as hearing, seeing, touching, tasting, and smelling: the latter employed in perceiving, by means of bodily organs, material things and their qualities; the former exerted, with no dependence on the body that we can explain, in perceiving the human mind and its operations, and the ideas or thoughts that pass in succession before it.

* * *

Chap. I: Difference between Memory and Imagination

Some philosophers refer to memory all our livelier thoughts, and our fainter ones to imagination: and so will have it, that the former faculty is distinguished from the latter by its superior vivacity. We believe, say they, in memory; we believe not in imagination: now we never believe any thing, but what we distinctly comprehend; and that, of which our comprehension is indistinct, we disbelieve.[1] — But this is altogether false. The suggestions of imagination are often so lively, in dreaming, and in some intellectual disorders, as to be mistaken for real things; and therefore can-

---

[1] [Beattie is probably alluding to Hume: see *A Treatise of Human Nature*, I.iii.5 (ed. David Fate and Mary Norton, Oxford: Oxford University Press, 2000, pp. 59–60).]

not be said to be essentially fainter than the informations of memory. We may be conscious too of remembering that whereof we have but a faint impression. I remember to have read books, of which I cannot now give any account; and to have seen persons, whose features and visible appearance I have totally forgotten. Nor is it true, that we believe, or disbelieve, according to the vivacity, or the faintness, of our ideas. No man will say, that he has a distinct idea of eternity; and yet, every rational being must believe, that one eternity is past, and another to come. I have a livelier idea of Parson Adams,[2] than of the impostor Mohammed; and yet I believe the former to be an imaginary character, and the latter to have been a real man. I read, not long ago, Vertot's *Revolutions of Sweden*, and *The Adventures of Tom Jones*: I believe the history, and I disbelieve the novel; and yet, of the novel I have a more lively remembrance, than of the history.

Memory and imagination, therefore, are not to be distinguished, according to the liveliness or faintness of the ideas suggested by the one, or by the other. The former may be faint, while the latter is lively: nay, a great Poet has observed, that,

> Where beams of warm imagination play,
> The memory's soft figures melt away:[3]

A maxim, which, though not always, will sometimes be found to hold true. — Besides, belief may be said to imply disbelief. If I believe the existence of Julius Cesar, I disbelieve his non-existence. If I admit the history of that commander to be true, I reject every suspicion of its being false. And yet, of Julius Cesar, and his actions, my ideas are equally clear, whether I believe or disbelieve. The faculties in question I would therefore distinguish in the following manner.

'I remember to have seen a lion; and I can imagine an elephant, or a centaur, which I have never seen': — he, who pronounces these words with understanding, *knows* the difference between the two faculties, though perhaps he may not be able to *explain* it. When we remember, we have always a view to real existence, and to our past experience; it occurs to our minds, in regard to this thing which we now remember, that we formerly heard it, or per-

---

[2]   [A character in Henry Fielding's novel *Joseph Andrews*.]

[3]   Pope, *Essay on Criticism*, I, ll. 58–9.

ceived it, or thought of it; 'I remember to have seen a lion': — When we imagine, we contemplate a certain thought, or idea, simply as it is in itself, or as we conceive it to be, without referring it to past experience, or to real existence; 'I can imagine such a figure as that of the elephant, though I have never seen one; or a centaur, with the head and shoulders of a man joined to the body of a horse, though I know that there is no such animal on earth'. I remember what has actually happened, and what, in consequence of my remembering, I believe to have happened: I can imagine a series of adventures, which never did, or which never can, happen. He who writes the history of his own life, or who compiles a narrative from the books he has read, is guided by the informations of memory: he who composes a romance, puts those things in writing, which are suggested by his imagination.

A friend describes an adventure, in which he says that he and I were engaged twenty years ago, and informs me of what I said and did on the occasion: I tell him, that I can distinctly imagine every thing he relates, but that I remember nothing of it. He mentions a circumstance, which on a sudden brings the whole to my memory. You are right, I then say; for now I remember it perfectly well. At first, I could only imagine the facts he spoke of: but, though I might believe his word, I could not recall any experience of mine, by which, in this particular case, it might be verified. But now, my memory informs me, that the adventure was real, and that I was an agent in it, and an eyewitness. Hence it appears, that in some cases imagination may become remembrance. And it may be further observed, that remembrance will sometimes decay, till it be nothing more than imagination: as when we retain the appearance of an object, without being able to affirm with certainty, where we perceived, or whether we ever perceived it: a state of mind, which one is conscious of, when one says, 'I either saw such a thing, or I dreamed of it'.

Chap. II: Phenomena and Laws of Memory

I: General account of this Faculty. — Whether we have reason to think that it is connected with the Brain.

I proceed, in the second place, to take notice of some of the more remarkable phenomena of Memory.

This is a faculty, which, if it were less common, and we equally qualified to judge of it, would strike us with astonishment. That we should have it in our power to recall past sensations and thoughts, and make them again present, as it were: that a circumstance of our former life should, in respect of us, be no more; and yet occur to us, from time to time, dressed out in colours so lively, as to enable us to examine it, and judge of it, as if it were still an object of sense: — these are facts, whereof we every day have experience, and which, therefore, we overlook as things of course. But, surely, nothing is more wonderful, or more inexplicable. If thoughts could occupy space, we might be tempted to think, that we had laid them up in certain cells or repositories, to remain there till we had occasion for them. But thoughts cannot occupy space; nor be conceived to have any other existence, than what the mind gives them by meditating upon them. Yet, that which has been long forgotten, nay, that which we have often endeavoured in vain to recollect, will sometimes, without any effort of ours, occur to us, on a sudden, and, if I may so speak, of its own accord. A tune, for example, which I hear today, and am pleased with, I perhaps endeavour to remember tomorrow, and next day, and the day following, without success: and yet, that very tune shall occur to me, a month after, when my mind is taken up with something else. Where, if I may ask the question, were my ideas of this tune, when I wished to recollect them, and could not? How comes it, that they now present themselves, when I am not thinking of them at all? These questions no man can answer: but the fact is certain.

Often, when we do not immediately call to mind what we wish to remember, we set ourselves, as it were, to search for it; we meditate on other things or persons, that seem to be like it, or contrary to it, or contiguous, or to bear any other relation to what we are in quest of; and thus, perhaps, we at last remember it. This continued effort of voluntary remembrance is called Recollection. It resembles the procedure of those, who, missing something valuable, look for it in every place where they think they might have been when they dropped it; and thus recover what they had lost. For the last mentioned fact it is easy to account. A jewel, or a piece of coin, is a visible, tangible, and permanent thing, and must remain in its place till it be removed: and, if we come to that place, and examine it with attention, we can hardly fail to find what we are in quest of. But, where a thought should be, when it is forgotten; how it should have any permanency or any existence, when it is no longer in the mind; and what should restore it to our memory, after a long interval of forgetfulness; are points, whereon human wisdom can determine nothing.

Is it not wonderful, that old men should remember more accurately what happened fifty years ago, than the affairs of last week? And yet that, in many cases, our remembrance of any fact should be accurate in proportion to its recency? It may be said, indeed, that the more we attend, the better we remember; and that old men are forgetful of those things only, to which they are inattentive; for that not one of them ever forgot the place where he had deposited his money. All this is true, as Cicero remarks in his book on old age:[4] but how we come to remember that best, to which we are most attentive, we can no otherwise explain, than by saying, that such is the law of our nature.

To account for this, and other phenomena of memory, by intermediate causes, many authors, both ancient and modern, were fain to suppose, that every thing perceived by us, whether a thought of the mind, or an external object, every thing, in a word, that we remember, makes upon the brain a certain impression, which, remaining for some time after, is taken notice of by the mind, and recognized, as the mark of that particular sensation or idea; and that this sensation or idea, thus obtruded upon us anew, gives rise to remembrance. They supposed further, that attention to the thing perceived deepens this impression, and, consequently, makes it more durable; while that, to which we slightly attend, makes but a slight impression that soon wears out. When the brain itself is disordered, by disease, by drunkenness, or by other accidents, these philosophers are of opinion, that the

---

[4] [Cicero, *On Old Age* (*De Senectute*), vii.]

impressions are disfigured, or instantly erased, or not at all received; in which case, there is either no remembrance, or a confused one: and they think, that the brains of old men, grown callous by length of time, are, like hard wax, equally tenacious of old impressions, and unsusceptible of new. Many plausible things may indeed be said, for solving the difficulties above mentioned, if we will only admit this theory. But it must, notwithstanding, be rejected; and that for several good reasons.

The human brain is a bodily substance; and sensible and permanent impressions made upon it must so far resemble those made on sand by the foot, or on wax by the seal, as to have a certain shape, length, breadth, and deepness. Now such an impression can only be made by that, which has solidity, magnitude, and figure. If then we remember thoughts, feelings, and sounds, as well as things visible and tangible, which will hardly be denied; those sounds, thoughts, and feelings, must have body, and, consequently, shape, size, and weight. What then is the size or weight of a sound? Is it an inch long, or half an inch? Does it weigh an ounce, or a grain? Does the roar of a cannon bear any resemblance to the ball, or to the powder, in shape, in weight, or in magnitude? What figure has the pain of the toothache, and our remembrance of that pain? Is it triangular, or circular, or a square form? The bare mention of these consequences may prove the absurdity of the theories that lead to them.

Moreover; supposing impressions to be made on the brain, I would ask, *how* the mind perceives them, and why at one time more than at another? Does the human soul go up to the *pia mater*,[5] as a housewife does to her garret, only at certain times? Or, if she make it her place of abode, are there any corners of it which she is acquainted with, or neglects to look into? Nay, admitting this supposition, we should be apt to conclude, from the facts already specified, that some of these impressions do occasionally force themselves into notice, when the soul is differently employed; and that she often looks for others, without being able to find them, as if they were lost, or mislaid. — To all which we may add, that the theory in question ought not to find a place in philosophy, because incapable of proof from experience; it being impossible,

---

[5] [The *pia mater* is a fine membrane that envelops the brain and spinal cord.]

with bodily eyes, to discover, in what way the human brain may be affected by thinking and perceiving. — And therefore, without employing more time in vain inquiries after the *cause* of remembrance, let us be satisfied, if, from what we certainly know of this faculty, we can propose any rules for its improvement.

But, before I proceed to a more particular account of its appearances and laws, it may be proper to remark, that a sound state of the brain does in fact seem to be necessary to the right exercise of memory, as well as of our other intellectual powers. Memory is often suspended during sleep, and is also impaired by distemper, by old age, and by sudden and violent accidents. Thucydides, in his account of the plague at Athens, relates, that some persons survived that dreadful disease, with such a total loss of memory, that they forgot their friends, themselves, and every thing else. I have read of a person, who, falling from the top of a house, forgot all his acquaintance, and even the faces of his own family; and of a learned author, who, on receiving a blow on the head by a folio dropping from its shelf, lost all his learning, and was obliged to study the alphabet a second time. There goes a story of another great scholar, who, by a like accident, was deprived, not of all his learning, but only of his Greek. — One may question some of these facts: but what follows is certainly true. I know a clergyman, who, upon recovering from a fit of apoplexy about fifteen years ago, was found to have forgotten all the transactions of the four years immediately preceding; but remembered as well as ever what had happened before that period. The newspapers of the time were then a great amusement to him; for almost every thing he found in them was matter of surprise: and, during the period I speak of, some very important events had taken place, particularly the accession of his present Majesty, and many of the victories of the last war. By degrees he recovered what he had lost; partly by the spontaneous revival of his memory, and partly by information. He is still alive, though old and infirm; and as intelligent as people of his age commonly are. — I may further mention, that I have several times in my life been in a swoon: twice, as I remember, by falls from a horse; and once, on going suddenly to a great fire, from the damp air of a winter night: and that, on each occasion, I observed, as others in like cases have done, that, when I recovered, I had utterly forgotten what happened just before the deliquium came on, and was not a little surprised when the persons present told me of the circumstances. A like failure of memory I have once and again been conscious of, when awake and in health, on being startled at some alarming incident. — These facts prove, that our soul and body are closely united, and do mutually affect each other; and that by disorders in the brain and the other contiguous parts, the intellectual powers may be discomposed. But from these facts we are not warranted to infer, either that the brain is the organ of memory, or that impressions are made on it by what we externally or internally perceive; or that, supposing them to be made, they are at all necessary to remembrance.

II: The Subject continued. — Laws of Memory. — Importance of Attention.

The most lively remembrance is not so lively as the sensation from which it is derived: and, for the most part, memory becomes more faint, as the original sensation becomes more remote in time. What I saw last year, I remember more distinctly than what I did not see these seven years. This, however, is not always the case. Old men can give a more exact account of what happened in their youth, than of more recent events. And any man remembers better the face of a dear friend whom he has not seen for many days, than that of an indifferent stranger whom he chanced to see yesterday. Of the books, too, which we read, and of the narratives which we hear, every one knows, that some we forget immediately, and that others we retain long.

That is likely to be long remembered, which at its first appearance affects the mind with a lively sensation, or with some pleasurable or painful feeling. Thus we remember more exactly what we have seen, than what we have only heard of; and that which awakened any powerful emotion, as joy, sorrow, wonder, surprise, love, indignation, than that which we beheld with indifference. Here we discern the reason of a cruel piece of policy, which is said to be practised in some communities, and was once, I believe, in this; that of going round the lands once a year, and at every landmark scourging one or two boys, who were taken along for that purpose. For it was presumed, that those boys could never forget the places they had suffered pain; and would of course be able, when grown up, or grown old, to give testimony concerning the boundaries, if any dispute should arise on that subject. We all know the difference between a discourse or narrative which we forget as soon as we hear, and one that leaves a lasting impression. The former gives no entertainment, and awakens no passion: the latter amuses with a variety of examples and images, or by the force or beauty of the style; or gives rise to wonder, hope, fear, pity, laughter, or other lively emotions.

The ancient moralists were at pains to illustrate their precepts by examples, parables, and other allusions to things external. This made the hearer both understand their meaning, and retain it: for in those days, recourse could seldom be had to books; and it was necessary for the people to remember what was delivered to them, if they intended to profit by it. Religious, political, and moral doctrines, when enforced by facts and apposite examples, lose their abstract nature, and become, as it were, objects of sense; and so engage attention, are easily understood, make a deep impression on the mind, and produce a durable remembrance. This ought to be carefully attended to, by those whose business it is to instruct mankind by speaking to them. What is written is permanent, and may be reviewed at leisure; but what is addressed to the ear is immediately gone; and, if it take no hold of the memory, is good for nothing.

The force wherewith any thing strikes the mind, is generally in proportion to the degree of attention we bestow upon it. And therefore, what we attend to, is better remembered, than what we consider superficially. Inattentive people have always bad memories. At least, their memory is bad in regard to those things to which they are inattentive: — for there is no person of a sound mind, who has not some pursuit, and some favourite sphere of observation. If our attention is engaged by matters of importance; by the duties and decorums of life; by historical facts; by philosophical researches; by the trade, manufactures, and other political concerns of our country; our memory will be stored with matters of importance: but if we are captivated by trifles only, we shall remember only trifles. It is therefore of great moment, that the views and attentions of young people be properly directed. Where parents are given to foolish talk, or insipid storytelling, children often acquire the same propensity. For it is certain, that the bent of the genius is partly determined by those early habits of attention or inattention, whereby the memory is either enriched with what is valuable, or encumbered with what is frivolous.

The great art of memory is attention. Without this, one reads, and hears, to no purpose. And we shall be more or less profited by what we read or hear, as the objects of our attention are more or less important. To read in haste, or without reflecting on what we read, may amuse a vacant hour, but will never improve the understanding. And therefore, while we peruse a good author, let us, from time to time, lay the book aside, and propose to ourselves the following queries. What is it this author aims at? What is his general plan? How far has he proceeded in his subject? If I were to give without book a summary of the last chapter, how should I express myself? Is the author quite clear and satisfactory in what he has hitherto advanced? If he is not, what are his principal defects? How much of his subject is still before him? From what I know of his plan, of the parts he has already gone through, of his principles, and of his method of illustration, may I not form conjectures in regard to what is to follow? — It is this sort of intellectual exercise, that improves both the memory and the judgment, and makes reading equally agreeable and beneficial. — And, in like manner, after hearing a discourse, or bearing a part in conversation, it may be of use to recollect the heads of it: taking care to treasure up those sentiments that were remarkable for their truth or beauty, or that came recommended by the piety or benevolence of the speaker; and overlooking every levity, sophistry, and ill-natured observation, that seemed to betray depravity of principle, or hardness of heart. By cherishing habits of attention, and of recollection, in the various circumstances of life, the mind is continually improved; but idleness, inadvertence, and inaccuracy, extinguish genius, and eradicate virtue.

When we are engrossed by a multiplicity of affairs, new objects command but a slight attention, unless they be very striking. And therefore, those things are most attended to, and best remembered, which occur when the mind is at ease, and unemployed; as in the early part of life, or in the morning. Hence, that is well remembered, of which we have had a previous expectation: for this disengages the mind from other concerns, and prepares us to attend to that which we look for, as soon as it shall appear. When, therefore, we take up a book, with a view to profit by it, we ought to lay all other business aside, and prevent, as much as possible, the intrusion of impertinent ideas. This will not only assist memory, but also give such a variety to our thoughts as may prove very salutary to the soul. For the same train of thinking too long pursued is often detrimental to health, and sometimes even to reason.

The rule here hinted at should never, on any occasion, be forgotten. It is a matter of no small importance, that we acquire the habit of doing only one thing at one time: by which I mean, that while employed on any one object our thoughts ought not to wander to another. When we go from home in quest of amusement, or to the fields for the sake of exercise, we shall do well to leave all our speculations behind: if we carry them with us, the exercise will fatigue the body without refreshing it; and the amusement, instead of enlivening, will distract, the soul: and both in the one case, and in the other, we shall confirm ourselves in those habits of inattention, which, when long persisted in, form what is called an *absent man*. In conversation too, let us always mind what is saying and doing around us, and never give the company ground to suspect, that our thoughts are elsewhere. Attention is a chief part of politeness. An absent man, provided he is good-natured, may be born with, but never can be agreeable. He may command our esteem, if we know him to be wise and virtuous; but he cannot engage our love. For inattention implies negligence, and neglect often proceeds from contempt: if, therefore, we find that we are not attended to, we shall fancy that we are neglected, and to a certain degree despised: and how is it possible to repay contempt with kindness! And when unkindness and dissatisfaction prevail in any society, all the comforts of it are at an end. — Besides, if we are not strictly observant of every thing that passes in company, we cannot be either amused by it, or instructed: in other words, we deprive ourselves of much innocent pleasure, and useful information. For a great deal of our best knowledge is obtained by mutual intercourse: and for the most valuable comforts of life we are indebted to the social and benevolent attentions of one another.

But, must one mind the insipid prattle of those who can neither instruct, nor entertain? — Provided it be inoffensive, I answer, yes: particularly, if they are, by their rank, or sex, or age, or other circumstances, entitled to more than ordinary regard. Avoid their company, if you please, and as much as you conveniently can; but, when you are in it, be attentive and civil. If you are, you contribute to their happiness, which it is your duty to do; and you ensure their good-will, which is better than their hatred: you may, at the same time, improve yourself in benevolence and patience; you contract no evil habits of inattention; you will find entertainment in the discovery of their characters, and so enlarge your acquaintance with the human heart; and it will be strange indeed, if you do not gather something from them, which may either inform by its novelty, or divert by its singularity.

Let it not be objected, that some great men, as Newton, have been remarkably absent in company. Persons, who are engaged in sublime study, and who are known to employ their time and faculties in adorning human nature by the investigation of useful truth, may be indulged in such peculiarities of behaviour, as in men of common talents neither are, nor ought to be, tolerated. For, in regard to the former, we are willing to suppose, that, if they overlook us, it is because they are engrossed by matters of greater importance: but this is a compliment, which we should not think ourselves obliged to pay the latter, at least in ordinary cases. And I scruple not to say, that it would have been better for Newton himself, as well as for society, if he had been free from the weakness abovementioned. For then, his thoughts, and his amusements would have been more diversified, and his health probably better, and his precious life still longer than it was: and a mind like his, fully displayed in free and general conversation, would have been, to all who had the happiness to approach him, an inexhaustible source of instruction and delight.

If, therefore, we wish to have a due regard for others, or for ourselves, let us endeavour to acquire a habit of strict attention at all times, and in all circumstances; of attention, I mean, to that, whatever it is, in which we happen to be engaged. It is true, that some of our customary actions may be well enough performed, even when we are thinking of something else. We may put on our clothes, or (when alone) eat our victuals, or play an easy tune on a musical instrument, and our mind be all the while taken up with other matters. But this we ought not to do often, lest we contract a habit of doing it; which will be, as far as it goes, a habit of inattention, and therefore faulty; and which, though it take its rise from trivial things, may gain upon us, till it come to affect our behaviour in things of moment.

Great, indeed, and many are the advantages of habitual attention. Clearness of understanding, extensive knowledge, and exact memory, are its natural consequences. It is even beneficial to health, by varying the succession of our ideas and sensations; and it gives us the command of our thoughts, and enables us at all times to act readily, and with presence of mind. As they who live retired are disconcerted at the sight of a stranger; as he whose body has never been made pliant by exercise cannot perform new motions either gracefully or easily; so the man, who has contracted a habit of ruminating upon a few things and overlooking others, is fluttered, and at a loss, whenever he finds himself, as he often does, in unexpected circumstances. He looks round amazed, like one raised suddenly from sleep. Not remembering what happened the last moment, he knows nothing of the cause of the present appearance, nor can form any conjecture with respect to its tendency. If you ask him a question, it is some time before he can recollect himself so far as to attend to you; he hesitates, and you must repeat your words before he understand them: and when he has with difficulty made himself master of your meaning, he cannot, without an effort, keep out of his usual track of thinking, so long as is necessary for framing an explicit reply. This may look like exaggeration; but nothing is more certain, than that habits of inattention, contracted early, and long persisted in, will in time form such a character.

* * *

Chapter IV: Remarks on the Brutes. — Inferences

I shall now make a few remarks on the memory of brutes. That many of them have this faculty, is undeniable. We find that whelps, as well as children, once burned, avoid the fire; and that horses, oxen, and dogs, and many other animals, not only have their knowledge of nature enlarged by experience, but also derive from man various arts and habits, whereby they become useful to him, in war, hunting, agriculture, and other employments. Most of these creatures know their fellows, and keepers: nay dogs and horses learn to do certain things, on hearing certain words articulated. Beagles obey the voice of the hunter, and pursue, or desist from pursuit, as he commands; and the war-horse is acquainted, not only with the voice of his rider, but also with the summons of the drum and trumpet; as hunting coursers are, with the opening of the hounds, and the sound of the horn. Goats, sheep, and oxen, and even poultry, of their own accord, repair in the evening to their homes: parrots acquire the habit of uttering words; and singing birds, of modulating tunes: and bees, after an excursion of several miles (as naturalists affirm) return, each to her hive; nor does it appear that they mistake another for their own, even where many are standing contiguous. Lions spare him who attends them, when they would tear in pieces every thing else: doves fly to the window where they have been fed; and the elephant is said to possess a degree of remembrance not many removes from rationality. I might mention too the dog of Ulysses, who knew his master after twenty years absence; for the story is probable, though it may not be true: as well as what is recorded in Aulus Gellius, of Androclus and his lion, who, having received mutual civilities from each other in the deserts of Africa, renewed their acquaintance when they met in the circus at Rome, and were inseparable companions ever after.[6] That the inhabitants of the water have memory, we cannot doubt, if we believe, what Pliny, in his *Natural History*, Bernier, in his account of Indostan, and Martial, in some of his epigrams, have mentioned, of fishes kept in ponds, that had learned to appear in order to be fed, when called by their respective names.[7] Whether shellfishes, and snails, and worms, and other torpid animals, have at any time given signs of memory, I am not able to determine.

In some particulars requisite to the preservation of brutes, instinct seems to supersede the necessity of remembrance. Young bees, on the first trial, extract honey from flowers, and fashion their combs, as skilfully as the oldest; and the same thing may be remarked of birds building their nests; and of brute animals, in general, adopting, when full grown, the voice and the manner of life, which nature has appropriated to the species. Some late

---

[6] Aulus Gellius, *The Attic Nights* (*Noctium Atticarum*), v. 14.

[7] Pliny, *Natural History* (*Naturalis Historia*), x. 89; François Bernier, *Voyages dans les Etats du Grand Mogol* (1723); Martial, *Epigrams*, iv. 30, x. 30.

authors pretend, that birds learn to sing from their parents; and that a lark, for example, which had never heard the lark's song, would never sing it. But this I cannot admit, because my experience leads to a different conclusion; though I allow, that many animals have the power of imitating, by their voice, those of another species. If this theory be just; then a bird gets its note, as a man does his mother-tongue, by hearing it; and, therefore, the songs of individual birds will be as various nearly, as the languages of individual men; so that the larks of France would have one sort of note, those of Italy another, and those of England a third. I would as soon believe, that a dog, which had never heard any other voice, than that of a man, or of a swine, would not bark, but speak, or grunt. — Man is taught by experience, what is fit to be eaten, or to be drank. But brutes seem to know this by instinct. The mariner, who lands in a desert island, is cautious of tasting such unknown fruits, as are not marked by the pecking of birds. Dogs, and other animals, may be poisoned by the superior craft of men; but leave them to themselves, and they are seldom in danger of taking what is hurtful, though they sometimes suffer from swallowing too much of what is good. And some of these creatures, when their health is disordered, are directed by instinct to the proper medicine.

Without memory, brutes would be incapable of discipline; and so, their strength, sagacity, and swiftness, would be in a great measure unserviceable to man. Nor would their natural instincts guard them sufficiently against the dangers they are exposed to, from one another, and from things inanimate. Memory is also to them, as to us, a source of pleasure. For to this in part must be owing the satisfaction that many of them take, in the company of their fellows, in the friendship of man, and in the care of their offspring; of which last, however, their love and remembrance last no longer, than is necessary to the preservation of the young. — But such joys, as we derive, from the idea of danger escaped, of opposition vanquished, or of pleasure formally possessed, seem peculiar to rational nature, and not within the sphere of the inferior creation: for to produce them, not only memory, but also consciousness and recollection are necessary. Brutes are engrossed, chiefly or only, with what is present: their memory being rather a necessary and instantaneous suggestion, than a continued or voluntary act. For the sorrow, that a dog feels for the loss of his master, a cow for that of her calf, and a horse for that of his companion, is nothing more perhaps, though it may continue for some time, than an uneasiness arising from the sense of a present want. We can hardly suppose, that any thing then passes in the animal, similar to what we experience, when we revolve the idea of a departed friend. In a word, I do not find sufficient ground to believe, that they are capable of recollection, or active remembrance; for this implies the faculty of attending to, and arranging, the thoughts of one's own mind; a power, which, as was formerly remarked, the brutes have either not at all, or very imperfectly.

Yet, let me not be quite positive in this affirmation. Some of the more sagacious animals, as horses, dogs, foxes, and elephants, have occasionally displayed a power of contrivance, which *would seem* to require reflection, and a more perfect use of memory, than I have hitherto allowed that they possess. When a rider has fallen from his horse in a deep river, there have been instances of that noble creature taking hold with his teeth, and dragging him alive to land by the skirts of the coat. And let me here, for the honour of another noble creature, mention a fact, which was never before recorded, and which happened not many years ago within a few miles of Aberdeen. — As a gentleman was walking across the Dee, when it was frozen, the ice gave way in the middle of the river, and down he sunk; but kept himself from being carried away in the current, by grasping his gun, which had fallen athwart the opening. A dog, who attended him, after many fruitless attempts to rescue his master, ran to a neighbouring village, and took hold of the coat of the first person he met. The man was alarmed, and would have disengaged himself: but the dog regarded him with a look so kind and so significant, and endeavoured to pull him along with so gentle a violence, that he began to think there might be something extraordinary in the case, and suffered himself to be conducted by the animal; who brought him to his master, in time to save his life. — Was there not here, both memory and recollection, guided by experience, and by what in a human creature we should not scruple to call good sense? No: rather let us say, that here was an interposition of heaven; who, having thought fit to employ the animal as an instrument of this deliverance, was pleased to qualify him for it by a supernatural impulse. Here, certainly, was an event so uncommon, that from the known qualities of a dog no person would have expected it: and I know not, whether this animal ever gave proof of extraordinary sagacity in any other instance.

It is said by Aristotle, and generally believed, that brute animals dream. Lucretius describes those imperfect attempts at barking and running, which dogs are observed to make in their sleep; and supposes, agreeably to common opinion, that they are the effects of dreaming; and that the animal then imagines himself to be pursuing his prey, or attacking an enemy. But, whether this be really the case; or whether those appearances may not be owing to some mechanical twitches of the nerves or muscles, rendered by long exercise habitual, is a point on which nothing can be affirmed with certainty. — Infants a month old smile in their sleep: and I have heard good women remark, that the innocent babe is then favoured with some glorious vision. But that a babe should have visions or dreams, before it has ideas, can hardly be imagined. This is probably the effect, not of thought, but of some bodily feeling, or merely of some transient contraction or expansion of the muscles. Certain it is, that no smiles are more captivating. And Providence no doubt intended them as a sort of silent language to engage our love; even as, by its cries, the infant is enabled to awaken our pity, and command our protection.

Memory is in some brutes accompanied with unaccountable circumstances. When a horse, an ox, or a goat, returns home of his own accord from the pasture, it is not wonderful; being an effect of memory similar in all respects to what we experience in ourselves. But when a bee, whose eyes from their extreme convexity cannot see a foot before them, returns to her hive from a wide excursion; or when a dog, that has been carried in a basket thirty miles through a country which he never saw, finds his way a week after to his former dwelling, (of which I have known an instance) — what can we say, but that the smell of these animals, or some other faculty unknown to us, recalls to their memory past perceptions, in a way that we cannot conceive! Indeed, where there are perceptive powers different from, or more exquisite than, any we enjoy, it is reasonable to think, that there must be modes of remembrance equally surpassing our comprehension. And in bees, and dogs, and some other animals, there seem to be faculties, of the nature of smell, as far beyond ours in accuracy, as the informations conveyed by the finest microscope are superior to those we receive by the naked eye.

Yet, with all the helps he derives from instinct, or from more acute organs of sense, how inferior is the memory of the most intelligent brute to that of reasonable beings! The disproportion is almost infinite. Many of the irrational tribes are unsusceptible of discipline: — how narrow must the sphere be of their remembrance! Even the most docile soon reach the summit of improvement; and the arts, or rather the habits, attainable by them, and within the power of human industry to impress upon them, are very few. Wholly destitute of science, and of the powers of contemplation, they are also deficient in the recollective faculty; without which we know how little our memory would avail us: and all seem unable to follow even the shortest train of thought, or attend to any thing that does not affect the senses.

But of a human memory, improved to no extraordinary pitch, how vast is the comprehension! With what an endless multitude of thoughts is it supplied, by reflection, reading, and conversation, inlets of ideas denied to the inferior animals; and by an experience incomparably more diversified than theirs, and withal so modelled by our powers of arrangement and invention (which are also peculiar to man) as to be far more useful in itself, and much more distinctly remembered! Things natural; as animals, vegetables, minerals, fossils, mountains and valleys; land and water; earth and heaven; the sun, moon, and stars, with their several appearances, motions, and periods; the atmosphere and meteors, with all the vicissitudes of weather: — things artificial; as towns, streets, houses, highways, and machines, with their various appendages: — abstract notions in regard to truth and falsehood, beauty and deformity, virtue and vice, proportions in quantity and number, religion, commerce, and policy, whereof the brutes know nothing, and which are the chief materials of human conversation: these are some of the general heads, under which may be arranged the manifold treasures of human memory. And under each of these heads, what an infinity of individual things are comprehended! — Let a person, who has been as much in the world, as men of enterprise commonly are, revolve in his mind, how many human creatures he has been, and is, acquainted with; how much he remembers of their features, shape, voice, size, character, and sentiments, of their relations, connections, and history: let him then think of those men and women, whom he never saw, but has heard and read of; and of the characters he may have seen exemplified in plays, poems, and other fabulous writings; and will he not be amazed, that his memory should retain so many particulars relating to human creatures only; who yet, in the general distribution of human knowledge, do not perhaps form the most copious class of things? How numerous are the words even of one language! He, who is master of four, must be supposed to retain two hundred thousand words at least, with all the different ways of applying them according to rule, and innumerable passages in books to illustrate their meaning. And that four languages do not exceed the capacity of an ordinary man, will not be denied by those, who believe, with Pliny and Quintilian, that Mithridates understood two and twenty.

But who can reckon up, or even give a general arrangement of, all the objects, notions, and ideas, that one human mind may remember! And, is it not remarkable, and truly wonderful, that, the more an improved memory retains, the greater is its capacity? Was it ever said, by any person of a sound mind; my memory has received all it can receive, and I never from this hour desire to hear any new thing? — Let us hence learn to set a proper value on the dignity of the human soul; and to think of its intellectual faculties as inexpressibly superior, both in kind and in degree, to those of the animal world. If we be capable of endless improvement (and what reason is there to believe that we are not?), surely our definition must be different from theirs; for the Author of nature does nothing in vain: and an understanding, far more limited than that of man, would be sufficient for all the purposes of a creature, whose duration is circumscribed by the term of a hundred years. Our minds, therefore, must have been destined for scenes of improvement more extensive and glorious, than these below; and our being to comprehend periods more durable, than those which are measured out by the sun. This speculation forms a proof, by which the wiser heathens were led to believe in the immortality of the soul. Thus reasoned Tully, in the person of the elder Cato: 'Why should I enlarge?' says he, 'since the activity of the mind is so great; since it remembers so much of what is past, anticipates so wisely what is to come, and is capable of so many arts, sciences, and inventions; of this I am persuaded, and thus I believe, that the being possessed of such endowments cannot be mortal'.[8]

These reflections lead me to animadvert a little on two strange conceits of the modern philosophy. The first is, that human faculties are so like those of other animals, that, if the form of their bodies were but a little more familiar, we might characterize men, by calling them sagacious brutes; and brutes, by saying, that they are imperfect men.[9] For the writers I allude to will hardly admit, that there is one original faculty in the former, which is not in some degree in the latter; insinuating, that the difference, where there is any, is owing rather to habits and experiences obtained by means of a more or less exquisite formation of bodily organs, than to any thing essential in the frame of the mind. Nay, some have gone so far as to say, or at least to make us suppose it is their belief, that man's primitive state was a state of brutality; that in it he enjoyed more health and happiness than he does now; that he becomes the more imperfect, the more he deviates from the brutal character; and that, if he did as he ought to do, and as nature intended he should, he would go naked, and on all four. — As long as men believe history and their senses, it will not be necessary to combat the latter part of this doctrine. Of the former I shall only say, Let those acquiesce in it who can. He, who is ambitious to claim consanguinity with the beasts, will not be much inclined to read any thing I write; and therefore I may leave him to himself. — Brutes, no doubt, as well as men, have the power of retaining past perceptions: but, after what has been said, I presume it will appear, that they who compare this power, as it is in man, with what is called memory in a brute, and discern no essential difference, may as well find out, that gnats and whales are the same sort of animal, and that the hissing of a goose is an exact imitation of the thunder of a sea-engagement.

That there is in the universe a scale rising, by gradual ascent, from nothing up to Deity, is another modern conceit, not less absurd than the former; though, on account of certain names who have patronized it, somewhat more respectable. If brutes come

---

[8] Cicero, *On Old Age*, xxi.

[9] [Hume insists upon the similarities between men and animals: see especially *Treatise of Human Nature*, I.iii.16.]

next to men in this imaginary scale, sure it cannot be said to rise gradually. I allow indeed, that horses are swifter and stronger than men; and that many animals have faculties of perception and action that we have not; the swallow, for example, which can fly; the dolphin, which can live under water; and the bee, which can extract honey from flowers. But in every respect wherein they can be compared, how far is the rational nature above the irrational! We have seen, that even in regard to memory, which is common to both, the distance is inconceivably great. What then shall we think of this distance, when we consider it with a view to those powers, which form the glory, and indeed the distinguishing character of man; I mean, our capacities of speech, invention, and science, and those particulars in our frame, that entitle us to the denomination of moral, political, and religious beings? There is indeed a boundless variety in nature: and a scale gradually ascending might possibly be traced in some classes of being; as in the degrees of sagacity which belong to different brutes, and of intelligence as it appears in different men. But, how absurd is it to talk of a universal scale of things, when many of those things or ideas, that are mentioned as contiguous, are known to be separated by intervals of infinite extent! For such we must suppose the interval to be, between existence and nothing; between plants and animals; between a creature unconscious and irrational, and such a creature as man; and, which is still more apparent, between the highest order of created things, and the supreme, independent, and infinitely perfect being, who is the Author of all. In a scale of beings, or a series of ideas, said to rise, one above another, by gradual ascent, we must imagine (if the words have any meaning) the contiguous beings or ideas to have some qualities in common, or at least to have similar qualities, differing, not so much in kind, as in degree. But in existence, for example, what quality is there, which can be understood, in any degree, or in any kind, to belong to non-existence? In what respect can that which is not organized be said to approach to that which is; or dry, barren mould to resemble the *fabric* of a vegetable? Again, animals have sensation; plants have not: how can sensation, and the want of it, be confined as degrees of the same, or of kindred qualities! Moreover, man is capable of science, and endowed with consciousness, and a moral principle: can he, then, be supposed, in these respects, to be elevated, one degree only, above animals, that are destitute of a moral principle, and incapable of contemplation? Or does the wealth of him who has no wealth (if I may so speak) bear any proportion to that of a rich man? — And, lastly, is it possible to imagine, that any created being, the most glorious that can be conceived, should ever, after innumerable ages of improvement, approach within any distance less than infinite, of the almighty, eternal, and self-existent Creator?

Humble as we ought to be, under a sense of our great and many imperfections, let us however entertain a right idea of human nature; remembering, that it was made in the image of God, and that it is destined for immortality. And, in all our inquiries, let it be our care, to guard against prejudice and vain theory, and confine our views to matters of fact, and to plain and practical truth.

Six
Beattie's Division of Moral Philosophy

Human knowledge has been divided into history, philosophy, mathematics, and poetry or fable. History records the actions of men, and the other appearances of the visible universe. Poetry or fable is an imitation of history, according to probability, and exhibits things, not as they are, but as we might suppose them to be. Philosophy investigates the laws of nature, with a view to the regulation of human conduct, and the enlargement of human power. The mathematical sciences ascertain relations and proportions in quantity and number. — History and philosophy are founded in the knowledge of real things. Mathematical truths result from the nature of the quantities or numbers compared together. Poetical representations are approved of, if they resemble real things, and are themselves agreeable.

These parts of knowledge are not always kept distinct or separate. Philosophical investigation may find a place in history, and historical narrative is often necessary in philosophy. Many things in natural philosophy are ascertained and illustrated by mathematical reasoning. Poetical description may contribute to the embellishment of history; as may be seen in many passages of Livy, Tacitus, and other great historians. And true narrative and sound reasoning may in poetry be both ornamental and useful, as we see in many parts of *Paradise Lost*.

History is referred to memory, because it records what is past, whereof without memory men would have no knowledge. Poetry is the work of fancy or imagination, that is, of the inventive powers of man; which however must be regulated by the knowledge of nature. Philosophy and mathematics are improved and prosecuted by a right use of reason: but there is this difference between them, that to the discovery of mathematical truth reason is alone sufficient; whereas, to form a philosopher, reason and knowledge of nature are both necessary. Mathematics, therefore, though an instrument of philosophy, and an appendage to it, cannot with propriety be called a part of it.

Of philosophy different definitions and descriptions have been given, according to the different views which have been taken of it. As improved by Bacon, Boyle, Newton, and other great men, it may now be defined: the knowledge of nature applied to practical and useful purposes. It is useful in these four respects: first, because it exercises, and consequently improves, the rational powers of man: secondly, because it gives pleasure by gratifying curiosity: thirdly, because it regulates the opinions of men, and directs their actions: and fourthly, because it enables us to discover in part the existence and attributes of the Supreme Being, the Creator of all things, who has established those general principles, which are called the laws of nature, and according to which all the phenomena of the universe are produced.

Without some acquaintance with nature, we could not act at all, either in pursuing good, or in avoiding evil; we should not know that fire would burn or food nourish us. In brutes, whose experience, compared with ours, is very limited, the want of this knowledge is supplied, as far as may be necessary for them or beneficial to us, by natural instinct. — We discover causes by comparing things together, and observing the relations, resemblances, and connections that take place among them, and the effects produced by their being applied to one another. And, by comparing several causes together, we may sometimes trace them up to one common cause, or general principle; as Newton resolved the laws of motion into the *vis inertia* of matter.

As all philosophy is founded in the knowledge of nature, that is, of the things that really exist; and as all the things that really exist, as far as we are concerned in them and capable of observing them, are either bodies or spirits, philosophy consists of two parts, the philosophy of body, and the philosophy of spirit or mind. The latter, which is our present business, has been sometimes called the abstract philosophy, because it treats of things abstracted or distinguished from matter; and sometimes it is called moral philosophy, on account of its influence on life and manners. It consists, like every other branch of science, of a speculative and a practical part: the former being employed in ascertaining the appearances, and tracing out the laws, of nature; the latter, in applying this knowledge to practical and useful purposes. But to keep these two parts always, and entirely, distinct, would, if at all practicable, occasion no little inconvenience.

The speculative part of the philosophy of mind has been called pneumatology. It inquires into the nature of those spirits or minds, whereof we may have certain knowledge, and wherewith it concerns us to be acquainted; and those are the Deity and the human mind. Of other spirits, as good and evil angels, and the vital principle of brutes (if this may be called spirit), though we know that such things exist, we have not from the light of nature any certain knowledge, nor is it necessary that we should. Pneumatology, therefore, consists of two parts, first, natural theology, which evinces the being and attributes of the Deity, as far as these are discoverable by a right use of reason; and, secondly, the philosophy of the human mind, which some writers have termed psychology. We begin with the latter, because it is more immediately the object of our experience.

The mind of man may be improved, in respect, first of action, and secondly, of knowledge. The practical part, therefore, of this abstract philosophy consists of two parts, moral philosophy (strictly so called), which treats of the improvement of our active or moral powers; and logic, which treats of the improvement of our intellectual faculties. Thus we see that the moral sciences may be reduced to four, psychology, natural theology, moral philosophy, and logic. These, with their several divisions and subdivisions, I shall consider in that order which may be found the most convenient.

Seven

Of the Existence of God

That we ourselves and innumerable other things exist, may be taken for granted, as a first principle, as evident as any axiom in Euclid. Hence we infer, that something must always have existed. For if ever there was a time when nothing existed, there must have been a time when something began to be; and that something must have come into being without a cause; since, by the supposition, there was nothing before it. But that a thing should begin to exist, and yet proceed from no cause, is both absurd and inconceivable; all men, by the law of their nature, being necessarily determined to believe, that whatever begins to exist proceeds from some cause. Therefore some being must have existed from eternity. — This being must have been either dependent on something else, or not dependent on any thing else. Now an eternal succession of dependent beings, or a being which is dependent and yet exists from eternity, is impossible. For if every part of such a succession be dependent, then the whole must be so; and, if the whole be dependent, there must be something on which it depends; and that something must be prior in time to that which depends on it; which is impossible, if that which is dependent be from eternity. It follows, that there must be an eternal and independent being, on whom all other beings depend.

Some atheists seem to acknowledge a first cause, when they ascribe the origin of the universe to *chance*. But it is not easy to guess what they mean by this word. We call those things *accidental*, *casual*, or the *effects of chance*, whose immediate causes we are unacquainted with; as the changes of the weather, for example;

which however every body believes to be owing to some adequate cause, though we cannot find it out. Sometimes, when an intelligent being does a thing without design, as when a man throwing a stone out of his field happens to strike a man whom he did not see; it is called *accidental*. In affirming that the universe proceeds from chance, it would appear, that atheists mean, either that it has no cause at all, or that its cause did not act intelligently, or with design, in the production of it. That the universe proceeds from no cause, we have seen to be absurd. And therefore, we shall overturn all the atheistical notions concerning chance, if we can show, what indeed is easily shown, and what no considerate person can be ignorant of, that the cause of the universe is intelligent and wise, and in creating it, have acted with intelligence and wisdom.

Wherever we find a number of things, complex in their structure, and yet perfectly similar, we believe them to be the work of design. Were a man to find a thousand pairs of shoes, of the same shape, size, and materials, it would not be easy to persuade him that the whole was chance-work. Now the instances of complex and similar productions in nature are so very numerous as to exceed computation. All human bodies, for example, though each of them consists of almost an infinite number of parts, are perfectly uniform in their structure and functions; and the same thing may be said of all the animals and plants of any particular species. To suppose this the effect of undesigning chance, or the production of an unintelligent cause, is as great an absurdity as it is possible to imagine.

Further: a composition of parts mutually adapted we must always consider as the work of design; especially if it be found in a great variety of instances. Suppose a body, an equilateral prism, for example, to be formed by chance; and suppose a certain quantity of matter accidentally determined to resolve itself into tubes of a certain dimension. It is as infinite to one, that these tubes should have orifices equal to the base of the prism; there being an infinity of other magnitudes equally possible. Suppose the orifices equal, it is as infinite to one that any of the tubes should be prismatical; infinite other figures being equally possible. Suppose one of them prismatical, there is, for the same reason, an infinity of chances, that it shall not be equilateral. Suppose it equilateral, there are still infinite chances that the tube and prism shall never meet. Suppose them to meet, there are innumerable chances that their axes shall not be in the same direction. Suppose them to have the same direction, there are still may chances that the angles of the prism shall not coincide with those of the tube: and supposing them to coincide, there are innumerable chances that no force shall be applied in such a direction as to make the prism enter the tube.

How many millions of chances, then, are there against the *casual* formation of one prism inserted in a prismatic tube! Which yet a small degree of design could easily accomplish. Were we to find, in a solitary place, a composition of this kind, of which the tube was iron and the prism of wood, it would not be easy for us to believe, that such a thing was the work of chance. And if so small a thing cannot be without design, what shall we say of the mechanism of a plant, an animal, a system of plants and animals, a world, a system of worlds, an universe! No person, who has any pretensions to rationality, and is not determined to shut his eyes against the truth, will ever bring himself to believe, that works so stupendous could be the effect of undesigning chance.

To set this argument in a proper light, it would be necessary to take a survey of the works of nature; in which the vast number of systems, the artful union of parts, the nice proportions established between every part and system and its respective end, the innumerable multitudes of species, and the infinite numbers of forms in every species, are so conspicuous as to prove, beyond all doubt, that the Creator of the world is infinitely wise, powerful and good. Let a man examine only a grain of corn, by cutting it open and viewing it with a microscope; and then let him consider another grain as planted in the earth, and by the influence of heat, soil, air, and moisture, springing up into a plant, consisting of a great number of vessels that disperse the vital sap into every part, and endowed with the power, or susceptibility, of growing in bulk, till in due time it produce a number of other grains of the same kind, necessary to the existence of man and other creatures; — let a rational being attend to this fact, and compare it with the noblest efforts of human art; and if he is not struck with the infinite superiority of the one to the other, — what can we say of him, but that he is void of understanding! And yet the mechanism and growth of a vegetable seems an inconsiderable thing, when we think of the wisdom and power displayed in many other works of nature.

What a fabric is our solar system! Wherein bodies of such enormous magnitude accomplish their revolutions through spaces immense; and with a regularity, than which nothing can be more perfect. The distance of the planets from the sun, and their several magnitudes, are determined with the utmost wisdom, and according to the nicest geometrical proportion. The central orb, whether we consider its glorious appearance, its astonishing greatness, or the beneficial influence of its light and heat, is such an object as no rational being can contemplate without adoring the Creator. We have good reason to believe, that there are thousands of other suns and systems of worlds, more glorious perhaps and more extensive than ours; which form such a stupendous whole, that the human soul, labouring to comprehend it, loses sight of itself and of all sublunary things, and is totally overwhelmed with astonishment and veneration. With such thoughts in our view, we are apt to forget the wonders that lie immediately around us, and that the smallest plant or animal body amounts to a demonstration of the divine existence. But God appears in all his works, in the least as well as in the greatest; and there is not, in the whole circle of human sciences, any one truth confirmed by so many irresistible proofs, as the existence of the Deity.

The diurnal motion of the planets is the easiest way possible of exposing all their parts to the influence of light and heat. Their globular form is the fittest for motion, and for the free circulation of atmosphere around them; and at the same time supplies the most capacious surface. The principle of gravitation, prevailing through the whole system, and producing innumerable phenomena, is a most amazing instance of unbounded variety united with strictest uniformity and proportion. — But it is impossible in a few pages to give such an enumeration of particulars, as would do any justice to the subject. The man, who should suppose a large city, consisting of a hundred thousand palaces; all finished in the minutest parts, and furnished with the greatest elegance and variety of ornament, and with all sorts of books, pictures, and statues, executed in the most ingenious manner; to have been produced by the accidental blowing of winds and rolling of sands, would justly be accounted irrational. But to suppose the universe, or our solar system, or this earth, to be the work of undesigning chance, is an absurdity incomparably greater.

And now, — from a particular survey of the terraqueous globe; of the atmosphere, so necessary to light and life and vegetation; of the different productions of different countries, so well adapted to the constitution and use of the inhabitants: from the variety of useful minerals to be found in all parts of the earth; from the wonderful mechanism and still more wonderful growth of vegetables, their vast number and variety, their beauty and utility, and the great abundance of such as are most useful, particularly grass and corn; from the structure, life, motion, and instincts of animals; from the exact correspondence of their instincts to their necessities; from the different kinds of them and of vegetables having been so long preserved; from the similitude between all the individuals of each species; from the body and soul of man so replete with wonders; from his intellectual and moral faculties; and from innumerable other particulars that come under the cognizance of man; — we might proceed to set the Divine Existence in a still clearer light, if that were necessary: but the subject is so copious that we cannot enter upon it. We should injure it by a brief summary; and a full detail would comprehend astronomy, geography, natural history, natural philosophy, and several other sciences. I therefore refer you to what has been written on it, by Xenophon, in the fourth chapter of his first book of *Memorabilia*; by Cicero, in his second book *De natura deorum* [*Of the Nature of the Gods*]; by Derham, Ray, Fénelon, Nieuwentyt; by Clarke, Bentley, Abernethy, &c. in their sermons; and by other ingenious authors.[1]

Some have urged, that there are in the universe many marks of irregularity and want of design, as well as regularity and wisdom; and that therefore we have no evidence, that the being who made

---

[1] [William Derham, *Physico-Theology: or, A Demonstration of the Being and Attributes of God, from his works of Creation* (1713); John Ray, *The Wisdom of God manifested in the works of Creation* (1691); François Fénelon, *Démonstration de l'existence de Dieu* (1713); Bernard Nieuwentyt, *L'existence de Dieu démontrée par les merveilles de la nature* (1727); Samuel Clarke, *A Demonstration of the Being and Attributes of God* (1705); Richard Bentley, *The Folly and Unreasonableness of Atheism* (1693); John Abernethy, *Discourses concerning the Being and Natural Perfections of God* (1740).]

all things is perfectly good and wise. — But though we were to admit the fact, the inference would not be fair. The wonderful contrivance which appears in the arrangement of the solar system, or even in the human body, abundantly proves the Creator to be infinitely wise. That he has not thought fit to make all things equally beautiful and excellent, can never be an imputation on his wisdom and goodness: for how absurd would it be to say, that he would have displayed more wisdom, if he had endowed all things with life, perception, and reason! Stones and plants, air and water, are most useful things, and would have been much less useful if they had been percipient beings; as the inferior animals would have been both less useful and less happy, if they had been rational. Their existence, therefore, and their natures, are proofs of the Divine goodness and wisdom, instead of being arguments against it.

Besides, no man of sense accounts himself a complete judge of any work, even of a fellow-creature, unless he understands its end and structure, as well as the workman himself does. When we wish to know with certainty the value of a ship, or a house, or any complex machine, we consult those who are skilled in such things; for them only we hold to be competent judges. In a complex contrivance there may be many parts, of the greatest importance, which and unskilful observer would not perceive the use of, or would perhaps declare to be useless. Now in the course of providence, a vast number of events and objects may be employed to accomplish one great end; and it is impossible for us to pronounce reasonably of any one event or object, that it is useless or improper, unless we know its tendency, and connection with other things both past and future; which in cases innumerable we cannot do. For of the past we know but little, the present we know imperfectly, and of the future we have no certain knowledge beyond what is revealed. The system of providence relating to us and to our final destination, extends through thousands of years, as we have good reason to believe; but our life is short, and our views are bounded by our experience, which is very limited. That therefore may be a most wise and beneficent dispensation, which to a captious mind and fallible judgement may appear the contrary.

Moreover, the Deity intended, that the nature of all created things should be progressive. Many years pass away before a man arrives at maturity; and many days, before a plant can yield good fruit. Every thing is imperfect, while advancing to perfection; and we cannot say of any thing, whether it be well or ill-contrived for answering its end, till we know what its state of maturity will be, and what the effects are whereof it may be productive. Physical evils may, as will be shown by and by, be improved into blessings; and it will also be shown, that moral evil is a consequence of that law of nature which makes us capable of virtue and happiness. Even in this world, providence often brings good out of evil; and every man of observation must have perceived, that certain events of his life, which when they happened seemed to be great misfortunes, have been found to be great blessings in the end.

If, then, that which seems evil may really be good, for any thing we know to the contrary; and if that which is really evil often does, and always may, produce good: how can man be so presumptuous as to suppose, because he cannot distinctly see the nature and use of some things around him, that therefore the Creator of the world is not supremely good and wise! No man can draw this conclusion, unless he believe himself infallible in his knowledge of all things past, present, and future; and he who believes so, if there be any such, is a fool.

Eight

A First Lesson in Religion

From Beattie's Life of his son, James Hay Beattie[1]

... The doctrines of religion I wished to impress on his mind, as soon as it might be prepared to receive them; but I did not see the propriety of making him commit to memory theological sentences, or any sentences, which it was not possible for him to understand. And I was desirous to make a trial how far his own reason could go in tracing out with a little direction, the great first principle of all religion, the being of God. The following fact is mentioned, not as a proof of superior sagacity in him (for I have no doubt that most children would in like circumstances think as he did), but merely as a moral or logical experiment.

He had reached his fifth or sixth year, knew the alphabet, and could read a little; but had received no particular information with respect to the Author of his being: because I thought he could not yet understand such information; and because I had learned from my own experience, that to be made to repeat words not understood is extremely detrimental to the faculties of a young mind. In a corner of a little garden, without informing any person of the circumstance, I wrote in the mould, with my finger, the

---

[1] [James Hay Beattie was born in 1768, and died in 1790. He was his father's favourite, and in 1787 became Joint Professor of Moral Philosophy at Marischal College with his father.]

three initial letters of his name; and, sowing garden cresses in the furrows, covered up the seed, and smoothed the ground. Ten days after, he came running to me, and with astonishment in his countenance told me, that his name was growing in the garden. I laughed at the report, and seemed inclined to disregard it; but he insisted on my going to see what had happened. Yes, said I carelessly, on coming to the place, I see it is so; but there is nothing in this worth notice; it is mere chance: and I went away. He followed me, and, taking hold of my coat, said with some earnestness, it could not be mere chance; for that some body must have contrived matters so as to produce it. — I pretend not to give his words, or my own, for I have forgotten both; but I give the substance of what passed between us in such language as we both understood. — So you think, I said, that what appears so regular as the letters of your name cannot be by chance. Yes, said he, with firmness, I think so. Look at yourself, I replied, and consider your hands and fingers, your legs and feet, and other limbs; are they not regular in their appearance, and useful to you? He said, they were. Came you then hither, said I, by chance? No, he answered, that cannot be; something must have made me. And who is that something, I asked. He said, he did not know. (I took particular notice, that he did not say, as Rousseau fancies a child in like circumstances would say, that his parents made him). I had now gained the point I aimed at: and saw, that his reason taught him, (though he could not so express it) that what begins to be must have a cause, and that what is formed with regularity must have an intelligent cause. I therefore told him the name of the Great Being who made him and all the world; concerning whose adorable nature I gave him such information as I thought he could in some measure comprehend. The lesson affected him greatly, and he never forgot either it, or the circumstance that introduced it . . .

Nine

Of the Nature of Virtue

This word [i.e, *virtue*], in its most general acceptation, denotes *power* or *ability*. As applied to man, and characterized by the epithet *moral*, (to distinguish it from other sorts of virtue which will be specified afterwards), it signifies some quality, disposition, or habit, which fits a man for answering his *end*, that is, for living as he ought to live, and being what he ought to be; or, more explicitly, for living as the Author of his nature intended that he should live, and being what the Author of his nature intended that he should be. — But, can human reason discover what the Author of nature intended in making men such beings as they are? Yes: reason can discover this, in the same way in which it discovers, (and with the same degree of certainty), that an artist, in making a clock such a thing as we see it is, intended that it should measure time, and announce the hour. — For what end was man made, is, therefore, the first inquiry in ethics. Till we know this, we cannot know what is suitable to his end, or what is unsuitable; that is, we cannot know what is his virtue, or what is not his virtue.

Human nature is a very complex object, and confessedly in a state of lamentable degeneracy. But neither from its degeneracy, nor from its complexness, can any reasonable supposition arise of the impossibility of discovering its end. From many appearances in a ruinous building it might be easy to see the intention of the builder; whether he meant it for a church or a storehouse, a dwelling for men, or a shelter for cattle. And a person moderately skilled in mechanics might find out the use of a very complex machine, even though every part of it were new to him: which it cannot be pretended that any part of human nature is to us. And when, from the structure and relations of the parts, the end of any system is fairly investigated, the complex nature of that system proves nothing against the certainty of the investigation, but is an argument for it.

Man was made for two ends or purposes, action and knowledge. This will be readily admitted by every person who has observed, that all the powers of our nature fit us (as was formerly intimated) for action, for knowledge, or for both. That of these two ends action is the nobler, and that, by consequence, action is man's chief end, will appear, when we consider, that our happiness depends rather on what we do, than on what we know; that extensive knowledge falls to the share of but few, whereas action is the business of all men; and that knowledge is valuable only as it serves to promote or assist action, — those speculations being of no value, which can be applied to no practical purpose. Now we are capable of various sorts of action. The next inquiry therefore is: for what sort of action was man made?

We discover the end for which a system is made, by examining its fabric or constitution. In this way one might find out for what end a clock or watch was made, though one had never seen or heard of such a thing before. But the mere knowledge of the parts taken and examined separately would not be enough; the wheels and pegs lying in a heap, or detached from one another, would, to a person unskilled in the art, convey no idea of a clock or watch, or of the use of either: they must be put together according to the intention of the maker, and examined in their connected state, and as operating on one another: and that circumstance in the structure must be particularly attended to, that they are all subservient to, and regulated by the balance, or the pendulum. Human nature, though not a machine, is a most curious system, more so than any other that this sublunary world can exhibit, and consists of many parts or faculties mutually operating upon, or influencing one another; one of which, in common language called conscience, has a natural supremacy over all the rest: — as I shall endeavour to prove, when I have first given a brief account of this faculty.

Every man must be conscious, that he approves of some actions, because they seem to him to be good, and right, and what ought to be done; and disapproves of other actions, because he thinks them bad, wrong, and what ought not to be done. Now it is this faculty of conscience, that gives rise to these sentiments of approbation and disapprobation; and so enables us to distinguish between virtue and vice, between moral good and moral evil, between what is our duty and what is contrary to duty. This faculty is peculiar to rational nature; brutes have nothing like it: the being who is destitute of it we cannot consider rational. It is this faculty which makes man capable of virtue, and consequently of happiness; for without virtue rational beings cannot be happy. Some modern philosophers are willing to believe, that of every human faculty the inferior animals participate in some degree; and, because a dog loves and fears his master, infer, that brutes are not quite destitute of moral and religious notions. With equal reason it might be inferred, because dogs bark at the moon, and wolves *behold* or *behowl* it, as Shakespeare says, (either reading will serve in this place), that they are also studious of astronomy.[1]

Actions performed through compulsion, or against our will, conscience does not approve, even though they may tend to good; nor disapprove, though they may have an evil tendency: those only are approved as morally good, or disapproved as immoral, in the performance of which man is understood to be a free agent. Nor is it the action merely, that we either approve or disapprove. A man may kill another by accident, or may kill another by design: and in both cases the *action* may be the same; the firing of a musket may do either. But in the former case, the manslayer may be entirely innocent, in the latter, he may be guilty of murder: for in the latter there may be a criminal purpose, in the former there is or may be none. Our affections, therefore, dispositions, motives, purposes, or intentions, are the real objects of moral approbation or disapprobation.

The actions we consider as the signs and proofs of what was in the mind of the agent. For man cannot see the heart; and we call an action immoral or virtuous, according as it seems to us to manifest a criminal or a virtuous intention. In our intentions themselves, though not exerted in action, there may be virtue, or there may be

---

[1] [Beattie is alluding to a disputed passage in Shakespeare's *A Midsummer Night's Dream*: see Act V, l. 358.]

vice. He who intends to murder, is really, and in the sight of God, who knows the heart, a murderer. And he who does all the good he can, and wishes he were able to do more, is virtuous in proportion to the extent of his wishes, however small his ability may be.

In this notion of moral approbation, suggested to every man by his conscience, several notions or sentiments are comprehended, similar indeed in their nature, but which may be verbally distinguished. A generous or good action delights us when we think of it; and we say, that it is fit, right, and what ought to be done, and that he who has done it deserves reward or praise. A wicked action gives us pain when we think of it; and we say, that it is improper, wrong, and what ought not to be done, and that he who has done it deserves punishment or blame. These notions are universal among mankind. We are conscious of them in some degree, and frequently in a great degree, when the good or evil is done by others: we are conscious of them in a very great, and often in a most intense degree, when it is done by ourselves. — A man's moral judgement, applied to the consideration of his own conduct, is in common language called his conscience; when applied to the consideration of moral good or evil in general, it may be called the moral faculty; and has sometimes, both by modern and by ancient philosophers, been termed the moral sense. Disputes have been raised about the propriety of these appellations; but, if the thing be understood, the name is of small importance.

* * *

Conscience being proved to be the supreme regulating principle of human nature, it follows that *virtuous action* is the ultimate end for which man was made. For virtue is that which conscience approves; and what contradicts the supreme principle of any system must be contrary to the end of that system. It is true, that in most men for a little, and in bad men for a long time, conscience may lose its power, when born down by evil habit, or tumultuous passion: even as the strongest man, by being kept long in fetters, may lose the use of his limbs; and as the most lively genius, if doomed to slavery, may sink into inactivity and stupefaction. But though conscience may lose its power, it still retains its authority, that is, its right to govern. A good king may be dethroned by the rebellion of a wicked subject, and may for a time be unable to enforce his own laws; but he still retains that *right* to govern, which is secured to him by the constitution of his country. He however may die without being restored: but sooner or later, in the next world if not in this, conscience will resume its rights, and cover the guilty head with confusion.

We act, therefore, according to the end and law of our nature, when we act according to conscience. By doing so, we may, and indeed often must, control our inferior appetites; but then we promote the happiness and perfection of our *whole nature*. So a medicine may do good to the whole body, though it be offensive to the taste, or even to the stomach. By complying with an appetite in opposition to conscience, we may obtain a slight gratification; but then we introduce disorder and unhappiness into our nature, and make it more imperfect than it was before. So things may please the palate, and give momentary comfort to the stomach, which yet have poisonous qualities.

And now, we see in what respects a life of virtue may be said to be, what some ancients moralists called it, a life according to nature. The indulgence of any natural appetite may be called a natural indulgence; but, to act suitably to the dictates of the moral faculty, is according to the general tendency of our *whole nature*, because agreeable to the supreme principle of the human system. Some vices may be called natural; because there are in us passions that prompt to them, and a principle of corruption or degeneracy that urges our compliance: but no vice can be said to be according to our whole nature; because nothing is so but what conscience, our supreme regulating principle, approves. What pleases the palate may hurt health, and be therefore pernicious to the human constitution. That only can be called natural food, which preserves or promotes the health of the whole body.

Yet it has been said, that a life of virtue is a life of mortification and warfare. And nothing is more true; notwithstanding that, upon the whole, such a life must be the most happy. The nature of man is miserably corrupted. Criminal passions crave indulgence; and it requires great efforts to resist them: criminal habits must be overcome; and this is a work of long and difficult labour. Things, that by their agreeable qualities attract our notice, and engage our liking, often prove a snare; and it requires incessant watchfulness to keep aloof from them, or, when they fall in our way, to prevent their gaining on our affections. The best men fall into transgression, which in a good man is always followed by repentance; and repentance, though most salutary in its effects, is attended with great anguish of mind. How many dangers and disappointments must they encounter who engage in active life! Yet such a life is incomparably happier than security with idleness. Even so, virtue may be a warfare; but it is, upon the whole, happy as well as honourable, and never fails to be crowned with victory and eternal peace. Vice is a warfare too; but it is neither honourable nor happy, and necessarily ends in shame and punishment.

We may further learn, from what has been said, how foolishly those men argue, who give way to all their passions without reserve, and excuse themselves by saying, that every passion is natural, and that they cannot be blamed for doing what nature prompts them to do. The fallacy of this plea must be very apparent to those who, in their notions of man, can distinguish between the whole and a part. Partial indulgence may no doubt be obtained by gratifying criminal propensity; as a man may please his palate while he is swallowing poison: but every indulgence is unnatural, or at least improper, which disorders the moral system, by counteracting its supreme regulating principle. From the wheels of a clock or watch, if you take off those restraints whereby the motion is made regular, the wheels must move irregularly. Such motion you may, if you please, call natural; because it is natural for bodies to move according to the force that impels them: but such motion you cannot call right, or agreeable to the purpose of the maker, because it is not governed by that principle which was intended to control and regulate the whole machine.

Few sentiments are more familiar to the human mind than this, that vice deserves punishment, and virtue reward. But, to prevent mistakes, it is necessary to add, that, in strict propriety of speech, our virtue is meritorious with respect to our fellow-creatures only. Considered in his relation to the Supreme Being, man, when he has done his best, is an unprofitable servant. To enter into some particulars on this subject. — Life is by all men accounted a great blessing; for, in the general intercourse of the world, few things are more valued than that which supports it. Now life is a blessing, which the Deity confers on his creatures gratuitously: we cannot say that our virtue gives us a title to it, or is an adequate return for it. Our reason, conscience, susceptibility of happiness, and capacity for virtue, are all the free gift of God: and who can imagine that there is merit in having received what has been given us! If we abuse his benefits, we deserve punishment; if we make a right use of them, (which no man of sense will say that he does), we do nothing more than what is incumbent on us in consequence of our having received them, and for which our enjoyment of them is more than an adequate recompense.

Besides: virtue, even in this life, obtains very considerable gratifications. It obtains peace of mind, and an approving conscience; blessings more precious than life. It generally obtains the esteem of good men, and some degree of respect even from the worthless: the advantages whereof will be allowed to be great by those who consider, that good reputation, which alone can procure us the esteem of others, is by every generous mind accounted invaluable. Now, let it not be forgotten, that this peace of mind, esteem of good men, and respect from all men, are the result of laws established by our beneficent Creator, for the comfort of the virtuous in this world of trial. These are high privileges: for what other terrestrial consolations would a wise man exchange them?

It is to be observed further, that all human virtue is very imperfect; and that the best man on earth can scarce be said to pass a day, without violating the divine law in thought, word, or deed. There are hardly any human actions, how virtuous so ever they may *seem*, and how meritorious so ever with respect to our fellow-creatures they may *be*, of which the agent, if a man of sense, will not readily acknowledge, that they must, in the sight of the Creator, appear tainted with imperfection; and that we have always reason to pray, with humility and contrition, that God would pardon what is wrong or wanting even in our best performances. We all know, that criminal habits pervert the understanding, and debase the moral faculty; and that we have contracted many evil habits, which, with proper attention, we might have avoided, and are of course accountable for those debasements and perversities which are owing to our inattention, and for all the errors and follies thence resulting.

Now, since all human excellence is so defective; since even the best men are so great offenders; and since the advantages that virtue may enjoy even in this life are so important; what man is there who can say, that his virtue *entitles* him to receive any other rewards from that God whom he is continually offending; to whose goodness he is every moment under unspeakable obligations; and compared with whose consummate purity all human attainments are in the proportion of weakness to omnipotence, of finite to infinite, of time to eternity! From the placability of our Judge, who knows our frailty, reason, unenlightened by revelation, might perhaps encourage the penitent to hope for pardon; but to pardon a criminal, and to receive him into favour, are different things: and what proportion is there between human virtue, debased as it is with vice and with error, and a state of never-ending felicity in the life to come? Can we merit such a reward! — We, whose goodness, if we have any, is even in this world rewarded beyond what it deserves!

These speculations might lead into a labyrinth of perplexity, if it were not for what revelation declares concerning the divine government. It declares, that man may expect, on the performance of certain conditions, not only pardon, but everlasting happiness; not on account of his own merit, which in the sight of God is nothing, but on account of the infinite merits of the Redeemer; who, descending from the height of glory, voluntarily underwent the punishment due to sin, and thus obtained those high privileges for as many as should comply with the terms announced by him to mankind. — So much for the supremacy, and general nature, of the faculty of conscience.

It was hinted, and partly proved, that man's chief happiness results from virtue. A more explicit proof of this point may now be proper, and is as follows. — If we could at once gratify all the propensities of our nature, that would be our highest possible happiness, and what we might call our *summum bonum*, or chief good. But that cannot be; for our propensities are often inconsistent, so that if we comply with one, we must contradict another. He who is enslaved to sensuality cannot at the same time enjoy the more sublime pleasures of science and virtue: and he who devotes himself to science, or adheres to virtue, must often act in opposition to his inferior appetites. The ambitious man cannot labour for the acquisition of power, and taste the sweets of indolence at the same time: and the miser, while he indulges himself in the contemplation of his wealth, must be a stranger to the pleasures of beneficence. The gratification of all our appetites at once, is therefore impossible. Consequently, some degree of self-denial must be practised by every man, whether good or bad, by the ruffian as well as the saint, the sensualist as well as the hermit: and man's greatest possible happiness must be, at least in the present state, not a complete gratification of all our propensities, but the most comprehensive gratification of which we are capable. Now some pleasures conduce more to happiness than others, and are therefore more important than those others. And if we sacrifice a less important to a more important one, we add to our sum of happiness; and we take away from that sum, when we sacrifice a more important pleasure to one of less importance.

In forming a judgement of the comparative importance of gratifications, the following maxims may be safely admitted. First: some are of greater dignity than others, because more suitable to our rational nature, and tending more to improve it: the pleasures of the glutton or the miser are surely of less dignity than those which we derive from the discovery of truth, from the study of nature, or from the performance of a generous action. Pleasures, therefore, which have more dignity are preferable to such as have less. And it will be readily allowed, in the second place, that a more intense pleasure is more valuable than one that is less intense; and that such as are not attended with pain are better than those that bring pain along with them. Thirdly: considering the manifold evils of life, it will hardly be doubted, that pleasures which alleviate distress are preferable to those that do not; and that those which give a relish to other pleasures are better than such as make others insipid. Fourthly: durable gratifications are preferable to such as are transient; and those that do not please on reflection are of less value than those that do. Fifthly: some grow more insipid the more we are used to them, others continually improve upon repetition; the last are undoubtedly preferable. And lastly, those which may be had at all times and in all places must contribute more to happiness, than such as depend on circumstances, and are not in our own power.

If we be satisfied of the truth of these remarks on the comparative value of human gratifications, and we can hardly call them in question if we allow experience to be a rational ground of knowledge, we must also be satisfied, that of man's chief good, or greatest possible happiness, the following is a just character. It must be something that gratifies the more dignified powers of his nature; — yields intense pleasure, unmixed, and unaccompanied, with pain; — alleviates the calamities of life; — is consistent with, and gives a relish to, other pleasures; — is in itself durable, and pleases on reflection; — does not pall upon the sense, but grows more exquisite the more we are accustomed to it; — is attainable by every man, because dependent on himself, and not on outward circumstances; — and is accommodated to all times and places. — Now, every gratification, whereof human nature is capable, may be comprehended under one or other of these three classes: — the pleasures of outward sense; — the pleasures of imagination and intellect, that is of taste and science; — and the pleasures that result from the right exercise of our moral powers. Let us see then in which of these classes we are likely to find our chief good, or greatest felicity.

First: that the pleasures of sense contribute not a little to our comfort, and that some of them are not momentary, is acknowledged. But they are confessedly, at least in the opinion of all the enlightened part of mankind, the lowest gratifications of our nature; for no man ever yet became respectable by attaching himself to them. They often bring disgust and even pain along with them; they please not upon reflection; and they tend to disqualify us for the nobler delights of science and virtue. They depend not on ourselves, but on other things and persons; they are attainable in certain circumstances only; and we lose all taste for them in adversity. To them therefore the character of man's chief good is not applicable.

Secondly: the pleasures of imagination and science have great dignity; the pursuit of them is honourable, though it may run to excess; and they are consistent both with moral and with sensual gratification, and in an eminent degree friendly to the former. They are not momentary; they please upon reflection: and they grow more exquisite by being frequent. But they do not alleviate the calamities of life: and so far are they from being accommodated to all times and places, that by all the uninstructed, that is, by the greater part of the human race, they are absolutely unattainable. Consequently, the character of man's chief good does not belong to them.

Thirdly: the delights that arise from the right exercise of our moral powers, and from the approbation of conscience, are of all gratifications the most dignified: the more a man attaches himself to them, the more respectable he becomes, and it is not possible for him to carry such attachment to excess: with disgust, or with pain, they are never attended: they give a relish for other pleasures, by preserving the mind cheerful, and the body in health: they are not inconsistent with any innocent gratification, that is, they are consistent with all pleasures except those which bring pain and misery: they please intensely on reflection; are a perpetual source of comfort in adversity; become more exquisite the more we are accustomed to them; are within the reach of every man, high and low, learned and ignorant; are suited to all times and places: and, so long as we retain our rationality, it is not in the power of malice or of fortune to deprive us of them. To virtue, therefore, which is the right exercise of our moral powers, the character of man's chief good *does* belong: which will appear still more evident when we consider, that the hope of future felicity is the chief consolation of the present life, and that the virtuous alone can reasonably entertain that hope. As, on the other hand, vice, in the most prosperous condition, is subject to the pangs of a guilty conscience, and to the dreadful anticipation of future punishment; which are sufficient to destroy all earthly happiness.

I am far from adopting, in its literal sense, that maxim of the poet, 'Virtue alone is happiness below'.[2] For though I say, with the Peripatetics, that virtue is the chief good, I do not say, with the Stoics, that it is the only good. That a virtuous man in health and prosperity may be happier than a man of equal virtue beset with adversity and disease, I see no reason to doubt; and if so, health and prosperity are good, and disease and adversity evil. — Besides, if destitute of the hope of immortality, the mind of a good man (especially if he were a man of sensibility and penetration) would not be happy in this world, but would, on the contrary, be a prey to perplexity and anguish. Such a man would be perpetually shocked with the confusion which would then appear in the universe, and of which he could foresee no end. The world to him would seem to be governed by a being, whose power was indeed

---

[2] [Pope, *Essay on Man*, IV, l. 310.]

great, but whose justice and goodness were not equally conspicuous. It is the belief of a future state of retribution that satisfies the rational mind of the infinite rectitude of the divine government; and it is this persuasion only, that can make the virtuous happy in the present life. And as we could not, without revelation, entertain a well-grounded hope of future reward, it is only the virtue of the true Christian that can obtain the happiness we now speak of.

Virtue being the chief good of individuals, it is hardly necessary to add, that it must be the chief good of society. For of individuals society is made up, and that is the happiest society in which there is most private happiness. We cannot conceive a community, or a nation, to be prosperous, if the people who compose it are miserable. Kingdoms in every age have been flourishing and happy no longer than they maintained their virtue.

And now it appears, that virtue is founded in our constitution, and agreeable to *our whole nature*, of which indeed it is the perfection; that it must therefore be conformable to the will of him who is the author of our nature; and that it is the only means of making mankind truly happy. Vice, consequently, is contrary to *our whole nature*, and tends to debase and destroy it, is contrary to the will of God, and contrary to our own interest. — I conclude the chapter with the following *description*, every part of which will be found to have been enforced and illustrated by the foregoing reasonings. 'Moral virtue is a disposition of the mind — voluntary and active — agreeable in itself, and praiseworthy — incumbent on all men — and tending to improve our whole nature, and promote our happiness both here and hereafter'. So much for the general nature of virtue. I shall proceed to the practical part of Ethics, when I have made a few miscellaneous observations.

* * *

It may be proper, before we proceed to practical ethics, to offer a few brief observations on some points relating to the moral faculty, which have been made matter of controversy among philosophers. — Some have maintained, that moral approbation is an agreeable feeling, and nothing more; and that moral disapprobation is merely a disagreeable feeling. The truth is, that moral approbation is both an agreeable feeling, and also a determination of judgement or reason; the former following the latter, as an effect follows the cause. For the conduct of others, or of ourselves, would not give us an agreeable *feeling*, if we did not first *judge* it to be right; nor any painful feeling, if we did not first judge it to be wrong. Feelings and determinations of judgement frequently accompany each other: and sometimes, as in the case just now mentioned, the judgement precedes the feeling, and gives rise to it: and sometimes the feeling precedes and gives rise to the judgement; as in the case of our judging, that external things, because they affect our senses in a certain way, (that is, raise in us certain feelings), do really exist, and are what they appear to be. In popular language feelings and judgements are too often confounded; but they are not the same. Feelings distinguish what is animated from what is inanimate; judgements, what is rational from what is irrational. In other words, all animals feel, rational beings alone can judge. Previously to their acquiring the use of reason, human creatures are not considered, by either the moralist or the lawgiver, as moral beings: which would hardly be the case, if moral approbation and disapprobation were understood to be feelings merely, and not also exertions of rationality.

Sensations and sentiments should also be distinguished, though they too have been confounded by some modern writers. Opinion, notion, judgement, is the true English meaning of *sentiment*, which of course implies the use of reason. Of *moral sentiment*, therefore, we may speak with strict propriety; but *moral sensation* is not proper English: and yet, if the suggestions of the moral faculty were understood to be mere feelings, it would seem captious to object to it. In French the word *sentiment* has greater latitude of signification than in English; and this may have led some of our writers into a licentious use of that term. It may be added, that the same word has been, and often is, used in another peculiar sense, to denote an opinion or thought which greatly affects or interests us. This, too, is an innovation in our language, and seems to have given rise to various modes of expression, which, though we frequently see and hear them, it is not easy to explain. We have heard, not only of men and women of sentiment, (where perhaps the word may mean *taste* or *delicacy*); and of *sentimental* men and women, (which I know not whether I understand); but also of *sentimental tales*; and, what is yet more extraordinary, of *sentimental journeys*, — which I think should be *advertised* in the same paragraph with *philosophical razors*.[3]

Conscience, like every other human faculty, and suitably to the whole analogy of animal and even of vegetable nature, arrives at maturity by degrees, and may be either improved by cultivation, or perverted by mismanagement. In our early years, it is improved by moral precept and good example; and, as we advance in life, by habits of consideration, and a strict adherence to truth and our duty. By different treatment; by want of instruction, bad example, inconsiderate behaviour, neglect of duty, and disregard to truth, it may be perverted, and almost destroyed. From this, however, we are not warranted to infer, as some have done, that it is not a natural faculty, but an artificial way of thinking superinduced by education; nor suppose, that opposite habits, and opposite modes of teaching, would have made us disapprove virtue and approve vice, with the same energy of thought, wherewith we now disapprove vice, and approve virtue.[4]

For, let it be observed, that even our outward senses may be made better or worse by good or bad management. Excessive light, or too long continuance in darkness, may hurt our eyes irrecoverably; and, from a companion who squints, it is neither difficult nor uncommon to learn a habit of squinting: fever may destroy taste and smell: even touch, or any other faculty, may be depraved by those disorders which we call *nervous*; and which, by injudicious conduct, in regard to food, study, or exercise, any man may bring upon himself. — Those powers also, which I took the liberty to call, (perhaps not very properly), *secondary senses*, may, in like manner, be either *debased*;[5] — a musical ear, for example, by continually hearing barbarous music; and a taste for elegance and sublimity, by long acquaintance with vulgar manners, vulgar lan-

---

[3] [Lawrence Sterne had published *A Sentimental Journey* in 1768.]

[4] [Beattie is perhaps alluding to Hume's claim that justice and other virtues are 'artificial' rather than 'natural': see *A Treatise of Human Nature*, Book III, Part ii.]

[5] [In an earlier part of the *Elements of Moral Science*, Beattie divides sensation into 'primary' and 'secondary': for example, a primary sense tells us what shape and colour an object is; a secondary sense tells us whether or not the object is beautiful.]

guage, and bad company; or *improved*; — the former, by hearing and studying good music; and the latter, by reading such books, and keeping such company, as may make good manners, good language, and elegant writing, familiar to us. — Yet it cannot be denied, that the external senses are original faculties of our nature: it cannot be denied, that there is in man, if in any degree enlightened, a capacity of distinguishing between beauty and deformity, meanness and dignity, grossness and delicacy, dissonance and harmony: nor can it be denied, that these distinctions have as real a foundation in nature, as any other that can be mentioned.

Even reason itself, (which, if we have *any* original faculties, is surely one of them), is subject to the same law of habit, as the means of improvement or of debasement. How different is this faculty in its cultivated state, as it appeared in Newton, Clarke, Butler, (for example), or as it appears in any man of learning and good sense, from the unimproved understanding of a peasant, who can hardly follow the shortest train of reasoning; or from the still ruder intellect of a savage, who has never been accustomed to argumentation at all! What care is taken, by judicious parents and teachers, to improve both the moral and the intellectual powers of children! Yet it will not be said, that reason is merely an artificial thing, a way of thinking superinduced by education; or that human beings could, by the most artful management, be taught to mistake the plainest truth for falsehood, or the most glaring falsehood for truth. Ignorant people believe many things which are not true; and may, no doubt, by those who can infuse prejudice, or work upon the passions, be prevailed on to acquiesce in very gross absurdities: — reason, in short, as well as sense and conscience, may be artificially, or may be accidentally, perverted to a certain degree, and in some minds, even to a great degree. But a total perversion of these faculties, needs not be apprehended. The most ignorant man will never, if he is not an idiot, be induced to reject the evidence of sense, to disbelieve the existence of the material world, to think all human actions equally right or equally wrong; or, in general, to doubt the truth of what is self-evident, or of what, by a few words of argument suited to his capacity, has been in his hearing demonstrated to be true.

To prove that moral sentiments are merely the effect of education, some authors have taken pains to collect, from the history of both civilized and savage men, a detail of singular customs and institutions, which are accounted lawful in some countries, and criminal in others. Something of this kind was attempted by Locke, in the first book of his *Essay concerning Human Understanding*. His examples, however, though they were all unexceptionable, could prove nothing more, than that conscience is liable to be, in some degree, influenced by habit; which nobody denies: but would be far from proving, that it is wholly subject to that influence. But of those examples it might easily be shown that some are so bare of circumstances, that they prove nothing; that some are quoted from writers of doubtful authority; and that some, when fairly stated, will be found to prove just the contrary of what they are brought to prove. Till the motives whence men act be known, one cannot with certainty determine whether they be actuated by a good or a bad principle: and to detect the motives of those savage men of whose customs and language little or nothing is known except to themselves, would in most cases be difficult, in many impossible; and require a degree of sagacity which few travellers possess, or are solicitous to attain.

Besides: it is a true as well as an old observation, that most travellers are fond of the marvellous; few of them having that candour, humanity, and philosophical acuteness, which so eminently distinguished that ornament of his country and profession, the incomparable James Cook.[6] And I fear it is no less true, that, in an age so addicted to paradox as the present, too many of the *readers* of travels may be well enough pleased to see the licentious theories of modern Europe countenanced by reports from the extremities of Asia. We should therefore, as long at least as this mode of thinking remains in fashion, be cautious of admitting with implicit faith the first accounts, that may be circulated among us, of the immoralities said to prevail in remote nations. Some particulars of this sort, which appeared in a late collection of late voyages, have already, if I am not misinformed, been

---

[6] [Captain James Cook (1728–79) circumnavigated the world three times, before being killed on Hawaii. He published several accounts of his voyages and discoveries.]

declared on good authority to be unwarrantably exaggerated: but, even supposing the worst accounts to be true, we shall not find that they prove virtue an indeterminate thing; or the moral faculty a bias, either artificially or accidentally, impressed upon the mind by education and habit.

We may with good reason suppose, that in savage life moral notions must be few, the sphere of human action and human intellect being there extremely limited. In childhood we see the same thing happen among ourselves, even where the mind has been in some degree expanded by education. But if savages have any moral notions at all, they are not destitute of a moral faculty. And if there be friendship among them, or natural affection, or compassion towards one another there must also be mutual confidence, gratitude, good-will, and some regard to equity; virtues which cannot be where moral principle is not. Nor can any thing favourable to the opposite side of the question be inferred from their untowardly treatment of strangers, even of such as visit them with benevolent purposes; for it is very natural for them to mistake strangers for enemies; and it is melancholy to consider how often they have found them so. And if they be, as probably they all are, enslaved more or less to superstition, the immoralities and other absurdities thence resulting need not raise wonder; for superstition ever was, and ever will be, productive of absurd and immoral behaviour.

Against the doctrine here maintained, of conscience being, as well as reason, a natural faculty implanted in man by his Creator, it is no argument, that, where the objects of duty are unknown, or where mistakes are entertained concerning their nature, man must be liable to misapprehend his duty with respect to those objects. The objects of duty are, the Deity, our fellow-creatures, and ourselves. Give a rational being right notions of these, and his moral faculty will not permit him to be ignorant of the duty he owes them. Convince him, for example, that God is infinitely wise, powerful, good, and holy, the source of happiness, and the standard of perfection; and he cannot fail to *know* (whether his *practice* be conformable or not) that it is his duty to love, fear, and obey so great and glorious a being. Teach him, on the contrary, that there are many gods, some capricious and foolish, others a little more intelligent; some as weak and wicked as men; not one of them free from imperfection; and not a few infamously profligate: and you will make him have the same absurd notions which the heathen vulgar formerly had, of the duties that men owe to those gods. Is this occasioned by a depravity of conscience, or by a total want of that faculty! Is it not owing to an understanding perverted by misrepresentation and ignorance?

Consider the following case, which, if not exactly, is nearly parallel. With the bodily eyes we cannot perceive what is situated beyond our sphere of vision, and through an impure or unequal medium we must see things discoloured or distorted. This does not prove, either that we have no eyes, or that they are fallacious: nor does this prove, that it is education, or habit, which teaches men to see rightly, or to see wrong. For, without making any change on the visual organ; without subduing any evil habit or prejudice of education; and merely by purifying the medium, and bringing the objects within our sphere of vision, we see them at once in their natural colours and proportions. — Similar mistakes, with respect to social virtue and the duties of self-government, may be either infused into the mind, by false information concerning the nature and end of man; or removed and rectified, by counteracting false information, and enforcing true. — Now, of the divine nature, of the end for which men are sent into this world, of their relation to God and their fellow-men, and of the dispensations of providence with respect to their present and future state, the heathen world were very imperfectly informed; much more imperfectly indeed, than many of them might have been, if they had rightly improved the rational and moral faculties that had been given them. Need we wonder then at the imperfection of the best systems of Pagan morality? Need we wonder, that Pagan nations, according as they make a better or a worse use of their mental powers, are some of them more and others less enlightened with the knowledge of moral truth?

Nor is it any objection to the present doctrine, that all sorts of wickedness are perpetrated in civilized nations. This is a proof, that there the moral faculty has not so much power as it ought to have; but this does not prove, that there the moral faculty does not exist, or is entirely born down by fashion and bad example. My argument requires me to speak here not of the *performance*, but of the *acknowledgement*, of duty: and nobody needs be informed, that men well instructed in all the duties of life act too often contrary to the dictates of their conscience, and the known will of God. *Video meliora proboque, Deteriora sequor* [*I see and approve the better course, but pursue the worse*],[7] is a confession which even the best men have frequent occasion to repeat. But while the faults of individuals are condemned by the general voice of a nation, or of the unprejudiced and considerate part of mankind, that general voice is prompted by the suggestions of a moral faculty, which, in spite of bad example, licentious opinion, and absurd education, has been able to retain both its authority, and its power. And the conscience of the criminal himself, however thoughtless or hardened he may be for a time, seldom fails, sooner or later, to bear such testimony against him, as he finds it misery to endure, and an impossibility to evade.

Were it necessary to bring further evidence, of conscience being not an artificial, but a natural, way of thinking, and that moral sentiments are among men as prevalent and permanent as rationality itself; I might remark, — that philosophers (*real* philosophers I mean) however they may have differed in their speculative notions concerning the foundation of morality, have not often disputed concerning the merit and demerit of particular virtues and vices: — that in writings composed by the wisest men of remote antiquity, and under the influence of governments and manners very unlike ours, moral notions are exhibited and exemplified, similar to, and in many particulars the same with, our own: — that in ancient poems and histories we seldom find those personages proposed as patterns for imitation whom *we* disapprove, or those actions condemned which *we* consider as meritorious: — and, that, though it might seem possible for us, after undergoing a certain course of discipline, to choose modes of life extremely different from those in which we have been educated, it seems not possible for us to reconcile our minds to such characters as Nero, Herod, Catiline, Muley Ishmael,[8] &c. — I may add, that moral sentiments seem to be necessary to the very existence of society; that no association of human beings, in which, invariably, that should be believed to be virtue which we account vice,

---

[7]   [Ovid, *Metamorphoses*, VII, ll. 20–21.]

[8]   [An eighteenth-century king of Morocco, famous for his brutality.]

and that to be vice which we account virtue, could subsist for a single day, if men were to do what in that case they would think their duty; and that, by consequence, wherever human societies are established, we may warrantably conclude that moral distinctions are there acknowledged. — I do not say, that any particular moral principle is innate, or that an infant brings it into the world with him: this would be as absurd as to say, that an infant brings the multiplication table into the world with him. But I say, that the moral faculty which dictates moral principles, and the intellectual faculty which ascertains proportions of quantity and number, are original parts of man's nature; which, though they appear not at his birth, nor for some time after, even as the ear of corn is not seen till long after the blade has sprung up, fail not however, provided outward circumstances be favourable, to disclose themselves in due season.

Much has been said, by writers on casuistry, concerning the merit or demerit of those actions which proceed from an erroneous conscience; that is, which are authorized by a conscience so perverted by education or habit, as in a particular case to approve what is wrong, or disapprove what is right. On this subject volumes might be written, and a thousand difficulties supposed which probably will never take place in fact: but the whole matter, as far as it may be expressed in general terms, amounts to little more than this. It is man's duty, not to debase his reason by prejudice, nor his moral faculty by criminal practice; but to do every thing in his power to improve his nature, and particularly to obtain, in all matters that affect the conscience, the fullest information. If the person who has done this shall mistake his duty after all, the error is unavoidable, and he is not to blame. But if he has not taken due pains to obtain information, or to improve his moral nature, he has no right, at least in ordinary cases, to urge the plea of an erroneous conscience. In fact, men seldom do so: which is a proof that, when we do evil, our conscience seldom fails to inform us, that it is evil which we are doing.

It has been the opinion of some respectable writers, that no action or affection is morally good, unless it have a benevolent tendency. And it is true, that every virtue tends to public as well as private good; and that whatever is done with a view to promote happiness, without doing injury, is well done, and a proof of goodness in the agent. It is also true, that every act of virtue, even the most secret that we can perform, tends eventually to the good of others; either by diffusing happiness immediately, or by improving our nature, and consequently making us more useful and more agreeable members of the community. But there are in the world many men, whose minds, from natural weakness or other unfavourable circumstances, have always remained in an uncultivated state, and who therefore must be very incompetent judges of public good, as well as of the tendency of their actions to promote it. Yet, if such men are industrious and sober, honest in their dealings, and regardful of their duty, it would be very hard to refuse them the character of virtuous men.

Every moralist allows, that there are duties which a man owes to himself: in the deepest solitude we are not exempted from religious and moral obligation. For if a man were in the condition in which, according to the fable, Robinson Crusoe is said to have been, and confined for many years in a desert island, without having it in his power to do either good or harm to others of his species, he would, according to the measure of rationality that had been given him, be as really a moral being, and accountable to God and his conscience for his behaviour, as if he were in the most crowded society. In such a solitude, it would be in his power to be in various ways virtuous or vicious. He might impiously repine at the dispensations of providence; or he might acquiesce in them with thankfulness and humility. He might lead a life of industry; or abandon himself to idleness and all other sensualities that were within his reach. He might envy the prosperity of others, and amuse himself with laying plans for their destruction; or pray for their happiness, and wish for opportunities of promoting it. — In a word, benevolence is not the only virtue: but I admit, that there can be no virtue without it.

The Stoics, who were much given to wrangling, and in many things affected to differ from popular opinion, maintained, that all virtues are equally meritorious, and all vices equally blameable. As one truth (said they) cannot be more true than another, nor one falsehood more false than another, so neither can one vice or virtue be greater or less than another vice or virtue. As he who is a hundred miles from Rome is not more really out of Rome than he who is one mile from it; so he who has transgressed the bounds of innocence is equally a transgressor, whether he has gone a great way beyond them, or a little way. — Some crimes, however, they allowed to deserve a heavier punishment than others: but that, they said, was owing, not to the comparative greatness of one crime above another, but to this consideration, that one crime might be more complex than another. For example: he who murders a slave is as really a murderer as he who commits parricide: but the former is guilty of one injurious act, the other is guilty of many; the one has killed a man; the other has killed a man, has killed his parent, has killed his benefactor, has killed his teacher.

Such a tenet may be useful to declaimers; as one may argue long, and plausibly, in behalf of it: but plausible declamation is of no weight, when counterbalanced by the general opinion of mankind, as warranted by conscience and reason. What would be thought of a lawgiver who should declare every violation of the law a capital crime; or who, because some transgressions are venial, should grant pardon to every transgressor? The best man on earth is every day guilty of sins of infirmity: but who will say, that all the sins of this sort, which a good man commits in the course of a long life, are equal in guilt to one single act of treachery or cruelty! Every vice is indeed blameable; and every virtue, which it is in our power to perform, we ought to perform: but it may be presumed, that the possible degrees of guilt, which one may incur even by single acts of transgression, are as many as the possible degrees of punishment; and that the possible degrees of virtue are as various as the possible degrees of reward. Though all men are sinners, yet some are highly respectable on account of their goodness: and there are crimes so atrocious, perjury for example, that one single perpetration makes a man infamous. The Scripture expressly declares, that, in the day of judgement, it will be more tolerable for some criminals than for others; and not obscurely insinuates, that the future exaltation of the righteous will be in proportion to their virtue.

Ten

Of the Origin of Civil Governments

... I proceed to consider the origin and nature of civil government, and the laws essential to the several forms of it. Civil government, or policy, or (as it was formerly and more properly called) polity is 'human society moulded into a certain form by human art'. Different forms of it are found in different nations; and one form of it is supported by one system of laws, and another by another. The study of politics, properly conducted, tends not a little to the improvement of the human mind. It makes history and law intelligible; enlarges our acquaintance with human nature and human affairs; and qualifies men for rational conversation. In this country it is peculiarly necessary; because, without some knowledge of politics, it is impossible for us to understand that system of government under which we live: the constitution of Great Britain being the most curious, the most complex, and the most excellent, form of human policy, that ever appeared in the world. This is said, not from any blind partiality to it, which however might be pardoned in a British subject: all this has been admitted by the most enlightened foreigners. Few foreigners indeed understand it; but those who do, unanimously admire it. That it is perfect, I do not affirm; I know of no work of man that is so. But its imperfections are fewer, and less grievous, than the discontented, the turbulent, and the visionary, are willing to believe; and their alleged bad consequences will, to a candid and intelligent observer, appear to exist rather in the imagination of the theorist, than in reality.

Man is the only political animal; that is, the only animal capable of government. Many sorts of beasts, birds, insects, and fishes, herd together, and take pleasure in one another; man only has a notion of public good, and legal subordination. Some brutes acquire pre-eminence among their fellows, by superiority of strength; man alone has an idea of authority, or a right to govern, and of the duties and obligations thence arising. Some animals, as ants and bees, are guided by instinct to live together and assist one another; and this, by a figure of speech, has been called their *government*. But, in the proper sense of this word, government is an art, which one learns in no other way than by studying it: it is the effect of reason, foresight, and moral principle united, and must therefore be peculiar to rational beings. — In treating of it, I shall consider, first, the origin and general nature of government; secondly, the several simple forms of it, and their fundamental laws; and thirdly, the structure and principles of that excellent system of policy, the British constitution.

Section I
Origin of Government

The origin of government is a subject which may be said to comprehend answers to these two questions. First; for what reasons, and by what steps is it probable, that men, not subject to government, would think of it, and submit themselves to it? Secondly; what may reasonably be presumed to have been the actual origin of government among men, according to the best lights that may be had from the history, tradition, or conjecture? — With respect to the first question, it is to be observed, that, before the institution of government, men would live in what is called 'the state of nature', perfectly independent, equal, and free. But some would have more strength, more activity, and more wisdom, than others; and it may be presumed, that they who were conscious of their own weakness in these particulars, would look up for advice and assistance to those who were able to assist and advise them; and would thus, gradually and voluntarily, confer on them some sort of authority, or lawful pre-eminence. Hence one motive to political union, arising from the diversity of human characters, and from our natural admiration of superior abilities. In respect of abilities, indeed, both of mind and of body, men are born so unequal, and their fortunes, with regard to the acquisition of property, are so different, that a variety of ranks and conditions, in social life, is plainly agreeable to the intentions of providence, as well as beneficial to mankind.

Another motive to political union would arise from the inconveniencies of the natural state; in which men, being fallible, must often mistake their rights, and disagree about them. When this happens in the political state, the law decides the matter, and the power of government enforces the decision. But, in the state of nature, man would have nothing but his own strength and caution to defend him from injury; and of course, when injured, would retaliate, which could hardly fail to produce more retaliation, and more injury, and so end in confusion. Suppose him to submit himself and his cause to an arbiter mutually chosen by him and his adversary, yet if either party prove refractory, the matter is just where it was; there being no power to enforce the sentence. Hence one source of evil in the natural state, arising from men's mutual independence, and perfect equality with respect to their rights. Of this evil the obvious and the only remedy is government, or political subordination.

But, men being wicked as well as fallible, the evils of the natural state must be much greater than I have hitherto supposed. We see them injure one another in spite of the sanctions of both divine and human law. Remove these, and they would be still more injurious. It is melancholy, but it is nevertheless true, that men are never so apt to throw off all regard to decency, as in the time of some great public calamity, when cities are overturned by earthquake, or depopulated by pestilence; for then the law loses its power, because the magistrate no longer retains that vigour of mind which is necessary to put it in execution. In short, we may presume the disorders incident to the natural state would be so great, that if it were to be at all, it could not be of any long continuance. Now as these would arise from the equality and independence of the members, they could be remedied in no other way, than by abolishing, or limiting, that equality and independence. Hence the necessity of men's divesting themselves of the freedom of the natural state, uniting in society, appointing a sovereignty, entrusting it with certain powers for the public good, and supporting it in the exercise of those powers. And all the members of a political body, thus uniting their strength, and acting in one direction, are able to repel injury, and defend one another, much more effectually, than it is possible to do in the state of nature.

Though we here set government in opposition to the natural state, we must not call the former unnatural: *artificial* is the epithet which it derives from the contrast. Man is born naked; but clothes, though artificial, are not unnatural. Government, being an art useful to man, and indeed necessary to civilized man, must be agreeable to the intention of providence, who made man what he is, and rendered him capable of moral and intellectual improvement. And those governments that most effectually promote human happiness are to be accounted the most sacred, and the most agreeable to the divine will.

All human arts are in some degree imperfect, and government as well as others: but its advantages greatly overbalance its imperfections. A subject of the best government must give some of his property in the way of tax, to defray the public expense; and in certain cases may be obliged to expose himself to danger in defending the community. But then his connection with government enables him to defend himself and his property at less expense, with less danger, and more effectually, than is possible in the state of nature. His right of punishing injury he must resign into the hands of the magistrate. But this cannot appear a hardship to those who consider, that revenge hardens the heart, exposes the soul to the ravage of tempestuous and painful passion, and tends to the confusion of society; that to inflict punishment seems to a generous mind to be a work equally tormenting and debasing; and that no man is an impartial judge in his own cause. Government promotes benevolence, justice, public spirit, security, and the cultivation of arts and sciences. People are generally civilized, in proportion as the arts of government are understood among them.

The independence and equality of men in the natural state, being alienable rights, may be parted with, for valuable considerations. Men quitting that state, in order to establish policy, would accordingly part with them; and either expressly or tacitly enter into a mutual agreement to the following purpose. First: every individual would engage to unite himself with the rest so as to form one community; whose conduct in matters of public concern is to be determined by the will of those who shall be entrusted with the sovereignty. Secondly: it must be further agreed, that the government shall be some one particular form; that is, that the sovereignty shall be lodged in the body of the people, which is democracy; or in the more distinguished citizens, which is aristocracy; or in one man, which is monarchy; or that the government shall be made up, as ours is, of two or more of these forms mixed together. For different forms of government are supported by different systems of law and therefore, till the form be ascertained, it cannot be distinctly known what laws would be expedient. Thirdly: the form being agreed on, they who are entrusted with the sovereignty would become bound to provide for the common interest, and the subjects would be bound to allegiance and obedience. And from this contract would arise the sovereign's right to command, and an obligation on the rest of the community to obey. — Observe, that I here use the word *sovereign* to denote the supreme power of a state wherever placed; whether it be in the hands of one, or of many; whether lodged in the whole people, as in democracy; or in a senate, as in aristocracy; or in a king, as in monarchy; or in a king and senate jointly, as in the constitution of Great Britain.

Observe further, that the foregoing, and some of the following reasonings, are purely *hypothetical*; that is, are founded on the *supposition* of what rational beings would probably do, if they were to make a transition from the state of nature to that of policy. But these reasonings are not on that account chimerical: for they do in fact lead us to discover the end, the utility, and the fundamental principles, of government. Geometry may be considered as a hypothetical science; but it is not for that reason the less useful. The geometer does not inquire, whether there be in nature mathematical lines, circles, or right-angled triangles; but on the *supposition* that there are or may be, he proves that such and such must be their properties. I do not inquire, whether men ever made such a transition, as is here supposed, from the natural to the civil state; but, *supposing* them to make it, and to make it rationally, and of choice, I say, that they would probably be determined by the views and motives above specified.

A community acts in one direction, and as one person; by agreeing that the will of the majority, or of a certain proportion greater than the majority, as two thirds or three fourths, shall determine the whole. If it were not for this, communities could never act but when they are unanimous; which in political matters is not often to be expected. — In all just government, the interests of the sovereign and of the people are the same; public good being the aim of both. Government will soon cease to be just, where an opposite maxim is adopted. Tyrannical governors cannot be happy, because they live in continual fear and danger: and people who licentiously invade the rights of the sovereign, must have an unsettled government, and therefore cannot enjoy security or peace.

Men, agreeing to quit the state of nature and establish policy, must be supposed to have the good of their children as much at heart, as their own. Their children, therefore, have a right to the privileges of their fathers; unless they declare, when grown up, that they do not acquiesce in the determination of their fathers, but choose rather to relapse into the state of nature, or to alter the form of government. If the whole or greater part of the community agree in this, it must be done. But if that is not the case, the right of self-defence, which belongs to all, and to societies as well as individuals, will authorize the government to lay such restraints on these refractory people, as the public safety may require; and even to punish them, if they should breed disturbance, or transgress the law. However, where public good is not concerned, it would be unreasonable to hinder inoffensive people from going away in peace, in order to better their fortune elsewhere. And thus we see, how laws and the obligations of government, though it were to be formed in the way here supposed, might be transmitted from generation to generation. Every man is under ties of gratitude to the government that protects him, and protected his forefathers: and whoever lives in a country, or retains property in it, obliges himself, in so doing, by a contract either express or tacit, to obey the laws of it. — Thus far, arguing hypothetically, I have considered, 'For what reasons, and by what steps, men, not subject to government, would probably think of it, and submit themselves to it'.

Of the *actual origin* of government, the second thing proposed to be considered, history gives little information. For policy is almost coeval with the world; and, in the first ages, it is not probable that men would think of writing history. Without written records, it is wonderful to observe, how soon human affairs are forgotten; and hence the history of every ancient people, the Jews excepted, becomes more uncertain the further back it goes, and ends at last, or rather begins, in fable. Ignorant nations have erected pillars, mounds of earth, and heaps of stones, to perpetuate the remembrance of great events. They thought perhaps, that those structures would always raise curiosity, and that tradition would never be wanting to gratify it: but posterity were too much engrossed by their own concerns, to inquire into those of their ancestors; the great events of the present time obliterated the memory of the past; and the monumental pile, having become familiar to the eye, was looked at with little wonder and less curiosity. And when people came afterwards to be improved by letters, to aspire after historical information, and to study the antiquities of their native land, they could learn very little from those rude memorials; which, having no definite meaning, could convey no distinct knowledge. In this country, there is not a province, there is hardly a parish, in which several of these monuments are not still to be seen; some whereof the neighbours endeavour to account for by fabulous tradition, while others baffle all conjecture.

That, in the first ages of the world, government may have arisen from parental authority, is very probable. The first man lived nine hundred and thirty years. In this long tract of time, his sons and daughters and their offspring, who were equally long-lived or nearly so, must have increased to an exceeding great number, and peopled all the adjoining regions, of those were sufficient for their accommodation. It was surely natural for them to look up with extraordinary veneration to their common ancestor, who having been created pure, and having no doubt received much knowledge by inspiration, would probably retain, notwithstanding his fall, a greater portion of wisdom and virtue than any other of his contemporaries. Equally reasonable it is to suppose, that, after his death, the oldest of his children, as being then the oldest man upon earth, would be considered as his successor in that part of the world where he resided; and among those, who had settled in remote parts, it would come to be a thing of course, that he, who had the pre-eminence in years and wisdom, should be the sovereign of those who were within his reach. The patriarchs, we find, in aftertimes exercised in their own household a sort of kingly authority; which was no doubt vested in them partly on account of their age and virtue, and partly because it had been customary before their time.

But to prevent mistakes on this subject, it is necessary to remark, that the authority of a parent is very different, both in kind and in degree, from that of a sovereign. In some respects, indeed, they are similar. The magistrate is bound, by the most sacred ties, to consult the happiness of his people, and it is equally a parent's duty to promote the good of his children. Both the one and the other are entitled to respect and obedience as long as their commands are reasonable; and no sound is more pleasing to the ear of a good sovereign, than to be called the father of his country. But, though children, through the whole of life, ought to reverence their parents, there is a time when the parental authority ceases, and the child becomes as free as the parent; namely when the former leaves his father's house to establish a family of his own. Whereas the sovereign may enact laws to continue in force through ages, and whose authority is indeed perpetual, unless they be abrogated by the same sovereign power that made them. — Besides, the legislature may both denounce and inflict capital punishment; but no man is supposed to have this right vested in him on his becoming a parent; and if fathers in ancient Rome had such a right, they derived it, not from the law of nature, but from the municipal law of their country. The sovereign may in all lawful cases *command*; the parent in many cases can only *entreat* or *advise*. The child becomes, or may become, a parent in his turn; the subject does not in the same manner grow up into a sovereign. If therefore parents have in the early ages become the sovereigns of their descendents for any *just* title, it must have been, not solely by virtue of their parental authority, but by the consent of their descendents, expressly or tacitly given for that purpose.

Many governments have been founded in conquest. Such were of old the Assyrian, Persian, and Macedonian empires; and such, though more gradual in its progress, was the Roman. Such in latter times was the Turkish tyranny; and such the first feudal governments established in the southern parts of Europe. England was conquered by the Romans, the Saxons, the Danes, and at last, in the eleventh century, by the Normans, under William Duke of Normandy, commonly called the Conqueror. The effects of this last conquest are still discernible in the British Constitution; and our Royal Family is descended from William; though indeed it justly claims an origin still higher and nobler: His Majesty being the great-grandson of George I; who was great-grandson of James VI of Scotland; who was descended from Malcolm III, commonly called Malcolm Ceanmore, by Margaret the sister of Edgar; whose ancestors had been kings in England several hundred years before the Norman Conquest.[1]

That conquest alone conveys no *just* right to sovereignty, is self-evident. Great Britain, for example, has no more right to conquer Spain, than Spain has to conquer Great Britain; or than any man has to plunder me, and make me a slave, merely because he is stronger than I. Yet all governments founded in conquest are not unlawful. Joshua's conquest of Canaan was lawful, because authorized by the Deity himself, who has the supreme disposal of all his creatures; and who commanded that the Canaanites should be destroyed in this manner, on account of their abominable wickedness. If a conquered nation, admiring the abilities of their conqueror, and in order to avoid greater evils, shall make choice of him for their king, he has a right to be so: and it was by a title of this kind that William the Conqueror, who was a man of abilities, became the rightful sovereign of England; Edgar, the only surviving heir to the crown, having relinquished his claim in favour of William; and all the people assembled at William's coronation having repeatedly declared, when the question was put to them by the archbishops of Canterbury and York, that they chose him to be their king.

If a nation be troublesome to its neighbours, and after frequent defeats refuse to be quiet, the victor may pursue his advantages till he has subdued them. But he must not punish the innocent with the guilty; and therefore he must not make them slaves, or establish among them arbitrary power. For that would be to inflict punishment, not only on the women and common people, many

---

[1] [Malcolm III, also known as Malcolm Ceanmore, ruled Scotland from 1057 to 1093. His wife, Margaret, was sister to Edgar Aetheling, who was Edward the Confessor's closest living relative when Edward died in 1066.]

of whom probably had no hand in the public injuries, but also on their young children, and unborn descendents, who certainly had no hand in them. All governments, therefore, founded in conquest, are not unlawful. But every government is unlawful in some degree, which deprives men of their *freedom*, or of that *Political Liberty*, which promotes prosperity and virtue. And here it is proper to ascertain what may reasonably be understood by the term Political Liberty; which is used in many different senses, and most used perhaps by those who least understand it. In this question I take it for granted that Britain is a free state: which no man of sense denies: which Montesquieu, the greatest political genius that ever lived, acknowledges; and which they, who are most dissatisfied with the administration of our affairs, seem to admit, when they say, that our liberty is in danger; for in danger that cannot be, which does not exist.[2]

Does liberty, then, consist in the power of doing what we please? No: for if every body had this power, there could be no liberty at all; because our life and property would be at the disposal of every man who was able and willing to take them from us. In a free country, every violation of law is an attack upon the public liberty. The laws of God and our country are our best and only security against oppression; and therefore liberty can exist among us no longer than while those laws are obeyed. Milton, who loved liberty as much, I believe, as any man ever did, has truly observed, when speaking of it, that 'Who loves that must first be wise and good'.[3]

Does liberty consist in our being governed by laws of our own making? I know not how many political writers have laid this down as a first principle, and a self-evident maxim: and yet, if Britain be a free government, this maxim is grossly absurd. Who are they who can be said to be governed by laws of their own making? I know of no such persons; I never heard or read of any such; except, perhaps, among pirates and other banditti, who, trampling on all laws divine and human, refuse to be governed in any

---

[2] [Montesquieu describes England as the one state in the world 'whose constitution has political liberty for its direct purpose': see *The Spirit of the Laws*, II.v, ed. and trans. Anne Cohler, Basia Miller, and Harold Stone, Cambridge: Cambridge University Press, 1989, p. 156.]

[3] [Sonnet XII, l. 12.]

other way than by their own licentious regulations. The greatest part of the laws by which we are governed were made long ago: I should be glad to know how a man co-operates in making a law before he is born. But are we not instrumental in making those laws; which are made in our own time? Granting that we are, which is by no means the case; these are not the only laws by which we are governed: we must obey the common law of the land, which of immemorial standing, as well as the statutes made in the last session of parliament.

The British laws are enacted by the King, Lords, and Commons, who may amount in all to about eight hundred persons: the inhabitants of Great Britain, who must obey these laws, are computed at eight millions. In Britain, therefore, not to mention the rest of the empire, are more than seven millions of persons who are governed by laws which they neither make, nor can alter: and even the King, Lords, and Commons, are themselves governed by laws which were made before they were born. Nay more: if the majority of the Lords and Commons agree to a bill, which afterwards receives the Royal assent, that bill is a law, though the minority vote against it; and the minority in both houses might comprehend three hundred and eighty persons. So that a law to bind the whole British nation might, according to the principles of our constitution, be made, even contrary to the will of three hundred and eighty members of the legislature. — Nay further: in the house of Commons, forty members, in ordinary cases of legislation, make a house, or quorum; the majority is twenty-one, which, deducted from five hundred and fifty-eight, the number of members in that house, leaves five hundred and thirty-seven. So that a bill might pass the house of Commons, if the house happened to be very thin, contrary to the will of five hundred and thirty-seven members of that house; and yet if such a bill were afterwards ratified by the Lords, and assented to by the King, it would be a law. — Surely, if we are a free people, liberty must be something, that does not consist in our being governed by laws of our own making.

It is said, indeed, that every British subject has influence in the legislature by means of his representative freely chosen, who appears and acts for him in parliament. But this is not true. There are not, in this island, one million of persons who have a vote in electing parliament-men: and yet, in this island, there are eight millions of persons who must obey the law. And for their conduct, as lawgivers, our parliament-men are not answerable to their electors, or to any other persons whatever. And it not often happens, that in making laws they are unanimous; yet the minority in both houses must obey the laws that are made against their will. — Besides, we are all subject to the law of God, and are free in proportion as we obey it; for his service is perfect freedom. But who will say that man is the maker of God's law! — We see then, that our liberty does not consist, either in the power of doing what we please, or in being governed by laws made by ourselves.

They, who are hindered from doing what the law allows, or who have reason to be afraid of one another, even while they are doing their duty, cannot be said to enjoy liberty. Where this is the case, there must be in the hands of certain individuals some exorbitant power productive of oppression, and not subject to law; or there must prevail in the state a spirit of licentiousness which the law cannot control. — Nor can men be said to be free, who are liable to have oppressive laws imposed on them, or to be tried by tyrannical or incompetent judges. In Great Britain, by a contrivance to be explained hereafter, our laws are made by men, whose interest it is to make them equitable; and who, with a very few exceptions of little moment, are themselves subject to the laws they make. In Britain, too, by the institution of juries, our judges in all criminal and in many civil causes, are our equals; men, who are acquainted with our circumstances, to whose prudence and probity we have no objection, and who are favourably inclined towards us, on account of being their equals. In Great Britain, therefore, an honest man has nothing to fear, either from the law, or from the judge. — Neither can those people be accounted free who dare not complain when they suffer injury, or who are denied the privilege of declaring their sentiments freely to one another. In both these respects our freedom is secured by the liberty of the press; of which I shall speak afterwards.

Political liberty, therefore, I would describe thus. 'It is that state in which men are so governed by equitable laws, and so tried by equitable judges, that no person can be hindered from doing what the law allows, or have reason to be afraid of any person so long as he does his duty'. This is true liberty; for this is the only sort of liberty that promotes virtue and happiness; and surely no wise or good man would ever wish for any other: and this is a degree and a perfection of liberty, which I know not that any other people on earth ever enjoyed. How the several parts of the British constitution are contrived, and adjusted, so as to secure this liberty, I shall afterwards endeavour to explain.

The Jewish policy was of divine origin, and some of the Jewish kings were appointed by a command from Heaven. Hence some writers have taught, that kingly government in general is of divine origin; and that kings, deriving their authority from God, are accountable to him alone, and must not be disobeyed or resisted by their people on any pretence whatever. This was called the doctrine of passive obedience and non-resistance. Formerly it made a noise in this country; but the minds of our people on the subject of government are now more enlightened; and the following brief remarks will be sufficient confutation of it.

First: Law is the declared will of a person who has a right to command. But no magistrate can have a right to violate the law to the oppression of his people, or to command them to do what God forbids. Were a sovereign to do either, his will, because not founded in right, would not be a law, nor, consequently, entitled to obedience. Secondly: The right of self-defence will justify a man in resisting that power which is unlawfully exerted to destroy him, or to deprive him of his perfect rights. Thirdly: Public good is the end of just government; and therefore that is not just government which promotes public evil. Fourthly: Kings and other lawful magistrates derive their authority immediately, though by divine permission, from the laws of their country; and no sovereign, some of the Jewish kings excepted, was ever appointed by express command from heaven.

But, fifthly, the person of a good sovereign is as sacred as any thing human can be; and while the king executes the law, he does what the law requires of him, and it is absolutely unlawful to resist or disobey him. And in all government there must be some supreme power, in whatever person or persons it may be lodged, which every subject must obey: for law cannot contradict itself; which, however, it would do, if it were to require obedience, and excuse disobedience. Let it be observed too, that resistance to government is always attended with danger and bloodshed, involves many an innocent man in ruin, and many a worthy family in misery, and may in the end produce anarchy, or tyranny, more intolerable than any of the evils which it might have been intended to remove. To a remedy so desperate a good man will not have recourse, unless both he, and the greater and wiser part of the nation, are morally certain, that it will be productive of good.

And therefore, when a government is established, and upon the whole tolerably mild, though it should fall far short of the perfection of that under which we have the happiness to live, a good man will be careful not to breed disturbance in it; but will, on the contrary, as far as he is able, promote concord and peace, even though he should have reason to disapprove of many things in the conduct of his superiors. To his relations, friends, and fellow-subjects he owes the great duty of benevolence; and would therefore be extremely sorry to see them involve themselves in civil war, which of all human calamities is the worst, which leads to the perpetration of innumerable crimes, and the event of which it is impossible to foresee. As to those who foment dissention in a state, in order to enrich or distinguish themselves, or to gratify the rancour of party spirit, what can be said of them, but that they are public incendiaries, and the enemies of their country and of mankind!

The doctrine, of the divine right of kings to do what they please, was no doubt contrived by their flatterers, who wanted to make their court to the monarch, by magnifying his power, and enslaving his people. When Alexander had murdered Clytus, and was in an agony of remorse for what he had done, Anaxarchus, a fellow, who attended the king, and called himself a philosopher, endeavoured to give him comfort by telling him, that whatever was done by the supreme power was right, and that is was unworthy of Alexander to be afraid of the law, or the tongues of men; for that his will was the law of his subjects, and ought to be to them the measure of right and wrong. By this doctrine, says Plutarch, he alleviated the king's grief, but made him withal more haughty and unjust; and insinuated himself into the royal favour much more than he had been able to do before. The same doctrine was taught in England, in the last century, by Mr Hobbes and others. But kings were never obliged to those who taught it. If it make them more tyrannical, which it will certainly do if they listen to it, it will also make them more insecure and more wretched. The only happy princes are they who govern according to law; for the law is their excuse for every thing that is done: and, if there should be dissatisfied persons, which, though an angel from heaven were to be king, there always would be, such princes are sure of the affection of the greater and more respectable part of their people. Cruel and arbitrary sovereigns are unhappy while they live, and often come to an untimely end. In no other country on earth is the deposition of princes so common as in Turkey, where the sovereign is despotical, and the people are slaves: and let it not be forgotten, that of the twelve Caesars eight were tyrants and usurpers, and six of the eight perished by assassination. — So much for the origin of government.

Eleven

On Slavery

... That I may not be thought a blind admirer of antiquity, I would here crave the reader's indulgence for one short digression more, in order to put him in mind of an important error in morals, inferred from partial and inaccurate experience, by no less a person than Aristotle himself. He argues, 'that men of little genius, and great bodily strength, are by nature destined to serve, and those of better capacity, to command; that the natives of Greece, and of some other countries, being naturally superior in genius, have a natural right to empire; and that the rest of mankind, being naturally stupid, are destined to labour and slavery'.[1] This reasoning is now, alas! of little advantage to Aristotle's countrymen, who have for many ages been doomed to that slavery, which, in his judgement, nature had destined them to impose on others; and many nations whom he would have consigned to everlasting stupidity, have shown themselves equal in genius to the most exalted of humankind. It would have been more worthy of Aristotle, to have inferred man's natural and universal right to liberty, from that natural and universal passion with which men desire it. He wanted, perhaps, to devise some excuse for servitude; a practice which, to their eternal reproach, both Greeks and Romans tolerated even in the days of their glory.

Mr Hume argues nearly in the same manner in regard to the superiority of white men over black. 'I am apt to suspect', says he, 'the negroes, and in general all the other species of men, (for there are four or five different kinds), to be naturally inferior to the whites. There *never was* a civilized nation of any other complexion than white, *nor even any individual* eminent either in action or spec-

[1] [This is not a quotation from, but a paraphrase of, Aristotle, *Politics*, Book I, Chapters 5–6.]

ulation. *No* ingenious manufactures among them, *no* arts, no sciences. — There are negro-slaves dispersed all over Europe, of which *none* ever discovered any symptoms of ingenuity'.[2] These assertions are strong; but I know not whether they have any thing else to recommend them. For, first, though true, they would not prove the point in question, except it were also proved, that the Africans and Americans, even though arts and sciences were introduced among them, would still remain unsusceptible of cultivation. The inhabitants of Great Britain and France were as savage two thousand years ago, as those of Africa and America are at this day. To civilize a nation, is a work which it requires long time to accomplish. And one may as well say of an infant, that he can never become a man, as of a nation now barbarous, that it never can be civilized. Secondly, of the facts here asserted, no man could have sufficient evidence, except from a personal acquaintance with all the negroes that now are, or ever were, on the face of the earth. Those people write no histories; and all the reports of all the travellers that ever visited them, will not amount to any thing like a proof of what is here affirmed. But, thirdly, we know that these assertions are not true. The empires of Peru and Mexico could not have been governed, nor the metropolis of the latter built after so singular a manner, in the middle of a lake, without men eminent both for action and speculation. Everybody has heard of the magnificence, good government, and ingenuity, of the ancient Peruvians. The Africans and Americans are known to have many ingenious manufactures and arts among them, which even Europeans would find it no easy matter to imitate. Sciences indeed they have none, because they have no letters; but in oratory, some of them, particularly the Indians of the Five Nations, are said to be greatly our superiors. It will be readily allowed, that the condition of a slave is not favourable to genius of any kind; and yet, the negro-slaves dispersed over Europe, have often discovered symptoms of ingenuity, notwithstanding their unhappy circumstances. They become excellent handicraftsmen, and practical musicians, and indeed learn every thing their masters are at pains to teach them, cruelty, perfidy, and debauchery not excepted.

---

[2]   [See Hume, 'Of National Characters', *Essays Moral, Political, and Literary*, revised edition, ed. Eugene F. Miller, Indianapolis: Liberty Fund, 1987, p. 208 fn.]

That a negro-slave, who can neither read nor write, nor speak any European language, who is not permitted to do any thing but what his master commands, who has not a single friend on earth, but is universally considered and treated as if he were of a species inferior to the human; — that such a creature should so distinguish himself among Europeans, as to be talked of through the world for a man of genius, is surely no reasonable expectation. To suppose him of an inferior species, because he does not thus distinguish himself, is just as rational, as to suppose any private European of an inferior species, because he has not raised himself to the condition of royalty.

Had the Europeans been destitute of the arts of writing, and working in iron, they might have remained to this day as barbarous as the natives of Africa and America. Nor is the invention of these arts to be ascribed to our superior capacity. The genius of the inventor is not always to be estimated according to the importance of the invention. Gunpowder, and the mariner's compass, have produced wonderful revolutions in human affairs, and yet were accidental discoveries. Such probably were the first essays in writing, and working in iron. Suppose them the effects of contrivance; they were at least contrived by a few individuals; and if they required a superiority of understanding or of species in the inventors, those inventors, and their descendents, are the only persons who can lay claim to the honour of that superiority.

That every practice and sentiment is barbarous which is not according to the usages of modern Europe, seems to be a fundamental maxim with many of our critics and philosophers. Their remarks often put us in mind of the fable of the man and the lion. If negroes or Indians were disposed to recriminate; if a Lucian or a Voltaire from the coast of Guinea, or from the *Five Nations,* were to pay us a visit; what a picture of European manners might be present to his countrymen at his return! Nor would caricature, or exaggeration, be necessary to render it hideous. A plain historical account of some of our most fashionable duellists, gamblers, and adulterers, (to name no more), would exhibit specimens of brutish barbarity and sottish infatuation, such as might vie with any that ever appeared in Kamschatka, California, or the land of Hottentots.

It is easy to see, with what views some modern authors throw out these hints to prove the natural inferiority of negroes. But let every friend to humanity pray, that they may be disappointed. Britons are famous for generosity; a virtue in which it is easy for them to excel both the Romans and the Greeks.

Let it never be said, that slavery is countenanced by the bravest and most generous people on earth; by a people who are animated with that heroic passion, the love of liberty, beyond all nations ancient or modern; and the fame of whose toilsome, but unwearied, perseverance, in vindicating, at the expense of life and fortune, the sacred rights of mankind, will strike terror into the hearts of sycophants and tyrants, and excite the admiration and gratitude of all good men, to the latest posterity.

Twelve

On Poetry

When we affirm, that every art or contrivance which has a meaning must have an end, we only repeat an identical proposition: and when we say, that the essential or indispensable rules of an art are those that direct to the accomplishment of the end proposed by the artist, we repeat a definition whereof it would be captious to controvert the propriety. And therefore, before we can determine any thing in regard to the essential rules of this art, we must form an idea of its end or destination.

Of the End of Poetical Composition

That one end of poetry, in its first institution, and in every period of its progress, must have been, to give pleasure, will hardly admit of any doubt. If men first employed it to express their adoration of superior and invisible beings, their gratitude to the benefactors of mankind, their admiration of moral, intellectual, or corporeal excellence, or, in general, their love of what was agreeable in their own species, or in other parts of nature; they must be supposed to have endeavoured to make their poetry *pleasing*; because, otherwise, it would have been unsuitable to the occasion that gave it birth, and to the sentiments it was intended to enliven. Or if, with Horace, we were to believe, that it was first used as a vehicle to convey into savage minds the principles of government and civility;[1] still we must allow, that one chief thing attended to in its composition must have been, to give it charms sufficient to engage the ear and captivate the heart of an unthinking audience. In latter times, the true poet, though in choosing materials he never lost sight of utility, yet in giving them form (and it is the

---

[1] *The Art of Poetry (Ars Poetica)*, ll. 391–407.

form chiefly that distinguishes poetry from other writings), has always made the entertainment of mankind his principle concern. Indeed, we cannot conceive, that, independently on this consideration, men would ever have applied themselves to arts so little necessary to life, and withal so difficult, as music, painting, and poetry. Certain it is, that a poem, containing the most important truths, would meet with a cold reception, if destitute of those graces of sound, invention, and language, whereof the sole end and aim is to give pleasure.

But is it not the end of this art, *to instruct*, as well as *to please*? Verses, that give pleasure only, without profit, — what are they but chiming trifles? And if a poem were to please, and at the same time, instead of improving, to corrupt the mind, would it not deserve to be considered as a poison rendered doubly dangerous and detestable by its alluring qualities? — All this is true: and yet pleasure is undoubtedly the immediate aim of all those artifices by which poetry is distinguished from other compositions, — of the harmony, the rhythm, the ornamented language, the compact and diversified fable: for I believe it will be allowed, that a plain treatise, destitute of all these beauties, might be made to convey more instruction than any poem in the world. As writing is more excellent than painting, and speech than music, on account of its superior usefulness; so a discourse, containing profitable information even in a rude style, may be more excellent, because more useful, than any thing in Homer or Virgil: but such a discourse partakes no more of the nature of poetry, than language does of melody, or a manuscript of a picture; whereas an agreeable piece of writing may be poetical, though it yield little or no instruction. To instruct, is an end common to all good writing, to all poetry, all history, all sound philosophy. But of these last the principal end is to instruct; and if this single end be accomplished, the philosopher and the historian will be allowed to have acquitted themselves well: but the poet must do a great deal for the sake of pleasure only; and if he fail to please, he may indeed deserve praise on other accounts, but as a poet he has done nothing. — But do not historians and philosophers, as well as poets, make it their study to please their readers? They generally do; but the former please, that they may instruct; the latter instruct, that they may more effectually please. Pleasing, though uninstructive, poetry may gratify a light mind; and what tends even to corrupt the heart may gratify profligates: but the true poet addresses his work, not to the giddy, nor to the worthless, nor to any party, but to mankind; and if he means to please the *general* taste, *must* often employ instruction as one of the arts that minister to this kind of pleasure.

* * *

But may not agreeable affections arise in the mind, which partake neither of vice nor of virtue; such as joy, and hope, and those emotions that accompany the contemplation of external beauty, or magnificence? And, if pastorals and songs, and Anacreontic odes, awaken these agreeable affections, may not such poems be pleasing, without being instructive? This may be, no doubt. And for this reason, among others, I take instruction to be only a secondary end of poetry. But it is only by short poems, as songs and pastorals, that these agreeable affections indifferent alike to vice and virtue, are excited, without any mixture of others. For moral sentiments are so prevalent in the human mind, that no affection can long subsist there, without intermingling with them, and being assimilated to their nature. Nor can a piece of real and pleasing poetry be extended to any great length, without operating, directly or indirectly, either on those affections that are friendly to virtue, or on those sympathies that quicken our moral sensibility, and prepare us for virtuous impressions. In fact, man's true happiness is derived from the moral part of his constitution; and therefore we cannot suppose, that any thing which affects not his moral part, should be lastingly and generally agreeable. We sympathize with the pleasure one takes in a feast, where there is friendship, and an interchange of good offices; but not with the satisfaction an epicure finds in devouring a solitary banquet. A short Anacreontic we may relish for its melody and sparkling images; but a long poem, in order to be pleasing, must not only charm the ear and the fancy, but also touch the heart and exercise the conscience.

Still perhaps it may be objected to these reasonings, that Horace, in a well known verse, declares the end of poetry to be two-fold, to please, or to instruct;[2] whereas, we maintain, that the ultimate end of this art is to please; instruction being only one of the means (and not always a necessary one) by which that ultimate end is to be accomplished. This interpretation of Horace has indeed been admitted by some critics: but it is erroneous; for the passage, rightly understood, will not appear to contain anything inconsistent with the present doctrine. The author is there stating a comparison between the Greek and Roman writers, with a view to the poetry of the stage; and, after commending the former for their correctness, and for the liberal spirit wherewith they conducted their literary labours, and blaming his countrymen for their inaccuracy and avarice, he proceeds thus: 'The ends proposed by our dramatic poets (or by poets in general) are, to please, to instruct, or to do both. When instruction is your aim, let your moral sentences be expressed with brevity, that they may be readily understood, and long remembered: where you mean to please, let your fictions be conformable to truth, or probability. The elder part of your audience (or readers) have no relish for poems that give pleasure only without instruction; nor the younger for such writings as give instruction without pleasure. He only can secure the universal suffrage in his favour, who blends the useful with the agreeable, and delights at the same time that he instructs the reader. Such are the works that bring money to the bookseller, that pass into foreign countries, and perpetuate the author's name through a long succession of ages'. — Now, what is the meaning of all this? What, but that to the *perfection* of dramatic poetry (or, if you please, of poetry in general) both sound morals and beautiful fiction are requisite. But Horace never meant to say, that instruction, as well as pleasure, is necessary to give to any composition the *poetical character*: or he would not in another place have celebrated, with so much affection and rapture, the melting strains of Sappho, and the playful genius Anacreon;[3] — two authors transcendently sweet, but not remarkably instructive. We are sure, that pathos, and harmony, and elevated language, were, in Horace's opinion, essential to poetry;[4] and of these decorations

---

[2] *The Art of Poetry*, ll. 333–47.

[3] *Odes* (*Carmina*), Book 4, Ode 9.

[4] *Satires*, Book 1, Satire 4, ll. 43–4.

no body will affirm, that instruction is the end, who considers that the most instructive books in the world are written in plain prose.

Let this therefore be established as a truth in criticism, that the end of poetry is, to please. Verses, if pleasing, may be poetical, though they convey little or no instruction; but verses, whose sole merit is, that they convey instruction, are not poetical. Instruction, however, especially in poems of length, is necessary to their *perfection*, because they would not be *perfectly agreeable* without it.

Of the Standard of Poetical Invention

Homer's beautiful description of the heavens and earth, as they appear in a calm evening by the light of the moon and stars, concludes with this circumstance, 'And the heart of the shepherd is glad'.[5] Madame Dacier, from the turn she gives to the passage in her version, seems to think, and Pope, in order perhaps to make out his couplet, insinuates, that the gladness of the shepherd is owing to his sense of the utility of those luminaries.[6] And this may in part be the case: but this is not in Homer; nor is it a necessary consideration. It is true, that, in contemplating the material universe, they who discern the causes and affects of things must be more rapturously entertained, than those who perceive nothing but shape and size, colour and motion. Yet, in the mere outside of nature's works (if I may so express myself), there is a splendour, and a magnificence, to which even untutored minds cannot attend, without great delight.

Not that all peasants, or all philosophers, are equally susceptible of these charming impressions. It is strange to observe the callousness of some men, before whom all the glories of heaven and earth pass in daily succession, without touching their hearts, elevating their fancy, or leaving any durable remembrance. Even of those who pretend to sensibility, how many are there to whom the lustre of the rising or setting sun; the sparkling concave of the midnight-sky; the mountain-forest tossing and roaring to the storm, or warbling with all the melodies of a summer-evening; the sweet interchange of hill and dale, shade and sunshine, grove,

---

[5] *Iliad*, Book 8, l. 555.

[6] [Anne Lefèvre Dacier published a French translation of the *Iliad* in 1711; Pope's translation appeared between 1715 and 1720.]

lawn, and water, which an extensive landscape offers to the view; the scenery of the ocean, so lovely, so majestic, and so tremendous, and the many pleasing varieties of the animal and vegetable kingdom, could never afford so much real satisfaction, as the steams and noise of a ballroom, the insipid fiddling and squeaking of an opera, or the vexations and wranglings of a card-table!

But some minds there are of a different make; who, even in the early part of life, receive from the contemplation of nature a species of delight which they would hardly exchange for any other; and who, as avarice and ambition are not the infirmities of that period, would, with equal sincerity and rapture, exclaim,

> I care not, fortune, what you me deny;
> You cannot rob me of free nature's grace;
> You cannot shut the windows of the sky,
> Through which Aurora shows her brightening face;
> You cannot bar my constant feet to trace
> The woods and lawns by living stream at eve.[7]

Such minds have always in them the seeds of true taste, and frequently of imitative genius. At least, though their enthusiastic or visionary turn of mind (as the man of the world would call it) should not always incline them to practice poetry or painting, we need not scruple to affirm, that without some portion of this enthusiasm, no person ever became a true poet or painter. For he who would imitate the works of nature, must first accurately observe them; and accurate observation is to be expected from those only who take great pleasure in it.

To a mind thus disposed, no part of creation is indifferent. In the crowded city, and howling wilderness; in the cultivated province, and solitary isle; in the flowery lawn, and craggy mountain; in the murmur of the rivulet, and in the uproar of the ocean; in the radiance of summer, and gloom of winter; in the thunder of heaven, and in the whisper of the breeze; he still finds something to rouse or to sooth his imagination, to draw forth his affections, or to employ his understanding. And from every mental energy that is not attended with pain, and even from some of those that are, as moderate terror and pity, a sound mind derives satisfaction; exercise being equally necessary to the body and the soul, and to both equally productive of health and pleasure.

---

[7] James Thomson, *The Castle of Indolence*, Canto II, Stanza 3.

This happy sensibility to the beauties of nature should be cherished in young persons. It engages them to contemplate the Creator in his wonderful works; it purifies and harmonizes the soul, and prepares it for moral and intellectual discipline; it supplies a never-failing source of amusement; it contributes even to bodily health; and, as a strict analogy subsists between material and moral beauty, it leads the heart by an easy transition from the one to the other; and thus recommends virtue for its transcendent loveliness, and makes vice appear the object of contempt and abomination. An intimate acquaintance with the best descriptive poets, Spenser, Milton, and Thomson, but above all with the divine Georgic,[8] joined to some practice in the art of drawing, will promote this amiable sensibility in early years; for then the face of nature has novelty superadded to its other charms, the passions are not pre-engaged, the heart is free from care, and the imagination warm and romantic.

But, not to insist longer on those ardent emotions that are peculiar to the enthusiastic disciple of nature, may it not be affirmed of all men, without exception, or at least of all the enlightened part of mankind, that they are gratified by the contemplation of things natural, as opposed to unnatural? Monstrous sights please but for a moment, if they please at all; for they derive their charm from the beholder's amazement, which is quickly over. I have read indeed of a man of rank in Sicily, who chooses to adorn his villa with pictures and statues of most unnatural deformity; but it is a singular instance: and one would not be much more surprised to hear of a person living without food, or growing fat by the use of poison. To say of any thing, that it is *contrary to nature*, denotes censure and disgust on the part of the speaker; as the epithet *natural* imitates an agreeable quality, and seems for the most part to imply, that a thing is as it ought to be, suitable to our own taste, and congenial with our own constitution. Think, with what sentiments we should peruse a poem, in which nature was totally misrepresented, and principles of thought and of operation supposed to take place, repugnant to every thing we had seen or heard of: — in which, for example, avarice and coldness were ascribed to youth, and prodigality and passionate attachment to

---

[8]   [I.e. Virgil.]

the old; in which men were made to act at random, sometimes according to character, and sometimes contrary to it; in which cruelty and envy were productive of love, and beneficence and kind affection of hatred; in which beauty was invariably the object of dislike, and ugliness of desire; in which society was rendered happy by atheism, and the promiscuous perpetration of crimes, and justice and fortitude were held in universal contempt. Or think, how we should relish a painting, where no regard was had to the proportions, colours, or any of the physical laws, of nature: — where the ears and eyes of animals were placed in their shoulders; where the sky was green and the grass crimson; where trees grew with their branches in the earth, and their roots in the air; where men were seen fighting after their heads were cut off, ships sailing on the land, lions entangled in cobwebs, sheep preying on dead carcasses, fishes sporting in the woods, and elephants walking on the sea. Could such figures and combinations give pleasure, or merit the appellation of sublime or beautiful? Should we hesitate to pronounce their author mad? And are the absurdities of madmen proper subjects either of amusement or of imitation to reasonable beings?

Let it be remarked too, that though we distinguish our internal powers by different names, because otherwise we could not speak of them so as to be understood, they are all but so many energies of the same individual mind; and therefore it is not to be supposed, that what contradicts any one leading faculty should yield permanent delight to the rest. That cannot be agreeable to reason, which conscience disapproves; nor can that gratify imagination which is repugnant to reason. — Besides, belief and acquiescence of mind are pleasant, as distrust and disbelief are painful; and therefore, that only can give solid and general satisfaction, which has something of plausibility in it; something which we conceive it possible for a rational being to believe. But no rational being can acquiesce in what is obviously contrary to nature, or implies palpable absurdity.

Poetry, therefore, and indeed every art whose end is to please, must be natural; and if so, must exhibit real matter of fact, or something like it; that is, in other words, must be, either according to truth, or according to verisimilitude.

And though every part of the material universe abounds in objects of pleasurable contemplation, yet nothing in nature so powerfully touches our hearts, or gives so great variety of exercise to our moral and intellectual faculties, as man. Human affairs and human feelings are universally interesting. There are many who have no great relish for the poetry that delineates only irrational or inanimate beings; but to that which exhibits the fortunes, the characters, and the conduct of men, there is hardly any person who does not listen with sympathy and delight. And hence, to imitate human action, is considered by Aristotle as essential to this art; and is indeed essential to the most pleasing and most instructive part of it, I mean to epic and dramatic composition. Mere descriptions, however beautiful, and moral reflections, however just, become tiresome, where our passions are not occasionally awakened by some event that concerns our fellow-men. Do not all readers of taste receive peculiar pleasure from those little tales or episodes, with which Thomson's descriptive poem on the seasons is here and there enlivened? And are they not sensible, that the thunderstorm would not have been half so interesting without the tale of the two lovers;[9] nor the harvest-scene, without that of Palemon and Lavinia;[10] nor the driving snows, without that exquisite picture of a man perishing among them?[11] It is much to be regretted, that Young did not employ the same artifice to animate his *Night Thoughts*.[12] Sentiments and descriptions may be regarded as the pilasters, carvings, gildings, and other decorations of the poetical fabric; but human actions are the columns and the rafters, that give it stability and elevation. Or, changing the metaphor, we may consider these as the soul which informs the lovely frame; while those are little more than the ornaments of the body.

Whether the pleasure we take in things natural, and our dislike of what is the reverse, be the effect of habit or of constitution, is not a material inquiry. There is nothing absurd in supposing, that between the soul, in its first formation, and the rest of nature, a

---

[9] *The Seasons*, 'Summer', verse 1171.
[10] 'Autumn', verse 177.
[11] 'Winter', verse 276.
[12] [Edward Young's *The Complaint: or Night Thoughts on Life, Death, and Immortality* was published 1742-4.]

mutual harmony and sympathy may have been established, which experience may indeed confirm, but no perverse habits could entirely subdue. As no sort of education could make man believe the contrary of a self-evident axiom, or reconcile him to a life of perfect solitude; so I should imagine, that our love of nature and regularity might still remain with us in some degree, though we had been born and bred in the Sicilian villa above mentioned, and never heard any thing applauded but what deserved censure, nor censured but what merited applause. Yet habit must be allowed to have a powerful influence over the sentiments and feelings of mankind. Objects to which we have been long accustomed, we are apt to contract a fondness for; we conceive them readily, and contemplate them with pleasure; nor do we quit our old tracts of speculation or practice, without reluctance and pain. Hence in part arises our attachment to our own professions, our old acquaintance, our native soil, our homes, and to the very hills, streams, and rocks in our neighbourhood. It would therefore be strange, if man, accustomed as he is from his earliest days to the regularity of nature, did not contract a liking to her productions, and principles of operation.

Yet we neither expect nor desire, that every human invention, where the end is only to please, should be an exact transcript of real existence. It is enough, that the mind acquiesce in it as probable, or plausible, or such as we think might happen without any direct opposition to the laws of nature: — or, to speak more accurately, it is enough, that it be consistent, either, first, with general experience; or secondly, with popular opinion; or, thirdly, that it be consistent with itself, and connected with probable circumstances.

First: If a human invention be consistent with *general* experience, we acquiesce in it as sufficiently probable. *Particular* experiences, however, there may be, so uncommon and so little expected, that we should not admit their probability, if we did not know them to be true. No man of sense believes, that he has any likelihood of being enriched by the discovery of hidden treasure; or thinks it probable, on purchasing a lottery-ticket, that he shall get the first prize; and yet great wealth has actually been acquired by such good fortune. But we should look upon these as poor expedients in a play or romance for bringing about a happy catastrophe. We expect that fiction should be more consonant to the *general* tenor of human affairs; in a word, that not possibility, but probability, should be the standard of poetical invention.

Secondly: Fiction is admitted as conformable to this standard, when it accords with received opinions. These may be erroneous, but are not often *apparently* repugnant to nature. On this account, and because they are familiar to us from our infancy, the mind readily acquiesces in them, or at least yields them that degree of credit which is necessary to render them pleasing. Hence the fairies, ghosts, and witches of Shakespeare, are admitted as probable beings; and angels obtain a place in religious pictures, though they do not now appear in the scenery of real life. Even when a popular opinion has long been exploded, and has become repugnant to universal belief, the fictions built upon it are still admitted as natural, because they were accounted such by the people to whom they were first addressed; whose sentiments and views of things we are willing to adopt, when, by the power of pleasing description, we are introduced into their scenes, and made acquainted with their manners. Hence we admit the theology of the ancient poets, their Elysium and Tartarus, Scylla and Charybdis, Cyclops and Circe, and the rest of those 'beautiful wonders' (as Horace calls them) which were believed in the heroic ages: as well as the demons and enchantments of Tasso, which may be supposed to have obtained no small degree of credit among the Italians of the sixteenth century, and are suitable enough to the notions that prevailed universally in Europe not long before. In fact, when poetry is in other respects true; when it gives an accurate display of those parts of nature about which we know that men in all ages must have entertained the same opinion, I mean those appearances in the visible creation, and those feelings and workings of the human mind, which are obvious to all mankind; — when poetry, I say, is thus far according to nature, we are very willing to be indulgent to what is fictitious in it, and to grant a temporary allowance to any system of fable which the author pleases to adopt; provided that he lay the scene in a distant country, or fix the date to a remote period. This is no unreasonable complaisance: we owe it both to the poet and to ourselves; for without it we should neither form a right estimate of his genius, nor receive from his works that pleasure which they were intended to impart. Let him, however, take care, that his system of fable be such, as his countrymen and contemporaries (to whom his work is immediately addressed) might be supposed capable of yielding their assent to; for otherwise we should not believe him to be in earnest: and let him connect it as much as he can with probable circumstances, and make it appear in a series of events consistent with itself.

For (thirdly) if this be the case, we shall admit his story as probable, or at least as natural, and consequently be interested in it, even though it be not warranted by general experience, and derive but slender authority from popular opinion. Caliban, in *The Tempest*, would have shocked the mind as an improbability, if we had not been made acquainted with his origin, and seen his character displayed in a series of consistent behaviour. But when we are told, that he sprung from a witch and a demon, a connection not contrary to the laws of nature, as they were understood in Shakespeare's time, and find his manners conformable to his descent, we are easily reconciled to the fiction. In the same sense, the Lilliputians of Swift may pass for probable beings; not so much because we know that a belief in pygmies was once current in the world (for the true ancient pygmy was at least thrice as tall as those whom Gulliver visited), but because we find, that every circumstance relating to them accords with itself, and with their supposed character. It is not the size of the people only that is diminutive; their country, seas, ships, and towns, are all in exact proportion; their theological and political principles, their passions, manners, customs, and all the parts of their conduct, betray a levity and littleness perfectly suitable: and so simple is the whole narration, and apparently so artless and sincere, that I should not much wonder, if it had imposed (as I have been told it has) upon some persons of no contemptible understanding. The same degree of credit may perhaps for the same reasons be due to his giants. But when he grounds his narrative upon a contradiction to nature; when he presents us with rational brutes, and irrational men; when he tells us of horses building houses for habitation, milking cows for food, riding in carriages, and holding conversations on the laws and politics of Europe; not all his genius (and he there exerts it to the utmost) is able to reconcile us to so monstrous a fiction: we may smile at some of his absurd exaggerations; we may be pleased with the energy of style; and accuracy of description, in particular places; and a malevolent heart may triumph in the satire: but we can never relish it as a fable, because it is at once unnatural and self-contradictory. Swift's judgement seems to have forsaken him on this occasion:[13] he wallows in nastiness and brutality; and the general run of his satire is downright defamation. Lucian's *True History* is a heap of extravagancies put together without order or unity, or any other apparent design, than to ridicule the language and manner of grave authors. His ravings, which have no better right to the name of fable, than a hill of rubbish has to that of palace, are destitute of every colour of plausibility. Animal trees, ships sailing in the sky, armies of monstrous things travelling between the sun and moon on a pavement of cobwebs, rival nations of men inhabiting woods and mountains in a whale's belly, — are liker the dreams of a bedlamite, than the inventions of a rational being.

If we were to prosecute this subject any further, it would be proper to remark, that in some kinds of poetical invention a stricter probability is required than in others: — that, for instance,

---

[13] There are improprieties in this narrative, which one would think a very slight attention to nature might have prevented; and which, without heightening the satire, serve only to aggravate the absurdity of the fable. *Houyhnhnms* are horses in perfection, with the addition of reason and virtue. Whatever, therefore, takes away from their perfection as horses, without adding to their rational and moral accomplishments, must be repugnant to the author's design, and ought not to have found a place in his narration. Yet he makes his beloved quadrupeds *dwell in houses* of their own building, and use *warm food* and the *milk of cows* as a delicacy: though these luxuries, supposed attainable by a nation of horses, could contribute no more to their perfection, than brandy and imprisonment would to that of a man. — Again, did Swift believe, that religious ideas, are natural to a reasonable being, and necessary to the happiness of a moral one? I hope he did. Yet has he represented his *houyhnhnms*, as patterns of moral virtue, as the greatest masters of reason, and with all as completely happy, without any religious ideas, or any views beyond the present life. In a word, he would make stupidity consistent with mental excellence, and unnatural appetites with animal perfection. These, however, are small matters, compared with the other absurdities of this abominable tale. — But when a Christian Divine can set himself deliberately to trample upon that nature, which he knows to have been made but a little lower than the angels, and to have been assumed by one far more exalted than they; we need not be surprised if the same perverse habits of thinking which harden his heart, should also debase his judgement.

comedy, whether dramatic or narrative, must seldom deviate from the ordinary course of human affairs, because it exhibits the manners of real, and even of familiar life; — that the tragic poet, because he imitates characters more exalted, and generally refers to events little known, or long since past, may be allowed a wide range; but must never attempt the marvellous fictions of the epic muse, because he addresses his work, not only to the passions and imagination of mankind, but also to their eyes and ears, which are not easily imposed on, and refuse to be gratified with any representation that does not come very near the truth; — that the epic poem may claim still ampler privileges, because its fictions are not subject to the scrutiny of any outward sense, and because it conveys information in regard both to the highest human characters, and the most important and wonderful events, and also to the affairs of unseen worlds, and superior beings. Nor would it be improper to observe, that the several species of comic, of tragic, of epic composition, are not confined to the same degree of probability; for that farce may be allowed to be less probable than the regular comedy; the masque, than the regular tragedy; and the mixed epic, such as *The Fairy Queen*, and *Orlando Furioso*, than the pure epopee of Homer, Virgil, and Milton. — But this part of the subject seems not to require further illustration. Enough has been said, to show, that nothing unnatural can please; and that therefore poetry, whose end is to please, must be according to nature.

And if so, it must be, either according to real nature, or according to nature somewhat different from the reality.

Thirteen

On Music

... Since imitation is so plentiful a source of pleasure, we need not wonder, that the imitative arts of poetry and painting should have been greatly esteemed in every enlightened age. The imitation itself, which is the work of the artist, is agreeable; the thing imitated, which is nature, is also agreeable; and is not the same thing true of the instrument of imitation? Or does any one doubt, whether harmonious language be pleasing to the ear, or certain arrangements of colour beautiful to the eye?

Shall I apply these, and the preceding reasonings, to the musical art also, which I have elsewhere called, and which is generally understood to be, imitative? Shall I say, that some melodies please, because they imitate nature, and that others, which do not imitate nature, are therefore unpleasing? — That an air expressive of devotion, for example, is agreeable, because it presents us with an imitation of those sounds by which devotion does naturally express itself? — Such an affirmation would hardly pass upon the reader; notwithstanding the plausibility it might seem to derive from that analogy which all the fine arts are supposed to bear to one another. He would ask: What is the natural sound of devotion? Where is it to be heard? When was it heard? What resemblance is there between Handel's *Te Deum*, and the tone of voice natural to a person expressing, by articulate sound, his veneration of the divine character and providence? — In fact, I apprehend, that critics have erred a little in their determinations upon this subject, from an opinion, that music, painting, and poetry, are all imitative arts. I hope at least I may say, without offence, that while this was my opinion, I was always conscious of some unaccountable confusion of thought, whenever I attempted to explain it in the way of detail to others.

But while I thus insinuate, that music is not an imitative art, I mean no disrespect to Aristotle, who seems in the beginning of his *Poetics* to declare the contrary. It is not the whole, but *the greater part* of music, which that philosopher calls imitative; and I agree with him so far as to allow this property to some music, though not to all. But he speaks of the ancient music, and I of the modern; and to one who considers how very little we know of the former, it will not appear a contradiction to say, that the one might have been imitative, though the other is not.

Nor do I mean any disrespect to music, when I would strike it off the list of imitative arts. I allow it to be a fine art, and to have great influence on the human soul: I grant, that, by its power of raising a variety of agreeable emotions in the hearer, it proves its relation to poetry, and that it never appears to the best advantage but with poetry for its interpreter: and I am satisfied, that though musical genius may subsist without poetical taste; yet these two talents united might accomplish nobler effects, than either could do singly. I acknowledge too, that the principles and essential rules of this art are as really founded in nature, as those of poetry and painting. But when I am asked, what part of nature is imitated in any good picture or poem, I find I can give a definite answer: whereas, when I am asked, what part of nature is imitated in Handel's *Water-music*, for instance, or in Corelli's *eighth concerto*, or in any particular English song or Scotch tune, I find I can give no definite answer: — though no doubt I might say some plausible things; or perhaps, after much refinement, be able to show, that music may, by one shift or other, be made an imitative art, provided you allow me to give any meaning I please to the word *imitative*.

* * *

How are the Pleasures We Derive from Music to be Accounted for?

It was said, that certain melodies and harmonies have *an aptitude* to raise certain passions, affections, and sentiments, in the human soul. Let us now enquire a little into the nature of this *aptitude*; by endeavouring, from acknowledged principles of the human constitution, to explain the cause of that pleasure which mankind derive from music. I am well aware of the delicacy of the argument, and of my inability to do it justice; and therefore I promise no complete investigation, nor indeed anything more than a few cursory remarks. As I have no theory to support, and as this topic, though it may amuse, is not of any great utility, I shall be neither positive in my assertions, nor abstruse in my reasoning.

* * *

... Pathos, or expression, is the chief excellence of music. Without this, it may amuse the ear, it may give a little exercise to the mind of the hearer, it may for a moment withdraw the attention from the anxieties of life, it may show the performer's dexterity, the skill of the composer, or the merit of the instruments; and in all or any of these ways, it may afford a slight pleasure: but, without engaging the affections, it can never yield that permanent, useful, and heartfelt gratification, which legislators, civil, military, and ecclesiastical, have expected from it. Is it absurd to ascribe utility, and permanence, to the effects produced by this noble art? ...

Music, however, would not have recommended itself so effectually to general esteem, if it had always been merely instrumental. For, if I mistake not, the expression of music without poetry is vague and ambiguous; and hence it is, that the same air may sometimes be repeated to every stanza of a long ode or ballad. The change of the poet's ideas, provided the subject continue nearly the same, does not always require a change of the music: and if critics have ever determined otherwise, they were led into the mistake, by supposing, what every musician knows to be absurd, that, in fitting verses to a tune, or a tune to verses, it is more necessary, that *particular words* should have *particular notes* adapted to them, than that the *general tenor* of the music should accord with the *general nature* of the sentiments.

It is true, that to a favourite air, even when unaccompanied with words, we do commonly annex certain ideas, which may have come to be related to it in consequence of some accidental associations: and sometimes we imagine a resemblance (which however is merely imaginary) between certain melodies and certain thoughts or objects. Thus a Scotchman may fancy, that there is some sort of likeness between that charming air which he calls

Tweedside, and the scenery of a fine pastoral country: and to the same air, even when only played on an instrument, he may annex the ideas of romantic love and rural tranquillity; because these form the subject of a pretty little ode, which he has often heard sung to that air. But all this is the effect of habit. A foreigner who hears that tune for the first time, entertains no such fancy. The utmost we can expect from him is, to acknowledge the air to be sweet and simple. He would smile, if we were to ask him, whether it bears any resemblance to the hills, groves, and meadows, adjoining to a beautiful river; nor would he perhaps think it more expressive of romantic love, than of conjugal, parental, or filial affection, tender melancholy, moderate joy, or any other gentle passion. Certain it is, that on any one of these topics an ode might be composed, which would suit the air most perfectly. So ambiguous is musical expression.

It is likewise true, that music merely instrumental does often derive significancy from external circumstances. When an army in battle-array is advancing to meet the enemy, words are not necessary to give meaning to the military music. And a solemn air on the organ, introducing or dividing the church-service, may not only elevate the mind, and banish impertinent thoughts, but also, deriving energy from the surrounding scene, may promote religious meditation.

Nor can it be denied, that instrumental music may both quicken our sensibility, and give a direction to it; that is, may both prepare the mind for being affected, and determine it to one set of affections rather than another; — to melancholy, for instance, rather than merriment, composure rather than agitation, devotion rather than levity, and contrariwise. Certain tunes, too, there are, which having been always connected with certain actions, do, merely from the power of habit, dispose men to those actions. Such are the tunes commonly used to regulate the motions of dancing.

Yet it is in general true, that poetry is the most immediate and most accurate interpreter of music. Without this auxiliary, a piece of the best music, heard for the first time, might be said to mean something, but we should not be able to say what. It might incline the heart to sensibility: but poetry, or language, would be necessary to improve that sensibility into a real emotion, by fixing the mind upon some definite and affecting ideas. A fine instrumental symphony well performed, is like an oration delivered with propriety, but in an unknown tongue; it may affect us a little, but conveys no determinate feeling; we are alarmed, perhaps, or melted, or soothed, but it is very imperfectly, because we know not why: — the finger, by taking up the same air, and applying words to it, immediately translates the oration into our own language; then all uncertainty vanishes, the fancy is filled with determinate ideas, and determinate emotions take possession of the heart.

* * *

Conjectures on Some Peculiarities of National Music

There is a certain style of melody peculiar to each musical country, which the people of that country are apt to prefer to every other style. That they should prefer their own, is not surprising; and that the melody of one people should differ from that of another, is not more surprising, perhaps, than that the language of one people should differ from that of another. But there is something not unworthy of notice in the particular expression and style that characterize the music of one nation or province, and distinguish it from every other sort of music. Of this diversity Scotland supplies a striking example. The native melody of the highlands and western isles is as different from that of the southern part of the kingdom, as the Irish or Erse language is different from the English or Scotch. In the conclusion of a discourse on music as it relates to the mind, it will not perhaps be impertinent to offer a conjecture on the cause of these peculiarities; which, though it should not (and indeed I am satisfied that it will not) fully account for any one of them, may however incline the reader to think that they are not unaccountable, and may also throw some faint light on this part of philosophy.

Every thought that partakes of the nature of passion, has a correspondent expression in the look and gesture: and so strict is the union between the passion and its outward sign, that, where the former is not in some degree felt, the latter can never be perfectly natural, but, if assumed, becomes awkward mimicry, instead of that genuine imitation of nature, which draws forth the sympathy of the beholder. If, therefore, there be, in the circumstances of particular nations or persons, any thing that gives a particularity to their passions and thoughts, it seems reasonable to expect, that they will also have something peculiar in the expression of their countenance, and even in the form of their features. Caius Marius, Jugurtha, Tamerlane, and some other great warriors, are celebrated for a peculiar ferocity of aspect, which they had no doubt contracted from a perpetual and unrestrained exertion of fortitude, contempt, and other violent emotions. These produced in the face of their correspondent expressions, which being often repeated, became at last as habitual to the features, as the sentiments they arose from were to the heart. Savages, whose thoughts are little inured to control, have more of this significancy of look, than those men, who, being born and bred in civilized nations, are accustomed from their childhood to suppress every emotion that tends to interrupt the peace of society. And while the bloom of youth lasts, and the smoothness of feature peculiar to that period, the human face is less marked with any strong character, than in old age: — a peevish or surly stripling may elude the eye of the physiognomist; but a wicked old man, whose visage does not betray the evil temperature of his heart, must have more cunning than it would be prudent for him to acknowledge. Even by the trade or profession the human countenance may be characterized. They who employ themselves in the nicer mechanic arts, that require the earnest attention of the artist, do generally contract a fixedness of feature suited to that one uniform sentiment which engrosses them while at work. Whereas, other artists, whose work requires less attention, and who may ply their trade and amuse themselves with conversation at the same time, have for the most part smoother and more unmeaning faces: their thoughts are more miscellaneous, and therefore their features are less fixed in one uniform configuration. A keen penetrating look indicates thoughtfulness and spirit: a dull torpid countenance is not often accompanied with great sagacity.

This, though there may be many an exception, is in general true of the visible signs of our passions; and it is no less true of the audible. A man habitually peevish, or passionate, or querulous, or imperious, may be known by the sound of his voice, as well as by his physiognomy. May we not go a step farther, and say, that if a man under the influence of any passion were to compose a discourse, or a poem, or a tune, his work would in some measure exhibit an image of his mind? I could not easily be persuaded, that Swift and Juvenal were men of sweet tempers; or that Thomson, Arbuthnot, and Prior were ill natured. The airs of Felton are so uniformly mournful, that I cannot suppose him to have been a merry, or even a cheerful man. If a musician, in deep affliction, were to attempt to compose a lively air, I believe he would not succeed: though I confess I do not well understand the nature of the connection that may take place between a mournful mind and a melancholy tune. It is easy to conceive, how a poet or an orator should transfuse his passions into his work: for every passion suggests ideas congenial to its own nature; and the composition of the poet, or of the orator, must necessarily consist of those ideas that occur at the time he is composing. But musical sounds are not the signs of ideas; rarely are they even the imitations of natural sounds: so that I am at a loss to conceive how it should happen, that a musician, overwhelmed with sorrow, for example, should put together a series of notes, whose expression is contrary to that of another series which he had put together when elevated with joy. But of the fact I am not doubtful; though I have not sagacity, or knowledge of music, enough to be able to explain it. And my opinion in this matter is warranted by that of a more competent judge; who says, speaking of church-voluntaries, that if the organist 'do not feel in himself the divine energy of devotion, he will labour in vain to raise it in others. Nor can he hope to throw out those happy instantaneous thoughts, which sometimes far exceed the best concerted compositions, and which the enraptured performer would gladly secure to his future use and pleasure, did they not as fleetly escape as they rise'.[1] A man who has made music the study of his life, and is well acquainted with all the best examples of style and expression that are to be found in the works of former masters, may, by memory and much practice, attain a sort of mechanical dexterity in contriving music suitable to any given passion; but such music would, I presume, be vulgar and spiritless, compared to what an artist of genius throws out, when under the power of any ardent emotion. It is recorded of

---

[1] Charles Avison, *An Essay on Musical Expression* (1752), pp. 88–9.

Lulli, that, once when his imagination was all on fire with some verses descriptive of terrible ideas, which he had been reading in a French tragedy, he ran to his harpsichord, and struck off such a combination of sounds, that the company felt their hair stand on end with horror.

Let us therefore suppose it proved, or, if you please, take it for granted, that different sentiments in the mind of the musician will give different and peculiar expressions to his music; — and upon this principle, it will not perhaps be impossible to account for some of the phenomena of a national ear.

The highlands of Scotland are a picturesque, but in general a melancholy country. Long tracts of mountainous desert, covered with dark heath, and often obscured by misty weather; narrow valleys, thinly inhabited, and bounded by precipices resounding with the fall of torrents; a soil so rugged, and a climate so dreary, as in many parts to admit neither the amusements of pasturage, nor the labours of agriculture; the mournful dashing of waves along the friths and lakes that intersect the country; the portentous noises which every change of wind, and every increase and diminution of the waters, is apt to raise, in a lonely region, full of echoes, and rocks, and caverns; the grotesque and the ghastly appearance of such a landscape by the light of the moon: — Objects like these diffuse a gloom over the fancy, which may be compatible enough with occasional and social merriment, but cannot fail to tincture the thoughts of a native in the hour of silence and solitude. If these people, notwithstanding their reformation in religion, and more frequent intercourse with strangers, do still retain many of their old superstitions, we need not doubt but in former times they must have been more enslaved to the horrors of imagination, when beset with bugbears of popery, and the darkness of paganism. Most of their superstitions are of a melancholy cast. That *Second Sight*, wherewith some of them are still supposed to be haunted, is considered by themselves as a misfortune, on account of the many dreadful images it is said to obtrude upon the fancy. I have been told, that the inhabitants of some of the Alpine regions do likewise lay claim to a sort of second sight. Nor is it wonderful, that persons of lively imagination, immured in deep solitude, and surrounded with the stupendous scenery of clouds, precipices, and torrents, should dream, even when they think themselves awake, of those few striking ideas with which their lonely lives are diversified; of corpses, funeral processions, and other objects of terror; or of marriages, and the arrival of strangers, and such like matters of more agreeable curiosity. Let it be observed also, that the ancient highlanders of Scotland had hardly any other way of supporting themselves, than by hunting, fishing, or war, professions that are continually exposed to fatal accidents. And hence, no doubt, additional horrors would often haunt their solitude, and a deeper gloom overshadow the imagination even of the hardiest native.

What then would it be reasonable to expect from the fanciful tribe, from the musicians and poets, of such a region? Strains, expressive of joy, tranquillity, or the softer passions? No: their style must have been better suited to their circumstances. And so we find in fact that their music is. The wildest irregularity appears in its composition: the expression is warlike, and melancholy, and approaches even to the terrible. — And that their poetry is almost uniformly mournful, and their views of nature dark and dreary, will be allowed, by all who admit of the authenticity of Ossian; and not doubted by any who believe those fragments of highland poetry to be genuine, which many old people, now alive, of that country, remember to have heard in their youth, and were then taught to refer to a pretty high antiquity.

Some of the southern provinces of Scotland present a very different prospect. Smooth and lofty hills covered with verdure; clear streams winding through long and beautiful valleys; trees produced without culture, here straggling or single, and there crowding into little groves and bowers; — with other circumstances peculiar to the districts I allude to, render them fit for pasturage, and favourable to romantic leisure and tender passions. Several of the old Scotch songs take their names from the rivulets, villages, and hills, adjoining to the Tweed near Melrose; a region distinguished by many charming varieties of rural scenery, and which, whether we consider the face of the country, or the genius of the people, may properly enough be termed the Arcadia of Scotland. And all these songs are sweetly and powerfully expressive of love and tenderness, and other emotions suited to the tranquillity of pastoral life . . .

Fourteen

Of Taste, and Its Improvement

Some ideas are too complex, to admit of logical definition. When this is the case, we must have recourse to description; and give a detail of the more important, if we should not be able to ascertain the essential qualities. And, if we can illustrate a subject, I believe it is not material, whether that be done by definition and syllogism, or by any other method equally brief, convincing, and intelligible.

It was said, that 'imagination, united with some other mental powers, and operating as a percipient faculty, in conveying suitable impressions of what is elegant, sublime or beautiful, in art or nature, is called taste'.[1] This account may be right as far as it goes; but it is not sufficiently comprehensive. By pointing out its defects, we make amends for them. They may be reduced to two.

First; sublimity, beauty, and elegance, are not the only things in art and nature, which gratify taste. There is also a taste in imitation, in harmony, and in ridicule. He who takes delight in truth, in virtue, in simplicity, may be said to have a taste for it. And, not to be charmed with such qualities; or to approve their opposites; to be insensible of harmony; to relish gross buffoonery; to prefer bad pictures to good, and financial ornament to manly simplicity, are proofs of bad taste; as disregard to truth, and indifference to virtue, are, of both a bad taste, and a bad heart.

Secondly; as elegance, sublimity, beauty, and the other qualities here mentioned as objects of taste, are all good and agreeable;

---

[1] [Beattie is quoting a definition he himself gave of taste earlier in the dissertation.]

we might, by trusting to the definition, be led to suppose, that taste, being an inlet to pleasure only, is not connected with painful emotions. But, in the works of human art, it is the office of taste, to discern, not only what is excellent, but also what is faulty; and to be delighted with the one, and dissatisfied with the other, according as that approaches to perfection, and this deviates from it. To read Blackmore and Milton with the same relish, or the same indifference; or, while we admire the latter, not to be disgusted with the former, would be a sign of bad taste, or of total insensibility.[2] A good-natured critic may confine his *remarks* to the beauties of his author: but, if he have true discernment, it is impossible for him not to perceive, and be offended with, the blemishes.

Since, then, that sort of mental sagacity, which we call taste, is too complex to be characterized in short definition; I proceed to enumerate those faculties or talents, which must be united in the person who possesses it.

To be a person of taste, it seems necessary, that one have, first a lively and correct imagination; secondly, the power of distinct apprehension; thirdly, the capacity of being easily, strongly, and agreeably affected, with sublimity, beauty, harmony, exact imitation, &c.; fourthly, sympathy, or sensibility of heart; and, fifthly, judgement, or good sense, which is the principal thing, and may not very improperly be said to comprehend all the rest.

I. Good taste implies lively imagination. This talent qualifies one, for readily understanding an author's purpose; tracing the connection of his thoughts; forming the same views of things which he had formed; and clearly conceiving the several images or ideas that the artist describes or delineates.

In this respect, the minds of different men are differently constituted. Some can enter into a description of what they have seen, or of what is familiar; and follow an author's train of thought; when he lays down a plan, and proceeds accordingly: but are not able to comprehend such thoughts or images as are uncommon; or to mark those delicacies of connection, which give surprise, or which imitate the desultory operations of enthusiasm, or any other ardent passion. Yet these delicate transitions are among the chief beauties of poetry. The philosopher lays down a plan; and

---

[2] [Sir Richard Blackmore (d. 1729) was the author of now forgotten works such as *Prince Arthur, an Heroick Poem in X books* (1695).]

follows it; his business being only, to instruct. But the orator sometimes; and the poet frequently, conceals his plan, and makes you expect something different from what he intends; because his aim is, to please, by working upon your passions, and fancy: which is never more effectually done, than when he exhibits what is at once natural and surprising. — In the end of Virgil's second *Georgic*, the praises of a country life are, by the poet's management, closely connected with the former part of the book, which treats of trees and vines: but the connection is not obvious to every eye; and they, who do not see it, blame the author for his want of method. The same delicate contrivance appears in the end of the first *Georgic*: where, from the precepts of agriculture, he makes a nice though natural transition to the prodigies that attended the death of Julius Cesar, and thence to the calamities of civil war; after which, he resumes with equal art the subject of agriculture, and so concludes the book.

The language of enthusiasm, and of all those passions that strongly agitate the soul, is naturally incoherent; and may appear even extravagant to those, who cannot enter into the views of the speaker, or form an idea of what is passing in his mind. Hence, in the odes of Pindar, and in some of the odes of Gray, which imitate the language of enthusiasm, many readers complain, that they are often at a loss to discover connection between the contiguous sentiments; while others, not more learned perhaps, find no difficulty in conceiving the progress of ideas, that lead these authors from one thought or image to another. The latter, surely, are the only persons qualified to judge of those odes: and this qualification they seem to derive from their superior liveliness of fancy. In a word, the imagination of a critic must, in respect of vivacity, be able to keep pace with that of the authors, whom he assumes the privilege of judging, or wishes to read with the true relish. Their powers of invention it is not necessary that he possess: but, in readily apprehending or imagining every thing they are pleased to set before him he cannot be in any degree inferior, without being in the same degree an incompetent judge. If we are unable to conceive a poet's imagery, or enter into his sentiments, we understand him as little, as if we were ignorant of his language.

The greatest liveliness of imagination will, however, avail but little, if it is not *corrected* and regulated by the knowledge of nature, both external or material, and internal or moral. Without this, there cannot be taste; because one cannot discern, whether the productions of art be natural or unnatural; that is, whether they be good or bad. In acquiring that knowledge of nature, which is necessary to taste, a man needs not descend to the *minutiæ* of natural history; but he must contemplate all the striking appearances of the world around him, surveying them in those picturesque attitudes, in which they most powerfully captivate the mind, and awaken the passions.

As means of promoting in young persons a taste for the beauties of external nature, I have in another place recommended frequent perusals of the best descriptive poets, particularly Virgil, Spenser, and Thomson;[3] together with some practice in drawing. I may now add, that Homer, Milton, and Shakespeare will improve that taste, and at the same time make them acquainted with moral nature, that is, with human passions and characters; which however, as Horace intimates, cannot be thoroughly understood, but by careful observation of men and manners, as they appear in the active scenes of real life.[4]

Liveliness of imagination, though a natural gift, is not unsusceptible of improvement. By studying the works of nature and art; by travelling into foreign countries, and conversing with people of different professions, capacities, and manners; by exploring new scenes of the inanimate world, mountains, valleys, and plains, whether distinguished by their wildness or regularity, by their beauty or grandeur; the memory may be stored with new ideas, which, if properly arranged and ascertained, will give vigour to all the mental powers, and to imagination among the rest. Milton is said to have quickened his fancy, by reading the old romances. And Leonardo da Vinci recommends it to the painter, to go into decayed buildings, and observe the stains on the broken and mouldy walls; where an eye accustomed to look at such things will frequently discern figures resembling clouds, battles, uncommon attitudes, draperies, ludicrous faces, and the like: agreeably to which idea, a pamphlet has been published, to show, how, from a few random strokes of a pencil dipped in Indian ink,

---

[3] [See above, p. 144.]

[4] *The Art of Poetry*, ll. 317–18.

Of Taste, and Its Improvement 165

hints may be obtained for the invention of landscapes.[5] Every thing, indeed, that puts us in the way of meeting with novelties, may be considered as a help to the fancy: but care must be taken to methodize those new ideas, lest they seduce from the love of nature, and give a taste for extravagant combinations. Liveliness and correctness of imagination are eminently and equally conspicuous in Homer: Spenser and Ariosto are not inferior in the first quality, but extremely defective in the second.

II. Sometimes, when one's imagination is lively, and regulated too by an acquaintance with nature, one may, notwithstanding, contract habits of indolence and irregularity in one's studies; which produce a superficial medley of knowledge very detrimental to the native vigour of the mind. And therefore I mentioned distinct apprehension, as the second thing necessary to good taste. There are men, who think with precision on every subject: and there are others, whose ideas are always inaccurate and obscure. The former make you understand their meaning at once, and may be known by their clearness of method and of style: the latter use indefinite and superfluous words, confusedly put together; which, though, on familiar topics, they may give a tolerable idea of what is intended, will often leave you at a loss, and perhaps, when any thing uncommon is to be expressed, make it impossible for you to find out what is in the mind of the speaker.

The former, it is obvious, are the only competent judges of what they read; because they are the only persons who perfectly understand it. How comes it, that, on every perusal of Homer, Virgil, or Milton, beauties are discovered, which never struck us before? Is it not, because, the more we are acquainted with these authors, we understand them the better? Elegant writing is distinguished by a thousand little graces, that escape the superficial reader, and are not immediately apparent even to the attentive. And therefore, habits of accurate study are indispensably requisite to form a true critic.

Besides, most performances in the fine arts are intended to raise, in the reader or beholder, certain emotions and sympathies. And it is generally true, that an emotion is lively in proportion to the clearness wherewith its object is perceived or apprehended by

---

[5] [Anon.], *An Essay to Facilitate the Inventing of Landscapes* (1759).

the mind. A man of obscure apprehension must, therefore, be a man of dull feeling, and so cannot possess true taste; because he is not susceptible of those ardent emotions, which the artist intended to raise, and which in sounder minds his work does actually raise.

It is remarkable, that in every language the most elegant authors are the most perspicuous. Such are Homer and Xenophon in Greek, and Caesar, Cicero, and Virgil, in Latin. A proof, that good taste and clearness of apprehension are inseparable: this last quality being the immediate cause of perspicuity in writing.

For attaining the faculty of distinct apprehension, the best rule that can be given is, to study with accuracy, and with method, every thing we apply to, whether books, or business. — But having already enlarged on this topic, I shall not now pursue it any further.

III. A board may be so shaped and painted, as that a dog shall mistake it for a man; but it does not appear, that he has any pleasure in it, as an *imitation*. Brutes no doubt perceive some of those things which we term ludicrous; but brutes never laugh, nor seem to have any notion of *incongruity*. All animals that see discern light, and probably colours; but man alone perceives, in colours and in figures, that pleasurable quality, which we term *beauty*. The *magnificence* of the starry firmament, of a lofty and craggy mountain, of a thundering cataract, of a tempestuous ocean, has no charms for any terrestrial creature, but man. *Novelty* yields pleasure to rational minds; but the inferior tribes seem rather to dislike it. Many brutes hear more acutely than we; and some of them may be soothed or alarmed by sound; but brutes have no sense of *harmony*: nay of those men, who hear with equal acuteness, some have a musical ear, and others have not.

In these and the like cases, there seems to be in the human mind a sort of double sensation: one conveyed immediately by the external organ; and the other depending, partly on that, and partly on some other faculty.

That there is in our constitution such a thing as a musical ear, a sense of beauty, a taste for sublimity and imitation, a love of novelty, and a tendency to smiles and laughter, will not be denied. And that these senses, or sensibilities, depend partly on the eye and the ear, and yet are to be distinguished from the outward senses of sight and hearing (for these may exist without the others), is evident from what has been said. They may therefore be called *secondary senses*. Some philosophers call them *reflex*, and some *internal*. And the pleasures derived from them are termed, by Addison, and Akenside, pleasures of imagination.[6]

Others have named them *emotions*, as if they were a sort of weaker passions. And the name is not improper. For all passions are attended with pleasure or pain, and produce sensible appearances both in the soul and in the body. And the feelings I speak of are all of the agreeable kind; and, where they operate without restraint, do all display themselves externally. The contemplation of beauty, for example, softens the features into a smile. Sublimity raises admiration and astonishment, and novelty often gives surprise; and these passions operate very sensibly on the countenance. Ludicrous objects call forth laughter, which is still more obvious to the eye, as well as to the ear. And the various pleasures that result from imitation do variously affect the face; according to the nature of the object imitated, and the skill displayed by the imitator.

But the name we assign to these modes of perception is not a matter of great moment. When I call them secondary senses, I would not be understood to find fault with the language of those authors, who in speaking of them have adopted a different phraseology.

Now a third thing necessary to good taste is, acuteness of (what is here called) secondary sensation; or, to express it in other words, 'a capacity of being easily, strongly, and agreeably affected, with sublimity, beauty, harmony, exact imitation', &c.

In this respect also the capacities of different men are very different. Some have no sense of harmony or modulation, either in language, or in music. Some, who are exceedingly delighted with the sublime and the beautiful, have little taste or genius in the way of ridicule: — Milton is an instance; who excels in grand and elegant description, but whose attempts at humour are nothing but quibble. Others have an exquisite relish for every sort of ludicrous

---

[6] See Francis Hutcheson's *System of Moral Philosophy* (1755); Alexander Gerard, *An Essày on Taste* (1759); the sixth volume of the *Spectator*; Mark Akenside's *Pleasures of the Imagination* (1744); and Lord Kames, *Elements of Criticism* (1762).

combination, who seem to be little affected with beauty, or with greatness: — Swift is one instance, and the author of *Hudibras* another.[7] To excel equally in the sublime and in the ludicrous, is a rare talent: Shakespeare, however, possessed it in a very high degree; and Pope, in a lower: Homer, too, is said to have been eminent in the comic, as well as in the solemn style; though that does not appear from any part of his works now extant. Some authors, of whom Homer is the most illustrious, give no delineations of moral or of material nature, but what bear an exact resemblance to reality; others, like Ariosto, abound in extravagant and unnatural fiction: the former, surely, have a better taste in imitation, as well as a better judgement, than the latter. The sense of harmony assumes various appearances. Pope, for all the smoothness of his numbers, had no musical ear; Milton, though his poetry is most harmonious, writes rugged prose: and Addison, whose prose is the sweetest that can be, is not distinguished as a melodious versifier.

Some of these varieties may be accounted for, from the power of habit. Of those, who have from nature a musical ear, many perhaps may never have thought of improving that talent, and many have never had the means of improving it: and we seldom acquire any true relish for music, unless we have been accustomed to it in our younger years. Besides, that sweetness of sound in prose, which is called harmony, is very different from musical harmony or melody: easy articulation belongs to the former; for we never call those words harmonious, which we find it hard to pronounce: but the latter has nothing to do with articulation: and therefore, one may have a taste for the one, who has none for the other. Nor is it to be wondered at, that a harmonious versifier should write in prose without harmony; for this may be the effect of haste or carelessness, or want of practice.

Further; the more we are accustomed, from our early years, to attend to what is great and beautiful; to read sublime poetry, or to associate with persons of a solemn deportment, the less we shall be inclined to give way to the levities of wit and humour. And from him, who is better pleased with the wildness of romance, than with the simplicity of nature and the ancients, a taste for cor-

---

[7] [The author of mock epic *Hudibras* (1662–78) was Samuel Butler.]

rect imitation is not to be expected. These various habits may be owing to various causes, too minute to be specified. Our way of life, our course of study, the company we keep, the taste of the age or of the society to which we belong, have great influence in perverting or improving all our intellectual faculties, and those of taste and genius in particular. I here join taste and genius together. They are kindred powers; and of so near affinity, that the first, perhaps, might be called *passive genius*, and the second *active taste*.

The human mind is always the same: but in one age one set of faculties are cultivated, and another in another; and the pursuits of men, the states of literature, the modes of taste, and the characters of nations, are varied accordingly. About the middle of the last century, the greater part of English authors were learned and serious, but not very attentive to elegant expression. Under Charles II, they ran into the opposite extreme, and became giddy, superficial, and indelicate; and none but wits and epigrammatists were accounted men of taste: so that, if the revolution had not taken place, our literature would probably have perished, as well as our laws and liberties. In the reign of Queen Anne, and George I, wit, learning, and elegance, were happily united. Of late the public taste seems to have been most effectually gratified by correct expression, and historical and philosophical inquiry.

But whatever influence habit may have in forming the taste and the genius, it must be repeated, that in minds, as well as in bodies, there are constitutional differences. There are men, who can never bring themselves to relish music; and some are equally disinclined to poetry. And of poets and musicians, as well as of painters, some excel in the grand style, and some in the ludicrous; nor will either class of artists admit, that the other is qualified to prescribe rules for both. And therefore, we are not to expect, that in different men taste should be precisely uniform, or that it should be absolutely perfect in any individual.

Any one of these secondary senses will form a sort of taste; but to the perfection of this talent the concurrence of them all is necessary. In a man thus accomplished, every object of his contemplation, whether fit to allure by its novelty, astonish by its grandeur, charm by its beauty, please by imitative elegance, or amuse by unexpected incongruity, will awaken that kind, and that degree, of internal satisfaction, which the most enlightened part of mankind would acknowledge to be adequate to the pleasurable qualities of the object. But such perfection of taste is imaginary: as there is not on earth a person, who is not a greater admirer, a more accurate observer, and of course a more competent judge, of some objects of taste, than of others. Rarely have we heard of one man completely skilled in music, painting, and poetry, or even in any two of those arts. The epic poet undervalues the epigrammatist, who in his turn pronounces all sublime writing to be affected or insipid; the architect is perhaps indifferent to both; and the composer of instrumental symphonies to all the three. There may be exceptions: but it is in general true, that

> One science only will one genius fit,
> So vast is art, so narrow human wit;
> Not only bounded to peculiar arts,
> But oft in those confin'd to single parts.[8]

It is easy to know, how far an author's taste may be deficient in this respect. If, while he aims at elevation, he disappoint the reader by mean language, or grovelling ideas, (which is generally the case with Blackmore) it is a sign, that he has no taste in sublimity. If he appear fond of describing what is unnameable or ungraceful, and disgust you with vile allusions and filthy images, (which is too often the case with Swift and Juvenal) he gives proof of an indelicate mind, that either has no sense or love of beauty, or, which is worse, does not choose to indulge it. If his views of nature be indefinite or inaccurate; if they be overcharged with unnecessary ornaments, or seem to be drawn not from his own observation, but from the works of other men, (which are faults common to all bad poets and bad painters) it is evident, that he has no distinct knowledge of nature, or, at least, that he has no talent or taste in imitation. If the sound of his verses offend, as in Donne and Hobbes, by its harshness; or, as in Waller and Lansdowne, proceed in one uniform tenor of smoothness, without changing according to the subject, or amusing the ear with those varieties of rhythm and cadence, which the most regular versification admits; it will be supposed, that he writes carelessly,

---

[8]   [Pope, *Essay on Criticism*, ll. 60–4.]

or that he has no true relish for harmonious composition.[9] If, in his comic scenes, he attempt to raise laughter by unnatural exaggeration; which is sometimes done by Sterne and Smollett: if, instead of humour, he obtrude upon you indecent buffoonery; which is frequent in Aristophanes and Rabelais: if, where he intends wit, he can only bring forth common-place jokes, or verbal quibbles; of which I am sorry to say that there is an example or two in Milton: or if, with Congreve and Vanburgh, he endeavour to make crimes and misfortunes matter of merriment; we must believe, either that he has no true sense of ridicule, or that he wilfully debases it, to gratify the taste of the times, or the singularity of his own temper.[10]

But let it be remembered, that the work of an artist is not to be characterized by incidental faults. These may be owing to the weakness of human nature; which in the best men is liable to transgression, in the wisest to error, and in the most attentive to inadvertence. Who can paint nature with the energy of Shakespeare? Who so sublime as Homer and Milton? Who more elegant than Horace? Yet Shakespeare is not always natural: Homer and Milton may, each of them, furnish more than one example of meanness: and Horace has written some verses that are equally unworthy of a good man and a good poet. If an author abound in beauties, let his blemishes be forgotten. If he give proof of good intention, and discover genius in any department of art or of science, he is entitled to honour. But when he falls continually into the same sort of fault, and persists in an undertaking which he is unable to execute, he justly incurs the censure of criticism.

It must also be remarked, that we ought not to expect, from any performance, a higher degree, or more varieties, of pleasure, than the author intended. Poets, who never attempt great things, may yet excel in elegy and pastoral, and other inferior branches of the art; and nobody blames Theocritus or Tibullus, because they possess not the sublimity of Homer: nay, they would have been really blameable, if they had endeavoured to introduce sublimity into

---

[9] [Hobbes published translations of the *Odyssey* and *Iliad* in 1675 and 1676. The poems of Edmund Waller (1606-87) and George Grenville, Baron Lansdowne (1667-1735) are no longer widely read.]

[10] [Sir John Vanburgh (1664-1720) is better remembered now for his architecture (he designed Blenheim Palace) than for his drama.]

poems that do not admit of it. Every work should be good in its kind; but every kind of work has a sort of goodness peculiar to itself.

Besides: though it is the aim of all the fine arts to give pleasure, by gratifying these secondary senses, it ought no less to be the aim of the artist, to promote the love of virtue; which may be done, by displaying the deformity of moral evil, as well as by painting the charms of moral goodness. And therefore, in Satire, and in such other writings, as are intended to move our indignation at vice, offensive images may be allowable. For though in themselves they could not give pleasure, they may yet be approved of, as evidences of good meaning in the author, and as tending to cherish good affections in the reader: even as harsh potions may warrantably be administered, and painful operations of surgery performed, in order to expel disease from the body. Yet, as we blame the physician, who gives more pain to his patient than is necessary; we must also blame the satirist, who, without observing any rule of moderation in this matter, introduces ideas, that are either too indelicate to be used on any occasion, or less delicate than the occasion requires. Flattery and witticism, bandied about from one courtier to another, are objects of satire, no doubt; but, surely, do not amount to a crime so very atrocious, as Pope would insinuate, when he vents his abhorrence of them in the filthiest allusion that ever was written: an allusion, which decency forbids me to transcribe, and of which the author himself supposes his friend to say —

> This filthy simile, this beastly line,
> Quite turns my stomach. — [11]

Most of our powers of perception are capable of improvement. The smell of a perfumer; the touch of a polisher; the sight of a painter, who studies the exact visible appearances of things; and the hearing of a blind man, who must often trust to his ear for his preservation; are generally more acute, than the same senses in other men: because they are more exercised, and the informations received by them more carefully attended to. A deviation from the square or the perpendicular is sooner perceived by the architect, or the joiner, than by the ordinary eye. Painters, in like man-

[11] ['Epilogue to the Satires: Dialogue II', ll. 181-2.]

ner, improve their ideas of sublimity, beauty, and elegant imitation, by studying the most admired pictures, and the best monuments of ancient art. And every musician knows, that, by the practice of music, our sense of harmony may be improved to a degree, which can hardly be conceived by those, who never cultivated that faculty. Delicacy of taste, in regard to wit and humour, is acquired by the same means. The vulgar are delighted with homely jokes, because they know no better: but one, who is accustomed to elegant conversation, and to the style of polite authors, will soon learn to distinguish between urbanity and rusticity, and undervalue that coarse buffoonery, to which, with less experience, he would perhaps have had no dislike.

The secondary senses are therefore to be improved by the study of nature, and of the best performances in art; and by keeping at a distance from every thing, in art, or in manners, that is inelegant, or indecent.

IV. A fourth requisite to good taste is sympathy; or that sensibility of heart, by which, on supposing ourselves in the condition of another, we are conscious in some degree of those very emotions, pleasant or painful, which in a more intense degree would arise within us, if we were really in that condition.

Human pleasures may be divided into those of the body, and those of the soul: the former common to us with the brutes; the latter peculiar to rational beings. Those are of short duration; these more permanent. By the first, an appetite may be gratified; but it is by the last only that we can be made happy.

The fine arts are intended to give pleasure rather to the mind, than to the bodily senses. For though sounds in music please the ear, and colours in painting the eye, they are little valued, if the soul receive no gratification. Now the human soul cannot be gratified, except by those things that raise in it certain passions or emotions: for a man unsusceptible of passion, who could neither hope nor fear, rejoice nor be sorry, desire nor dislike, would be incapable of happiness. And therefore, it must be the aim of all the fine arts, and of poetry in particular, to convey into the mind such passions, or affections, as bring pleasure along with them.

Tragedy gives pleasure, by infusing pity and imaginary terror, and other elevated emotions: and comedy, by displaying the follies of mankind in such a light as to provoke contempt and laughter. The epic poem, like tragedy, operates upon our sublimer affections; and inspires admiration of what is great, joy in the prosperity of the good, a tender sorrow for the unfortunate; and an agreeable agitation of mind, produced by the vicissitudes of hope and fear, as they are called forth by the circumstances of the story. True satire pleases, while it promotes the love of virtue and wisdom; and this it may do, by exposing the crimes of mankind to our indignation, or their follies to ridicule. Lyric poetry is applicable to a variety of matters, and gives scope to many passions: and these, by a pleasing extravagance in the choice of words and figures, and a peculiar wildness in the composition and harmony, it endeavours to work up to enthusiasm. Even when it paints inanimate nature, poetry is little esteemed, unless it touch the heart: and an author of sensibility knows, how to select those appearances that are most likely to captivate a reader's fancy, and lead his mind to such thoughts, as may awaken benevolence, piety, contentment, tenderness, admiration, surprise, and other pleasurable emotions.

In a word, every thing in poetry ought to be pathetic; that is, capable of moving the passions; not merely such as are melancholy and tender, but our affections in general. So that, if the reader want that gentleness of mind, which I have elsewhere described under the name of sympathy,[12] it will be impossible for him to receive any true pleasure from a good poem; however skilled he may be in language and versification, and however well acquainted with the ordinary appearances of nature.

And yet, a defect of this sensibility is not uncommon among the readers of poetry. One is wholly engrossed with the contrivance of the fable; another values nothing but the moral sentiments; a third attends chiefly to the style, and the numbers: I have heard of one, whose sole pleasure in reading Virgil arose from comparing Aeneas's voyage with the map; and of another, who could find nothing worth notice in the *Georgics*, but some precepts of agriculture. But the true poet touches the heart, whatever be his subject: and the true critic has a heart capable of being touched, with admiration, tenderness, joy, benevolence, piety, patriotism, or any other emotion that the author means to inspire; and of feeling

---

[12] [Beattie refers the reader to Chapter 7, 'Of Sympathy', of the essay 'Of Poetry and Music, as they affect the Mind'.]

the full effect of his harmony, and of those beautiful or sublime ideas that may adorn his composition.

V. The last thing mentioned as necessary to form good taste, is judgement, or good sense; which is indeed the principal thing; and which some would consider, as comprehending most of the foregoing particulars. By judgement, I here understand such a constitution of mind, as disposes a man to attend to the reality of things, and qualifies him for knowing and discovering the truth. It is by means of this faculty, as applied in criticism, that we compare poetical imitations with natural objects, so as to perceive in what they resemble, and in what they differ; that we estimate the rectitude of sentiments, the probability of incidents, and whether fictitious characters be similar to those of real life and consistent with themselves, and whether any *part* of a composition be unsuitable to the tendency of the whole. Hence too we discern, with respect to the plan of a work, whether it be simple and natural, or confused and unnatural; and whether the author have been careful to make it, both in the general arrangement, and in the structure of each part, conformable to rule.

Lest this should be misunderstood, I must repeat an observation, which I have elsewhere had occasion to make; that, in almost every art, two sorts of rules have obtained authority; the essential, and the ornamental. The former result from the very nature of the work, and are necessary to the accomplishment of the end proposed by the artist. The latter depend rather upon established custom, than upon nature; and claim no higher origin, than the practice of some great performer, whom it has become the fashion to imitate. To violate an *essential* rule, discovers want of sense in an author, and consequently want of taste: for where sense is not, taste cannot be. To depart from an *ornamental* or mechanical rule, may be consistent with the soundest judgement, and is sometimes a proof both of good taste and of great genius.

> Great wits sometimes may gloriously offend,
> And rise to faults true critics dare not mend:
> — From vulgar bounds with brave disorder part,
> And snatch a grace beyond the reach of art.[13]

---

[13] [Pope, *Essay on Criticism*, ll. 152-3.]

I am the more anxious to mark, and to dwell on this distinction, because the French critics in general seem to have no notion of it.[14] What is contrary to established rule, or to fashion, they condemn as contrary to taste, without enquiring further. The consequence is, that, according to them, French authors only can write in taste, because no other authors write in the French fashion: and Shakespeare's plays must be absurd farces, and their author a barbarian, because they happen to be framed, upon a plan, and in a style, which the critics of Paris have never acknowledged to be good. Criticism has been thought an entertaining, and useful part, of the philosophy of mind: but, upon this principle, is as much beyond the reach, or below the notice, of rational enquiry, as modes of hairdressing, or patterns of shoe buckles.

The following are some of the essential rules of composition, which must not be violated on any account.

1. In philosophy and history, the strictest regard is to be had to truth, in the detail of facts; and the inferences are to be made according to common sense, and the rules of sound reasoning.

2. In works of fiction, a like regard is to be had to probability, and no events are to be introduced, but such as, according to the general opinion of the people to whom they are addressed, may be supposed to happen.

3. Fictitious characters ought to speak and act suitably to their supposed condition, age, rank, and other circumstances; and to the passions, and sentiments, that are said to occupy their minds.

4. External objects are to be described, both in history, and in poetry, as they are found to be in nature. The poet, however, is not obliged to enumerate all their qualities, but those only that are necessary for his purpose.

5. An author's style must always be perspicuous, and fit to convey a full view of his meaning to an attentive reader; and so contrived, as not to hurt, but to please the ear, when it is pronounced. But in every sort of style, the same degree of perspicuity, or of harmony, is not to be expected.

---

[14] I should have said, the French critics of the present age. Few nations have produced more learned men than France. I speak here… of those writers, who have learned from Voltaire to censure because they envy, and to criticize what they do not understand.

6. Every composition, whether long or short, from an epic poem or tragedy, down to a sermon or short essay, ought to have some one end in view; and all its parts must be so disposed, as to promote that end. If it have no end, it has no meaning; if more ends than one, it may confound the attention by its multiplicity: if any of its parts be unserviceable, or repugnant to its final purpose, they are superfluous or irregular, and ought to have been lopped off, or corrected. Of this unity of design, Homer's two poems are perfect models. Each contains a great variety of action, conversation, and adventure: but everything, in the one, tends to the re-establishment of Ulysses in his kingdom, and, in the other, to display the anger of Achilles, and its lamentable consequences.

7. Every composition ought to have a moral tendency, or at least to be innocent. That mind is perverted, which can either produce an immoral book, or be pleased with one. Virtue and good taste are so nearly allied, that what offends the former can never gratify the latter.

8. As, in every nation, certain customs of long standing acquire in time the authority of law; so, in every art, there are rules, which, though one might have called them discretionary or indifferent at their first introduction, come at length, after having been invariably observed by the best authors, to be considered as essential. One example will explain this. Homer, who invented, or at least who perfected, epic poetry, adopted in both of his poems that measure of verse which is called hexameter. That *he* might without blame have adopted another, will hardly be questioned. His choice therefore was arbitrary. But, as it was a lucky choice; and as the practice of Homer became, in this respect, a law to the poets of antiquity; the hexameter is now, and was in the time of Horace, and probably long before, held to be indispensable in all Greek and Latin poems of the epic kind. — For the same reason, partly; and partly, as Aristotle observes, because it is too elaborate, and unlike the cadence of conversation, hexameter verse would not be tolerated in the Greek or Latin drama; the iambic, trochaic, and anapestic measures, having been adopted, by the best authors, in the ancient tragedy and comedy. And, in like manner, if an English author, in an epic or dramatic poem, were to attempt any other form of verse, than our iambic of five feet, he would be thought to transgress a rule, which, though at first a matter of indiffer-

ence, is now, after having been established by the practice of Chaucer, Spencer, Shakespeare, Milton, and all our great poets, become essential and unalterable.

I shall now give an instance or two, of the ornamental or mechanical laws of composition.

1. That a regular tragedy, or comedy, should consist of five acts, and neither more nor fewer, is a rule, for which it would be difficult to assign any better reason than this, that it has been followed by good authors, and is recommended by Horace. Nor has this rule been invariably followed. The Italian opera, which, as reformed by Metastasio, is a most beautiful species of dramatic poem, consists of but three acts: and we have, in English, many good plays, both serious and comical, divided in the same manner; and some of only two acts, and some even of one. It is true, that a dramatic piece ought not to be too long, because it would fatigue the spectator as well as the actor; nor too short, because it would not be sufficiently interesting: it is reasonable too, that some intervals should be allowed in the representation; for the relief both of the players, and of the audience: but that this purpose could not be answered by five intervals, or three, as well as by four, is a point, which I apprehend it would be difficult to prove.

2. Most of the French and Greek tragedians observe *the unities of time and place*: that is, they suppose every part of the action to have happened in the same place, because it is all represented on the same stage; and they limit the time of it to a few hours, because the representation is of no longer continuance. Unity of place is violated, when the scene changes from one place to another, from a house to the street, from the town to the country, or from one town or country to another. Unity of time is broken through, when the incidents of the fable are such, as could not have fallen out within a few hours, or a least within the space of one day and one night.

The observance of these unities may in some cases, no doubt, heighten the probability of the action: but they lay a mighty restraint upon an author's genius; and they may give rise to improbabilities as great as any of those that can be occasioned by the neglect of them. If the subject of the play be a conspiracy, for example, and the scene of action the street; then, if unity of place be held essential, the conspirators must conduct their affairs in the street, so as to be seen and heard by everybody: a very unlikely circumstance, and what, one may venture to say, can never happen. Surely, most audiences would be better pleased, and think the whole more natural, if, on such an emergency, the scene were to change from the street to a private apartment.

The improbabilities, occasioned by disregarding these unities, are not so great as some people imagine. While we sit in the theatre, it is easy for us to reconcile our minds to the shifting of the scene, from the town to the country, or from one country to another; as it is, at our entrance, to suppose the stage a certain place in Rome or Egypt. And, if we can persuade ourselves, that the player, whom we see, and whose name and person we know, has on a sudden become Cato, or Caesar, or any other ancient hero; we may as well believe, that the evening which we pass in the playhouse comprehends the space of several days or years.

But in fact, there is not, in dramatical representation, that strict probability which the critics talk of. We never mistake the actor for the person whose character he bears; we never imagine ourselves in a foreign country, or carried back into the ages of antiquity: our pleasure is derived from other sources; and from this chiefly, that we know the whole to be a fiction. — The unities of time and place are violated by Shakespeare, in every one of his plays. He often shifts the scene from one country to another: and the time of his action is not always limited to days or weeks, but extends frequently to months, and even to years. Yet these irregularities are not offensive to those who understand him. And hence, I think, we may infer, that the rule, which enjoins the dramatic poet to a rigid observance of the unities of time and place, is not an essential, but a mechanical rule of composition.

As to the improvement of taste in this particular; — I shall only remark, that whatever tends to correct, and methodize, our knowledge, either of men, or of things, is to be considered as a means of improving the judgement. History, geometry, and grammar; and those parts of philosophy, which convey clear ideas, and are attended with satisfactory proof, are eminently useful in this respect; — to which must be added such an acquaintance with life and manners, as fits a man for business and conversation. Idleness, and habits of superficial study, are ruinous to the understanding; as I have often remarked already, but can hardly repeat too often. And nothing is more detrimental to taste, and to judgement, than those subtleties of ancient and modern metaphysics, that encourage verbal controversy, and lead to nothing but doubt and darkness. They exhaust the vigour of the mind to no purpose; they extinguish the love of good learning; they withdraw the attention from the concerns of human life, and from those things in art and nature, that warm the heart, and elevate the fancy: they pervert the rational powers, they corrupt good principles, and they poison the sources of human happiness.

Taste, as far as it depends on the knowledge of rules, may be further improved, by reading good books of criticism, and comparing them with the authors whom they illustrate. Sound judgement, however, we must acknowledge to be in a great measure constitutional: and no person will ever acquire true taste, unless nature has made him a man of sense.

So much for *taste in general*, and its improvement. It is scarce necessary to add, because the thing is obvious, that, in order to be *completely* skilled in any of those *particular* branches of art, which are subject to the cognisance of this faculty, one must unite theory with practice. None but a painter is a competent judge of painting: no person who has never composed in prose or verse, can be an unexceptional critic in language and versification: and he who is truly a musical connoisseur must have practiced as a musician, and studied the laws of harmony. In every art, certain materials and instruments are employed; and they only, who have handled them, are entitled to decide upon the dexterity of the artist.

Yet, without having been a practitioner, one may acquire such taste in the fine arts, as shall yield a high degree, and a great variety, of entertainment. The pleasures of taste are worthy of our ambition: they are innocent and profitable. He, who employs his leisure in the study of nature and art, is esteemed on that very account; and has many sorts of liberal recreation in his power, which are unknown to those who devote themselves to sensuality, or the pursuit of riches.

But taste has a further use: it is friendly to virtue.[15] Nay, I might, and perhaps I ought to have mentioned the love of virtue as essential to it. Men of genius have too often employed their talents in

---

[15] [Here Beattie quotes a long passage from Joshua Reynolds, *Discourse at the Opening of the Royal Academy* (1769).]

corrupting and destroying mankind; but it may be questioned, whether a wicked heart be at all compatible with delicate taste. This will at least serve as a security against those vices that debase the soul; and, by directing our views to the observation of nature, must frequently lead us to contemplate that great being, who is the source of happiness, and the standard of perfection.

It has been said by some, that taste is wholly capricious; depending, not upon nature or reason, but upon fashion, and the fancies of men. And it is true, that the likings men contract to certain modes of dress and furniture are partly determined by custom, are different in different countries, and in one and the same country are perpetually changing. And that there should be diversities of taste in regard to beauty, has been shown to be natural: since in our own species, as well as in other things, that will always be the most agreeable, which brings along with it the most agreeable ideas; and supplies, or is connected with, the greatest variety of comforts and pleasures.

Yet in beauty we have seen that there is, and, in all things that admit the distinction of better and worse, we may affirm that there is, a standard of excellence; and taste, as opposed to caprice, has a real foundation in nature. To be pleased with novelty and imitation; to prefer good pictures to bad, harmony to harshness, and regular shape to distortion: to be gratified with accurate representations of human manners, especially in that state of primitive simplicity, in which they give a full display of the character: to be interested in a detail of human adventures: to look with delight on the sun, moon, and stars, the expanse of heaven, grand and regular buildings, huge rocks and cataracts, the scenery of groves and rivers, mountains and the ocean, the flowers and verdure of summer, and the pure splendour of winter snow: — is surely natural to every reasonable being, who has leisure to attend to these things, and is in any degree enlightened by learning or by contemplation. For this last clause must never be omitted; because, as I formerly observed, we cannot perceive at all without percipient faculties, nor accurately without improved faculties.

If it be denied, that these, and the like appearances in art and nature, have any intrinsic charm; for that other habits of education might have made us look upon them with indifference, or with disgust: I shall only ask, whence it comes, that the poems of every age and nation, which were certainly made for the purpose of pleasing, should abound in descriptions of these and the like objects; and why the fine arts have always been a matter of general attention in all civilized countries.

Truth is allowed to be uniform and unchangeable: yet what can be more absurd, than many of those opinions are, which have passed in the world for true! Was not the philosophy of Descartes admired, long after that of Newton was made public? Nay, in some parts of Europe, is not the former still considered as the true system? The existence of matter has been denied by one set of philosophers; that of motion, by another; that of spirit by a third; and that of every thing, by a fourth. How many theories of human nature have appeared, and disappeared, within these hundred years! What endless varieties of opinion among lawyers, and divines, physicians, and moralists! Nay, have we not seen, even in our days, the greatest of all intellectual depravities, a depravity whereof the devil himself is not capable, I mean atheism, patronized by some vain and worthless beings of the human form! Yet it will not be said, by any intelligent creature, that theological, philosophical, and moral truths are all destitute of foundation, or depend wholly upon fashion, and the fancies of men.

If, then, in regard to matters that admit of clear proof, ignorance, affectation, and error may prevail for a time among those, from whom better things might be expected; need we wonder, that bad taste should sometimes prevail; and Blackmore be preferred to Milton, Lucan to Virgil, and Pliny to Cicero? — But, whatever temporary infatuations may take place in the world of literature; simplicity and true taste sooner or later gain the ascendant, and prove their rectitude by their permanency. To the general suffrage of mankind if we were to oppose the cavils of Zoilus, Bavius, and Mevius, would Homer and Virgil lose any of their reputation? No. They were thought the greatest of poets two thousand years ago: they are thought so still, by all who understand them: nor can we conceive it possible, while nature remains unaltered, that the time will ever come, when they shall be considered as bad, or even as indifferent writers.

Fifteen

Illustrations of Sublimity

... What we admire, or consider as great, we are apt to speak of in such terms, as if we conceived it to be high in place: and what we look upon as less important we express in words that properly denote low situation. We go *up* to London; and thence *down* into the country. The Jews spoke in the same manner of their metropolis, which was to them the object of religious veneration. 'Jerusalem', says the Psalmist, 'is a city, to which the tribes go up': and the parable of the good Samaritan begins thus, 'A certain man went down from Jerusalem to Jericho'. Conformably to the same idiom, heaven is supposed to be above, and hell to be beneath; and we say, that generous minds endeavour to reach the *summit* of excellence, and think it *beneath* them to do, or design, any thing that is base. The terms *base*, *grovelling*, *low*, &c. and those of opposite import, *elevated*, *aspiring*, *lofty*, as applied in a figurative sense to the energies of mind, do all take their rise from the same modes of thinking. The Latins expressed admiration by a verb which properly signifies *to look up* (*suspicere*); and contempt by another (*despicere*) whose original meaning is *to look down*. A high seat is erected for a king, or a chief magistrate, and a lofty pedestal for the statue of a hero; partly, no doubt, that they may be seen at the greater distance, and partly also, out of respect to their dignity.

But mere local elevation is not the only source of sublimity. Things that surpass in magnitude; as a spacious building, a great city, a large river, a vast mountain, a wide prospect, the ocean, the expanse of heaven, fill the mind of the beholder with the same agreeable astonishment. And observe, that it is rather the relative magnitude of things, as compared with others of the same kind, that raises this emotion, than their absolute quantity of matter. That may be a sublime edifice, which in real magnitude falls far short of a small hill that is not sublime: and a river two furlongs in breadth is a majestic appearance, though in extent of water it is nothing when compared with the ocean.

Great number, too, when it gives rise to admiration, may be referred to the same class of things. Hence an army, or navy, a long succession of years, eternity, and the like, are sublime, because they at once please and astonish. In contemplating such ideas or objects, we are conscious of something like an expansion of our faculties, as if we were exerting our whole capacity to comprehend the vastness of that which commands our attention. This energy of the mind is pleasing, as all mental energies are when accompanied with pain: and the pleasure is heightened by our admiration of the object itself; for admiration is always agreeable.

In many cases, great number is connected with other grand ideas, which add to its own grandeur. A fleet, or army, makes us think of power, and courage, and danger, and presents a variety of brilliant images. A long succession of years brings to view the vicissitude of human things, and the uncertainty of life, which sooner or later must yield to death, the irresistible destroyer. And eternity reminds of that awful consideration, our own immortality; and is connected with an idea still more sublime, and indeed the most sublime of all, namely, with the idea of Him, who fills immensity with his presence; creates, preserves, and governs all things; and is from everlasting to everlasting.

In general, whatever awakens in us this pleasurable astonishment is accounted sublime, whether it be connected with quantity and number, or not. The harmony of a loud and full organ conveys, no doubt, an idea of expansion and of power; but, independently of this, it overpowers with so sweet a violence, as charms and astonishes at the same time: and we are generally conscious of an elevation of mind when we hear it, even though the ear be not sensible of any melody. Thunder and tempest are still more elevating, when one hears them without fear; because the sound is still more stupendous; and because they fill the imagination with the magnificent idea of the expanse of heaven and earth, through which they direct their terrible career, and of that almighty being, whose will controls all nature. The roar of cannon, in like manner, when considered as harmless, gives a dreadful delight; partly by the overwhelming sensation wherewith it affects the ear, and partly by the ideas of power and danger, triumph and fortitude, which it conveys to the fancy.

Those passions of the soul yield a pleasing astonishment, which discover a high degree of moral excellence, or are in any way connected with great number, or great quantity. Benevolence and piety are sublime affections; for the object of the one is the Deity himself, the greatest, and the best; and that of the other is the whole human race, or the whole system of percipient beings. Fortitude and generosity are sublime emotions: because they discover a degree of virtue, which is not everywhere to be met with; and exert themselves in actions, that are at once difficult, and beneficial to mankind. — Great intellectual abilities, as the genius of Homer, or of Newton, we cannot contemplate without wonder and delight; and must therefore refer to that class of things whereof I now speak. — Nay great bodily strength is a sublime object; for we are agreeably astonished, when we see it exerted, or hear of its effects. — There is even a sublime beauty, which both astonishes and charms: but this will be found in those persons only, or chiefly, who unite fine features with a majestic form; such as we may suppose an ancient statuary would have represented Juno, or Minerva, Achilles, or Apollo.

When great qualities prevail in any person, they form what is called a sublime character. Every good man is a personage of this order: but a character may be sublime, which is not completely good, nay, which is upon the whole very bad. For the test of sublimity is not moral approbation, but that pleasurable astonishment wherewith certain things strike the beholder. Sarpedon, in the *Iliad*, is a sublime character, and at the same time a good one: to the valour of the hero he joins the benignity of a gracious prince, and the moderation of a wise man. Achilles, though in many respects not virtuous, is yet a most sublime character. We hate his cruelty, passionate temper, and love of vengeance: but we admire him for his valour, strength, swiftness, generosity, beauty, and intellectual accomplishments, for the warmth of his friendship, and for his filial tenderness. In a word, notwithstanding his violent nature, there is in his general conduct a mixture of goodness and of greatness, with which we are both pleased and astonished. Julius Cesar was never considered as a man of strict virtue. But, in reading his *Memoirs*, it is impossible not to be struck with the sublimity of his character: that strength of mind, which nothing can bear down; that self-command, which is never discomposed; that intrepidity in danger; that address in negotiation; that coolness and recollection in the midst of perplexity; and that unwearied activity, which crowds together in every one of his campaigns as many great actions as would make a hero. Nay even in Satan, as Milton has represented him in *Paradise Lost*, though there are no qualities that can be called good in a moral view; nay, though every purpose of that wicked spirit is bent to evil, and to that only; yet there is the grandeur of a ruined archangel: there is force able to contend with the most boisterous elements; and there is boldness, which no power, but what is Almighty, can intimidate. These qualities are astonishing: and, though we always detest his malignity, we are often compelled to admire that very greatness by which we are confounded and terrified.

And be not surprised, that we sometimes admire what we cannot approve. These two emotions may, and frequently do, coincide: Sarpedon and Hector, Epaminondas and Aristides, David and Jonathan, we approve and admire. But they do not necessarily coincide: for goodness calls forth the one, and greatness the other; and that which is great is not always good, and that may be good which is not great. Troy in flames, Palmyra in ruins, the ocean in a storm, and Etna in thunder and conflagration, are magnificent appearances, but do not immediately impress our minds with the idea of good: and a clear fountain is not a grand object, though in many parts of the world it would be valued above all treasures. So in the qualities of the mind and body: we admire the strong, the brave, the eloquent, the beautiful, the ingenious, the learned; but the virtuous only we approve. There have been authors indeed, one at least there has been, who, by confounding admiration with approbation, laboured to confound intellectual accomplishments with moral virtues;[1] but it is shameful inaccuracy, and vile sophistry: one might as well endeavour to confound crimes with misfortunes, and strength of body with purity of

---

[1] [Beattie means Hume: see *A Treatise of Human Nature*, III.iii.4.]

mind: and say, that to be a knave and to lose a leg are equally worthy of punishment, and that one man deserves as much praise for being born with a healthy constitution, as another does for leading a good life.

But if sublime ideas are known by their power of inspiring agreeable astonishment, and if Satan in *Paradise Lost* is a sublime idea, does it not follow, that we must be both astonished at his character, and pleased with it? And is it possible to take pleasure in a being, who is the author of evil, and the adversary of God and man?

I answer; that, though we know there is an evil spirit of this name, we know also, that Milton's Satan is partly imaginary; and we believe, that those qualities are so in particular, which we admire in him as great: for we have no reason to think, that he has really that boldness, irresistible strength, or dignity of form, which the poet ascribes to him. So far, therefore, as we admire him for sublimity of character, we consider him, not as the great enemy of our souls, but as a fictitious being, and a mere poetical hero. Now the human imagination can easily combine ideas in an assemblage, which are not combined in nature; and make the same person the object of admiration in one respect, who in another is detestable: and such inventions are in poetry the more probable, because such persons are to be met with in real life. Achilles and Alexander, for example, we admire for their magnanimity, but abhor for their cruelty. And the poet, whose aim is to please, finds it necessary to give some good qualities to his bad characters; for, if he did not, the reader would not be interested in their fortune, nor, consequently, pleased with the story of it.

In the *picture* of a burning city, we may admire the splendour of the colours, the undulation of the flames, the arrangements of light and shade, and the other proofs of the painter's skill; and nothing gives a more exquisite delight of the melancholy kind, than Virgil's account of the burning of Troy. But this does not imply, that we should, like Nero, take any pleasure in such an event, if it were real and present. Indeed, few appearances are more beautiful, or more sublime, than a mass of flame, rolling in the wind, and blazing to heaven: whence illuminations, bonfires, and fireworks make part of a modern triumph. Yet destruction by fire is of all earthly things the most terrible.

An object more astonishing, both to the eye, and to the ear, there is hardly in nature, than (what is sometimes to be seen in the West Indies) a plantation of sugar-canes on fire, flaming to a vast height, sweeping the whole country, and every moment sending forth a thousand explosions, like those of artillery. A good description of such a scene we should admire as sublime; for a description can neither burn nor destroy. But the planter, who sees it desolating his fields, and ruining all his hopes, can feel no other emotions than horror and sorrow. — In a word, the sublime, in order to give pleasing astonishment, must be either imaginary, or not immediately pernicious.

There is a kind of horror, which may be infused into the mind both by natural appearances, and by verbal description; and which, though it make the blood seem to run cold, and produce a momentary fear, is not unpleasing, but may be even agreeable: and therefore, the objects that produce it are justly denominated sublime. Of natural appearances that affect the mind in this manner, are vast caverns, deep and dark woods, overhanging precipices, the agitation of the sea in a storm: and some of the sounds above mentioned have the same effect, as those of cannon and thunder. Verbal descriptions infusing sublime horror are such as convey lively ideas, of the objects of superstition, as ghosts and enchantments; or of the thoughts that haunt the imaginations of the guilty; or of those external things, which are pleasingly terrible, as storms, conflagrations, and the like.

It may seem strange, that horror of any kind should give pleasure. But the fact is certain. Why do people run to see battles, executions and shipwrecks? Is it, as an Epicurean would say, to compare themselves with others, and exult in their own security while they see the distress of those who suffer? No, surely: good minds are swayed by different motives. Is it, that they may be at hand, to give every assistance in their power to their unhappy brethren? This would draw the benevolent, and even the tender-hearted, to a shipwreck; but to a battle, or to an execution, could not bring spectators, because there the humanity of individuals is of no use. — It must be, because a sort of gloomy satisfaction, or terrific pleasure, accompanies the gratification of that curiosity which events of this nature are apt to raise in minds of a certain frame.

No parts of Tasso are read with greater relish, than where he describes the darkness, silence, and other horrors, of the enchanted forest: and the poet himself is so sensible of the captivating influence of such ideas over the human imagination, that he makes the catastrophe of the poem in some measure depend upon them. Milton is not less enamoured 'of forests and enchantments drear'; as appears from the use to which he applies them in *Comus*: the scenery whereof charms us the more, because it affects our minds, as it did the bewildered lady, and causes 'a thousand fantasies' —

— to throng into the memory,
Of calling shapes, and beckoning shadows dire,
And aery tongues, that syllable mens names
On sands, and shores, and desert wildernesses.[2]

Forests in every age must have had attractive horrors: otherwise so many nations would not have resorted thither, to celebrate the rites of superstition. And the inventors of what is called the Gothic, but perhaps should rather be called the Saracen, architecture, must have been enraptured with the same imagery, when, in forming and arranging the pillars and aisles of their churches, they were so careful to imitate the rows of lofty trees in a deep grove.

Observe a few children assembled about a fire, and listening to tales of apparitions and witchcraft. You may see them grow pale, and crowd closer and closer through fear: while he who is snug in the chimney corner, and at the greatest distance from the door, considers himself as peculiarly fortunate; because he thinks that, if the ghost should enter, he has a better chance to escape, than if he were in a more exposed situation. And yet, notwithstanding their present, and their apprehension of future, fears, you could not perhaps propose any amusement that would at this time be more acceptable. The same love of such horrors as are not attended with sensible inconvenience continues with us through life: and Aristotle has affirmed, that the end of tragedy is to purify the soul by the operations of pity and terror.

The mind and body of man are so constituted, that, without action, neither can the one be healthy, nor the other happy. And as

---

[2]   [*Comus*, ll. 205-9.]

bodily exercises, though attended with fatigue, as dancing, or with some degree of danger, as hunting, are not on that account the less agreeable; so those things give delight, which rouse the soul, even when they bring along with them horror, anxiety, or sorrow, provided these passions be transient, and their causes rather imaginary than real.

The most perfect models of sublimity are seen in the works of nature. Pyramids, palaces, fireworks, temples, artificial lakes and canals, ships of war, fortifications, hills levelled and caves hollowed by human industry, are mighty efforts, no doubt, and awaken in every beholder a pleasing admiration; but appear as nothing, when we compare them, in respect of magnificence, with mountains, volcanoes, rivers, cataracts, oceans, the expanse of heaven, clouds and storms, thunder and lightening, the sun, moon, and stars. So that, without the study of nature, a true taste in the sublime is absolutely unattainable. And we need not wonder at what is related of Thomson, the author of *The Seasons*; who, on hearing that a certain learned gentleman of London was writing an epic poem, exclaimed, 'He write an Epic poem! It is impossible: he never saw a mountain in his life'. This at least is certain, that if we were to strike out of Homer, Virgil, and Milton, those descriptions and sentiments that allude to the grand phenomena of nature, we should deprive these poets of the best part of their sublimity.

And yet, the true sublime may be attained by human art. Music is sublime, when it inspires devotion, courage, or other elevated affections: or when by its mellow and sonorous harmonics it overwhelms the mind with sweet astonishment: or when it infuses that pleasing horror abovementioned; which, when joined to words descriptive of terrible ideas, it sometimes does very effectually.

Architecture is sublime, when it is large and durable, and withal so simple and well-proportioned as that the eye can take in all its greatness at once. For when an edifice is loaded with ornaments, our attention to them prevents our attending to the whole; and the mind, though it may be amused with the beauty or the variety of the little parts, is not struck with that sudden astonishment, which accompanies the contemplation of sublimity. Hence the Gothic style of building, where it abounds in minute decorations, and where greater pains are employed on the parts, than in adjusting the general harmony of the fabric, is less sublime than the Grecian, in which proportion, simplicity, and usefulness, are more studied than ornament. It is true, that Gothic buildings may be very sublime: witness the old cathedral churches. But this is owing, rather to their vast magnitude, to the stamp of antiquity that is impressed on them, and to their having been so long appropriated to religious service, than to those peculiarities that distinguish their architecture from the Grecian.

The Chinese mode of building has no pretensions to sublimity; its decorations being still more trivial than the Gothic; and because it derives no dignity from associated ideas, and has no vastness of magnitude to raise admiration. Yet is it not without its charms. There is an air of neatness in it, and of novelty, which to many is pleasing, and which of late it has been much the fashion to imitate.

Painting is sublime, when it displays men invested with great qualities, as bodily strength, or actuated by sublime passions, as courage, devotion, benevolence. That picture by Guido Rheni, which represents Michael triumphing over the evil spirit, I have always admired for its sublimity, though some critics are not pleased with it. The attitude of the angel, who holds a sword in his right hand in a threatening posture, conveys to me the idea of dignity and grace, as well as of irresistible strength. Nor is the majestic beauty of his person less admirable: and his countenance, though in a slight degree expressive of contempt or indignation, retains that sweet composure, which we think essential to the angelic character. His limbs and wings are, it is true, contrasted: but the contrast is so far from being finical, that, if we consider the action, and the situation, we must allow it to be not only natural, but unavoidable, and such as a winged being might continue in for some time without inconvenience. Guido is not equally fortunate in his delineation of the adversary; who is too mean, and too ludicrous, a figure, to cope with an archangel, or to require, for his overthrow, the twentieth part of that force which appears to be exerted against him. — Painting is also sublime, when it imitates grand natural appearances, as mountains, precipices, storms, huge heaps of rocks and ruins, and the like.

At the time when Raphael began to distinguish himself, two styles of painting were cultivated in Italy. His master Pietro Perugino copied nature with an exactness bordering on servility: so that his figures had less dignity and grace than their originals. Michael Angelo ran into the opposite extreme; and, with an imagination fraught with great ideas, and continually aspiring to sublimity, so enlarged the proportions of nature, as to raise his men to giants, and stretch out every form into an extension that might almost be called monstrous. To the penetration of Raphael both styles seemed to be faulty, and both in an equal degree. The one appeared insipid in its accuracy, and the other almost ridiculous in its extravagance.[3] He therefore pursued a middle course; tempering the fire of Angelo with the caution of Perugino: and thus exhibited the true sublime of painting; wherein the graces of nature are heightened, but nothing is gigantic, disproportioned, or improbable. While we study his cartoons, we seem to be conversing with a species of men, like ourselves indeed, but of heroic dignity and size.

This great artist is in painting, what Homer is in poetry. Homer magnifies in like manner; and transforms men into heroes and demigods; and, to give the more grandeur to his narrative, sets it off with marvellous events, which, in his time, though not improbable, were however astonishing. But Ariosto, and the authors of the Old Romance, resemble Michael Angelo in exalting their champions, not into heroes, but into giants and monsters. Achilles, though superior to all men in valour, would not venture to battle without his arms: but a warrior of romance, whether armed or not, could fell a troop of horse to the earth at one blow, tear up trees by the root, and now and then throw a piece of a mountain at the enemy. The true sublime is always natural and credible: but unbounded exaggerations, that surpass all proportion and all belief, are more apt to provoke laughter than astonishment.

---

[3] I find that Sir Joshua Reynolds, from whose judgement there is no appeal, thinks more favourably of the sublime of Michael Angelo. I therefore retract part of what is said above ... The few pieces I have seen of Michael Angelo must have been in his worst manner.

Poetry becomes sublime in many ways: and this is the only fine art, which can at present supply us with examples, I shall from it select a specimen or two of the different sorts of sublimity.

1. Poetry is sublime, when it elevates the mind. This indeed is a general character of greatness. But I speak here of sentiments so happily conceived and expressed, as to raise our affections above the low pursuits of sensuality and avarice, and animate us with the love of virtue and of honour. As a specimen, let me recommend the account, which Virgil gives in his eighth book, of the person, family, and kingdom of Evander; an Arcadian prince, who, after being trained up in all the discipline of Greece, established himself and his people in that part of Italy, where a few centuries after was built the great metropolis of the Roman empire. In the midst of poverty, that good old man retains a philosophical and a royal dignity. 'This habitation (says he, to Eneas, who had made him a visit) has been honoured with the presence of Hercules himself. Dare, my guest, to despise riches; and do thou also fashion thyself into a likeness of God': or, as some render it, 'do thou also make thyself worthy of immortality'.

> Aude, hopes, contemnere opes; et te quoque dignum
> Finge Deo. —[4]

There is strength in the expression, whereof our language is not capable. 'I despise the world,' says Dryden, 'when I read it, and myself when I attempt to translate it.'

2. Poetry is sublime, when it conveys a lively idea of any grand appearance in art or nature. A nobler description of this sort I do not at present remember, than that which Virgil gives, in the first book of the *Georgic*, of a dark night, with wind, rain, and lightening: where Jupiter appears, encompassed with clouds and storms, darting his thunderbolts, and overturning the mountains, while the ocean is roaring, the earth trembling, the wild beasts fled away, the rain pouring down in torrents, the woods resounding to the tempest, and all mankind overwhelmed with consternation.[5]

---

[4] [*Aeneid*, Book 8, ll. 364-5.]

[5] The following is a more literal translation: but I know not how to imitate, in modern language, the awful, (I had almost said, the dreadful) simplicity of the original. 'High in the midnight storm enthroned,

> Ipse Pater, media nimborum in nocte, corusca
> Fulmina molitur dextra; quo maxima motu
> Terra tremit, fugere feræ, et mortalia corda
> Per gentes humilis stravit pavor. Ille flagranti
> Aut Atho, aut Rhodopen, aut alta Keraunia telo
> Deicit; ingeminant austri, et densissimus imber;
> Nunc nemora ingenti vento, nunc littora plangunt.[6]

This description astonishes, both by the grandeur, and by the horror, of the scene, which is either wrapt in total darkness, or made visible by the glare of lightning. And the poet has expressed it with the happiest solemnity of style, and a sonorous harmony of numbers. — As examples of the same sort of sublimity, namely of great images with a mixture of horror, I might call the reader's attention to the storm in the beginning of the *Aeneid*, the death of Cacus in the eighth book, to the account of Tartarus in the sixth, and that of the burning of Troy in the second. But in the style of dreadful magnificence, nothing is superior, and scarce any thing equal, to Milton's representation of hell and chaos, in the first and second books of *Paradise Lost*.

In the concluding paragraph of the same work, there is brought together, with uncommon strength of fancy, and rapidity of narrative, a number of circumstances, wonderfully adapted to the purpose of filling the mind with ideas of terrific grandeur: the descent of the cherubim; the flaming sword; the archangel leading in haste our first parents down from the heights of paradise, and then disappearing; and, above all, the scene that presents itself on their looking behind them.

> They, looking back, all th'eastern cliff beheld
> Of Paradise, so late their happy feat,
> Waved over by that flaming brand; the gate
> With dreadful faces throng'd and fiery arms.

To which the last verses form the most striking contrast that can be imagined.

Heaven's Sire/Hurls from his blazing arm the bolt of fire./Earth feels with trembling; every beast is fled;/And nations prostrate fall, o'erwhelm'd with dread./Athos rolls headlong, where his lightnings fly,/The rocks of Rhodope in ruin lie,/Or huge Keraunia. With redoubled rage/The torrent rain and bellowing wind engage;/Loud in the woods afar the tempests roar,/And mountain billows burst in thunder on the shore.'

[6]   *Georgics*, Book I ll. 328–34.

> Some natural tears they drop'd, but wiped them soon.
> The world was all before them, where to chuse
> Their place of rest, and Providence their guide.
> They, hand in hand, with wandering steps, and slow,
> Through Eden took their solitary way.

The final couplet renews our sorrow; by exhibiting, with picturesque accuracy, the most mournful scene in nature; which yet is so prepared, as to raise comfort, and dispose to resignation. And thus, while we are at once melting in tenderness, elevated with pious hope, and overwhelmed with the grandeur of description, the divine poem concludes. What luxury of mental gratification is here! Who would exchange this frame of mind (if nature could support it) for any other! How exquisitely does the faith of a Christian accord with the noblest feelings of humanity!

3. Poetry is sublime, when, without any great pomp of images or of words, it infuses horror by a happy choice of circumstances. When Macbeth (in Shakespeare) goes to consult the witches, he finds them performing rites in a cave; and, upon asking what they were employed about, receives no other answer than this short one, 'A deed without a name'. One's blood runs cold at the thought, that their work was of so accursed a nature, that they themselves had no name to express it by, or were afraid to speak of it by any name. Here is no solemnity of style, nor any accumulation of great ideas; yet here is the true sublime; because here is something that astonishes the mind, and fills it, without producing any real inconvenience.

Among other omens, which preceded the death of Dido, Virgil relates, that, when she was making an oblation of wine, milk and incense upon the altar, she observed the milk grow black, and found that the wine was changed into blood. This the poet improves into a circumstance of the utmost horror, when he adds, that she never mentioned it to any person, not even to her sister, who was her confidante on all other occasions: insinuating, that it filled her with so dreadful apprehension, that she had not courage even to attempt to speak of it. — Perhaps I may be more struck with this, than many others are; as I once knew a young man, who was in the same state of mind, after having been frightened in his sleep, or, as he imagined, by a vision, which he had seen about two years before he told me of it. With much entreaty I prevailed on him to give me some account of his dream: but there was one particular, which he said that he would not, nay that he durst not, mention; and, while he was saying so, his haggard eyes, pale countenance, quivering lips, and faltering voice, presented to me such a picture of horror, as I never saw before or since. I ought to add, that he was, in all other respects, in his perfect mind, cheerful, and active, and not more than twenty years of age.

Horror has long been a powerful, and a favourite, engine in the hands of the tragic poet. Eschylus employed it more than any other ancient artist. In his play called *The Furies*, he introduced Orestes haunted by a company of those frightful beings; intending thereby an allegorical representation of the torment which that hero suffered in his mind, in consequence of having slain his mother Clytemnestra, for the part she had taken in the murder of his father. But to raise the greater horror in the spectators, the poet was at pains to describe, with amazing force of expression, the appearance of the Furies; and he brought upon the stage no fewer than fifty of them; whose infernal looks, hideous gestures, and horrible screams, had such effects on the women and children, that, in the subsequent exhibitions of the play, the number of furies was by an express law limited, first to fifteen, and afterwards to twelve. There are, no doubt, sublime strokes in the poet's account of these furies; and there is something very great in the idea of a person haunted by his own thoughts, in the form of such terrific beings. Yet horror of this kind I would hardly call sublime, because it is addressed rather to the eyes, than to the mind; and because it is easier to disfigure a man so, as to make him have the appearance of an ugly woman, than, by a brief description, or well-chosen sentiment, to alarm and astonish the fancy. Shakespeare has, in my opinion, excited horror of more genuine sublimity, and withal more useful in a moral view, when he makes Macbeth, in short and broken starts of exclamation, and without any pomp of images or of words, give an utterance half-suppressed to those dreadful thoughts that were passing in his mind immediately before and after the murder of Duncan, his guest, kinsman, sovereign, and benefactor. The agonies of a guilty conscience were never more forcibly represented, than in this tragedy; which may indeed be said, in the language of Aristotle, to purify the mind by the operation of terror and pity; and which abounds more in that species of the sublime whereof I now speak, than any other performance in the English tongue....

4. Poetry is sublime, when it awakens in the mind any great and good affection, as piety, or patriotism. This is one of the noblest effects of the art. The Psalms are remarkable, beyond all other writings, for their power of inspiring devout emotions. But it is not in this respect only that they are sublime. Of the divine nature they contain the most magnificent descriptions that the soul of man can comprehend. The hundred and fourth psalm, in particular, displays the power and goodness of providence, in creating and preserving the world, and the various tribes of animals in it, with such majestic brevity and beauty, as it is vain to look for in any human composition. The morning song of Adam and Eve, and many other parts of *Paradise Lost*, are noble effusions of piety, breathed in the most captivating strains: and Thomson's Hymn on the Seasons, if we overlook an unguarded word or two, is not inferior.

Of that sublimity which results from the strong expression of patriotic sentiments, many examples might be quoted from the Latin poets, particularly Virgil, Horace, and Lucan: but there is a passage in Homer that suits the present purpose better than any other that now occurs. While Hector is advancing to attack the Greek entrenchments, an eagle lets fall a wounded serpent in the middle of his army. This Polydamas considers as a bad omen, and advises him to order a retreat. Hector rejects the advice with indignation. 'Shall I be deterred from my duty, (says he) and from executing the commands of Jupiter, by the flight of birds? Let them fly on my right hand or on my left, towards the setting or towards the rising sun, I will obey the counsel of Jove, who is the king of gods and of men.' And then he adds that memorable aphorism, 'To defend our country is the best of all auguries:'[7] or, as Pope has very well expressed it,

> Without a sign, his sword the brave man draws,
> And asks no omen, but his country's cause.[8]

---

[7]　*Iliad*, Book XII, l. 243.
[8]　[*The Iliad of Homer*, Book XII, ll. 283–4.]

If we attend to all the circumstances, and reflect that both Hector and Homer believed in auguries, we must own that the sentiment is wonderfully great.

I might also quote, from the same book of the *Iliad*, Sarpedon's speech to Glaucus; which contains the noblest lesson of political wisdom, and the most enlivening motives to magnanimity. I shall not translate it literally, but confine myself to the general scope of the argument; and I shall give it in prose, that it may not seem to derive any part of its dignity from the charm of poetical numbers. 'Why, O Glaucus, do we receive from our people in Lycia the honours of sovereignty, and so liberal a provision? Is it not in the hope, that we are to distinguish ourselves by our virtue, as much as we are distinguished by our rank? Let us act accordingly: that, when they see us encountering the greatest perils of war, they may say, we deserve the honours and the dignity which we possess. If indeed (continues he) by declining danger we could secure ourselves against old age and the grave, I should neither fight myself in the front of the battle, nor exhort you to do so. But since death is unavoidable, and may assail us from so many thousand quarters, let us advance, and either gain renown by victory, or by our fall give glory to the conqueror'. The whole is excellent: but the grandeur and generosity of the conclusion can never be too highly applauded.

5. Poetry is also sublime, when it describes in a lively manner the visible effects of any of those passions that give elevation to the character. Such is that passage, in the conclusion of the same twelfth book of the *Iliad*, which paints the impetuosity and terrible appearance of Hector, storming the entrenchments, and pursuing the enemy to their ships. Extraordinary efforts of magnanimity, valour, or any other virtue, and extraordinary exertions of strength or power, are grand objects, and give sublimity to those pictures or poems, in which they are well represented. All the great poets abound in examples.

Yet in great strength, for example, there may be unwieldiness, or awkwardness, or some other contemptible quality, whereby the sublime is destroyed. Polyphemus is a match for five hundred Greeks; but he is not a grand object. We hate his barbarity, and despise his folly, too much, to allow him a single grain of admiration. Ulysses, who in the hands of Polypheme was nothing, is incomparably more sublime, when, in walking to his palace, disguised like a beggar, he is insulted, and even kicked, by one of his own slaves, who was in the service of those rebels that were tempting his queen, plundering his household, and alienating the affections of his people. Homer tells us, that the hero stood firm, without being moved from his place by the stroke; that he deliberated for a moment, whether he should at one blow fell the traitor to the earth; but that patience and prudential thoughts restrained him. The brutal force of the Cyclops is not near so striking as this picture; which displays bodily strength and magnanimity united. For what we despise we never admire; and therefore despicable greatness cannot be sublime.

Homer and Virgil have, each of them, given a description of a horse, which is very much, and justly, celebrated. But they dwell rather upon the swiftness and beauty of the animal, or on such of his passions as have little or no dignity; and therefore their descriptions, though most elegant and harmonious, cannot properly be termed sublime. In the book of Job, we have the picture of a war-horse in the most magnificent style.[9] The inspired poet expatiates upon the nobler qualities of that animal, his strength, impetuosity, and contempt of danger: and several of the words made use of, being figurative, and in their proper meaning expressive of human emotions, convey uncommon vivacity and elevation to the whole passage . . . — Besides the grandeur of the animal, as here painted, the sublimity of the passage is heightened exceedingly by the landscape; which presents to our view an army in order of battle, and makes us think we hear the crashing of armour, and the shouts of encountering multitudes.

In describing what is great, poets often employ sonorous language. This is suitable to the nature of human speech: for while we give utterance to that which elevates our imagination, we are apt to speak louder, and with greater solemnity, than at other times. It must not however be thought, that high-sounding words are essential to the sublime. Without a correspondent dignity of thought, or grandeur of images, a sonorous style is ridiculous; and puts one in mind of those persons, who raise great expectation, and assume a look of vast importance, when they have either

---

[9] [Job, Chapter 39.]

nothing at all to say, or nothing that is worth notice. That style is sublime, which makes us conceive a great object, or a great effort, in a lively manner; and this may be done, when the words are very plain and simple. Nay, the plainest and simplest words have sometimes a happy effect in setting off what is intrinsically great; as an act of vast bodily strength is the more astonishing, when performed by a slight effort. This sort of sublimity we have in perfection in many of those passages of Holy Writ, that describe the operation of omnipotence: as, 'God said, Let there be light, and there was light: — He spoke, and it was done; he commanded, and it stood fast: — Thou openest thy hand, they are filled with good; thou hidest thy face, and they are troubled.'

It was observed, that the description of the horse in Job derives not a little of its dignity from those words, that properly signify human sentiments, and cannot be applied to an irrational animal, unless with a figurative meaning: 'he *rejoiceth in his strength*, he *mocketh at fear*; he *believeth not* that it is the sound of the trumpet; he *saith* among the trumpets, *ha, ha*'. It may now be remarked in general, that the sublime is often heightened, when, by means of figurative language, the qualities of a superior nature are judiciously applied to what is inferior. Hence we see in poetry, and in more familiar language, the passions and feelings of rationality ascribed to that which is without reason, and without life, or even to abstract ideas. — On Adam's eating the forbidden fruit,

> Earth trembled from her entrails, as again
> In pangs, and Nature gave a second groan;
> Sky lower'd, and, muttering thunder, some sad drops
> Wept, at compleating of the mortal sin
> Original.[10]

Who is not sensible of the greatness of the thought conveyed in these words; which represent the earth and heaven affected with horror at the sin then committed, and nature, or the universe, uttering in low thunder a groan of anguish? Had the poet simply said, that there was an earthquake, that the sky grew dark, and that some drops of rain fell, the account would no doubt have been sublime, as he would have given it. But is it not much more so, when we are informed, that this convulsion of nature was the effect of a sort of sensation diffused at that instant through the

---

[10] [Milton, *Paradise Lost*, Book IX, ll.1000–4.]

whole inanimate world? How dreadful must be the enormity of that guilt, which could produce an event so great, and withal so preternatural! Here are two sources of the sublime: the prodigy strikes with horror; the vastness of the idea overwhelms with astonishment.

In this place an unskilful poet would probably have brought on such a storm of thunder and lightning, and so violent an earthquake, as must have overturned the mountains, and set the woods on fire. But Milton, with better judgement, makes the alarm of that deep and awful kind, which cannot express itself in any other way, than by an inward and universal trembling: a sensation more affecting to the fancy, than those passions are, which vent themselves in outrageous behaviour; even as that sorrow is the most pathetic, which deprives one of the power of lamentation, and discovers itself only by fainting and groans. Besides, if this convulsion of the universe had been more violent, the unhappy offenders must have been confounded and terrified; which would not have suited the poet's purpose. For he tells us, and indeed the circumstances that follow in the narrative (which, by the by, are exquisitely contrived) do all suppose, that our first parents were so intent on gratifying their impious appetite, that they took no notice of the prodigies, which accompanied the transgression.

* * *

Most of the writers on this subject have considered our passion for what is great and elevated, as a proof of the dignity of the soul, and of the glorious ends for which it was made. The words of Longinus to this purpose are well translated by Dr Akenside. 'God has not intended man for an ignoble being; but, bringing us into life, and the midst of this wide universe, as before a multitude assembled at some heroic solemnity, that we might be spectators of all his magnificence, and candidates high in emulation for the prize of glory, has therefore implanted in our souls an inextinguishable love of every thing great and exalted, of every thing which appears divine beyond our comprehension. Whence it comes to pass, that even the whole world is not an object sufficient for the depth and rapidity of human imagination, which often sallies forth beyond the limits of all that surrounds us. Let any man cast his eye through the whole circle of our existence, and consider how especially it abounds with excellent and grand objects, and he will soon acknowledge for what enjoyments and pursuits we were created.'[11]

These are the sentiments of a Pagan philosopher. And how noble (I had almost said, how divine) they must appear, when compared with the selfish, sensual, and groveling ideas of the Epicurean, or with the narrow views and brutal insensibility of the ancient and modern Pyrrhonist! — I must not omit, that Addison has adopted the same turn of thinking; and, enlightened with the knowledge, and warmed with the piety, of a Christian, has greatly improved it. 'The Supreme Being', says he, 'has so formed the soul of man, that nothing but Himself can be its last, adequate, and proper happiness. Because therefore a great part of our happiness must arise from the contemplation of his being, that he might give our souls a just relish of such a contemplation, he has made them naturally delight in the apprehension of what is great and unlimited. Our admiration, which is a very pleasing emotion of the mind, immediately rises at the consideration of any object that takes up a great deal of room in the fancy; and, by consequence, will improve into the highest pitch of astonishment and devotion, when we contemplate his nature, who is neither circumscribed by time and place, nor to be comprehended by the largest capacity of a created being.'[12]

I shall only add, that our taste for the Sublime, cherished into a habit, and directed to proper objects, may, by preserving us from vice, which is the vilest of all things, and by recommending virtue for its intrinsic dignity, be useful in promoting our moral improvement. The same taste will also lead to the study of nature, which everywhere displays the sublimest appearances. And no study has a better effect upon the heart. For it keeps men at a distance from criminal pursuits, yields a variety of inoffensive and profitable amusement, and gives full demonstration of the infinite goodness and greatness of the adorable Creator.

---

[11] [Notes to Book I of *The Pleasures of the Imagination* (1744), quoting Longinus, *On the Sublime* (*De Sublimitate*), ch. xxiv.]

[12] [*Spectator*, no. 413 (24 June, 1712).]

Bibliography

Beattie's Philosophical Works

An Essay on the Nature and Immutability of Truth in Opposition to Sophistry and Scepticism, Edinburgh, 1770. (There were numerous subsequent editions; the last appeared in 1820. The *Essay* was also translated into French, Dutch and German.)
    Part I: Of the Standard of Truth
    Part II: Illustrations of the Preceding Doctrine, with Inferences
    Part III: Objections Answered

Essays: On Poetry and Music, As They Affect the Mind; On Laughter, and Ludicrous Composition; On the Usefulness of Classical Learning, Edinburgh, 1776. (Published with the 1776 edition of the *Essay on Truth*, and frequently reprinted in the late 1770s.)

Dissertations, Moral and Critical, Edinburgh, 1783. (Published in the same year also in London and Dublin; just one edition.)
    'On Memory and Imagination'; 'On Dreaming';
    'The Theory of Language'; 'On the Attachments of Kindred';
    'Illustrations of Sublimity'

Evidences of the Christian Religion, Briefly and Plainly Stated, Edinburgh, 1783. (In a third edition by 1788.)

Elements of Moral Science, 2 vols., Edinburgh, 1790–3. (Just one edition.)
    Vol. I: Part First: Psychology
           Part Second: Natural Theology
    Vol. II: Moral Philosophy
           Part First: Ethicks
           Part Second: Economicks
           Part Third: Politicks
           Part Fourth: Logick

Further Reading

Margaret Forbes, *Beattie and His Friends*, Westminster: Archibald Constable and Co., 1904.

Sir William Forbes, *An Account of the Life and Writings of James Beattie, LL.D.*, 2 vols., Edinburgh: Archibald Constable and Co, 1806.

James A. Harris, 'James Beattie, the Doctrine of Liberty, and the Science of the Mind', *Reid Studies* 5 (2002): 16–29.
   – *Of liberty and necessity: The free-will debate in eighteenth-century British philosophy*, Oxford: Oxford University Press, 2005, ch. 6.

Pierre Morère, *L'Oeuvre de James Beattie: tradition et perspectives nouvelles*, Paris: H. Champion, 1980.
David Fate Norton, 'Hume and His Scottish Critics', in David Fate Norton, Nicholas Capaldi and Wade L. Robison (eds), *McGill Hume Studies*, San Diego: Austin Hill Press, 1976.
N. T. Phillipson, 'James Beattie and the Defence of Common Sense', in Bernhard Fabian (ed.), *Festschrift für Reiner Gruenter*, Heidelberg, 1978.
Roger J. Robinson, Introductions to each of the 10 volumes of the Thoemmes Press edition of *The Works of James Beattie*, Bristol, 1996.
Ralph S. Walker (ed.), *James Beattie's London Diary 1773*, Aberdeen: Aberdeen University Press, 1946.
Paul Wood, 'Science and the Pursuit of Virtue in the Aberdeen Enlightenment', in M. A. Stewart (ed.), *Studies in the Philosophy of the Scottish Enlightenment*, Oxford: Clarendon Press, 1990.
— *The Aberdeen Enlightenment: The Arts Curriculum in the Eighteenth Century*, Aberdeen: Aberdeen University Press, 1995.

Textual Note

Selections 1, 2, 3 and 11 are from *An Essay on the Nature and Immutability of Truth, in opposition to Sophistry and Scepticism*, second edition, Edinburgh: A. Kincaird and J. Bell, 1771. (Selection 1: pp. 1–22; Selection 2: pp. 27–51; Selection 3: pp. 233–82; Selection 11: pp. 506–12.)
Selections 6, 7, 9 and 10 are from *Elements of Moral Science*, 2 vols., Edinburgh: T. Cadell, 1790–3. (Selection 6: vol. I, pp. ix–xv; Selection 7: vol. I, pp. 379–93; Selection 9: vol. II, pp. 8–16, 22–41, 54–77; Selection 10: vol. II, pp. 322–55.)
Selections 5, 14 and 15 are from *Dissertations Moral and Critical*, London: W. Strahan and T. Cadell, 1783. (Selection 5: pp. 1–20, 60–71; Selection 14: pp. 165–93; Selection 15: pp. 609–31, 654–5.)
Selections 12 and 13 are from *Essays: On Poetry and Music, as they affect the Mind; On Laughter, and ludicrous Composition; On the Usefulness of classical Learning*, third edition, London: E. and C. Dilly, 1779. (Selection 12: pp. 7–10, 24–43; Selection 13: pp. 118–20, 137, 145–50, 164–74.)
Selection 4 is from Sir William Forbes, *An Account of the Life and Writings of James Beattie, LL.D.*, 2 vols., Edinburgh: Archibald Constable and Co, 1806, vol. I, pp. 130–6.
Selection 8 is from James Hay Beattie, *Essays and Fragments in Prose and Verse . . . To which is prefixed an Account of the Author's Life and Character*, Edinburgh [no publisher given], 1794, pp. 11–13.

LIBRARY OF SCOTTISH PHILOSOPHY

full details overleaf

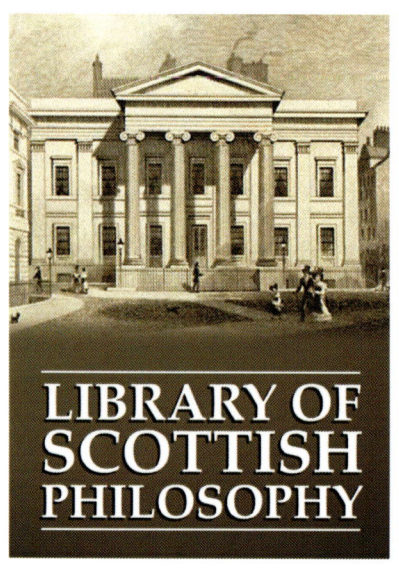

A major problem associated with the study of Scottish philosophy is access to the texts. Many simply are not available. Others are becoming so, but often in expensive reproductions or costly new editions. Through the *Library of Scottish Philosophy*, the Centre for the Study of Scottish Philosophy at the University of Aberdeen is sponsoring a series of inexpensive paperbacks comprising selections from both the better known and the less accessible Scottish authors, thus enabling both students and a wider public to read Scottish philosophy easily. The series has received generous financial support from the Carnegie Trust for the Universities of Scotland and Mr George S. Stevenson.

The series has two strands: (i) selections from individual authors; (ii) anthologies on particular themes. The series was launched in summer 2004 with the six volumes detailed below. The individual volumes are available in good bookshops or direct from the publisher, priced £12.95/$25.90; and at reduced price on subscription (enquiries to sandra@imprint.co.uk).

Vol 1: Scottish Philosophy: Selected Writings 1690-1960
edited and introduced by **Gordon Graham**. ISBN 0-907845-746

Vol 2: Adam Smith: Selected Philosophical Writings
edited and introduced by **James R. Otteson**. ISBN 1-84540-001-1

Vol 3: Art and Enlightenment: Scottish Aesthetics in the 18th Century
edited and introduced by **Jonathan Friday**. ISBN 0-907845-762

Vol 4: John Macmurray: Selected Philosophical Writings
edited and introduced by **Esther McIntosh**. ISBN 0-907845-738

Vol 5: The Scottish Idealists: Selected Philosophical Writings
edited and introduced by **David Boucher**. ISBN 0-907845-72X

Vol 6: James Beattie: Selected Philosophical Writings
edited and introduced by **James Harris**. ISBN 0-907845-711

Forthcoming titles from the Library of Scottish Philosophy:
Scottish Philosophical Theology, ed. David Fergusson. 0-907845-770
Politics and Society in Scottish Thought, ed. Shinichi Nagao. 0-907845-789

IMPRINT ACADEMIC, PO Box 200, Exeter EX5 5YX, UK
Tel: +44 (0)1392 841600   Fax: 841478   sandra@imprint.co.uk

full details & secure ordering: **www.imprint-academic.com/losp**